THE GOOD DIVORCE

THE GOOD DIVORCE
A Psychoanalyst's Exploration of Separation, Divorce, and Childcare

Arthur Leonoff

Routledge
Taylor & Francis Group
LONDON AND NEW YORK

First published 2015 by
Karnac Books Ltd.

Published 2018 by Routledge
2 Park Square, Milton Park, Abingdon, Oxon OX14 4RN
711 Third Avenue, New York, NY 10017, USA

Routledge is an imprint of the Taylor & Francis Group, an informa business

British Library Cataloguing in Publication Data

A C.I.P. for this book is available from the British Library

ISBN-13: 9781782202707 (pbk)

Typeset by V Publishing Solutions Pvt Ltd., Chennai, India

This book is dedicated to Lynda, Alison, Shayna, Emily, and Holly

CONTENTS

ACKNOWLEDGMENTS

Some books exist before they are written and *The Good Divorce* falls into this category. It was incubated through a creative synergy of psychology, psychoanalysis, family law and the family courts. I am very grateful for the privilege of doing the work I do—helping so many individuals and families over the length of a career. They have taught me so much and allowed for ideas to percolate and find form. My wife, Lynda, has been both supportive and patient. Her wisdom, affection and judgment are a constant source of strength. Jean Whieldon, a gem of an editor and kindred spirit, has been instrumental in bringing this text to press. It is her guidance, perseverance and stewardship that have made this work possible. Finally, thanks to Karnac for accepting this book for publication and bringing these ideas and experiences to a reading public that will hopefully find value and guidance in what is conveyed.

ABOUT THE AUTHOR

Dr. Arthur Leonoff is a psychologist and psychoanalyst in private practice in Ottawa, Canada. He is a supervising and training analyst with the Canadian Psychoanalytic Society and a member of the International Psychoanalytical Association. Apart from his work as an analyst and psychotherapist, Dr. Leonoff has a four-decade involvement studying and working in the area of divorce and family adjustment. In this regard, he has served as a court-appointed assessor, expert witness, and clinician working to resolve issues related to the care of children and their parents confronting and dealing with divorce with its manifold repercussions. In the capacity of expert, he has provided hundreds of court-mandated assessments over the years and has spoken frequently on the topic of divorce and its impact on children, adults, and families. Dr. Leonoff is co-author of *Custody and Access Assessments: A Practical Guide* (Toronto: Carswell, 1996).

AUTHOR'S NOTE

Plentiful clinical examples are instrumental to illustrating the important themes of this book. I view them as essential to giving form and life to the book's topics and ideas. Some are fictionalized although always relevant while others are amalgams of disguised and generalized case material absorbed from the clinic of experience. I am grateful to all who have crossed my path and to whom I could offer assistance, whether through court evaluation or treatment.

INTRODUCTION

They were an elegant couple, composed on the surface, well dressed and attractive—both professionals. They had been married for eleven years and had a nine-year-old daughter when Sean decided to leave Sally.

He had a plan and wanted shared care and joint custody of their daughter Sarah. Sally was confused. Sean was adamant. They could not seem to talk. She had many questions and no answers from Sean. How would they tell Sarah? "Daddy no longer loves mommy and wants to leave", was how Sean wanted to put it. Sally did not understand. What did it mean to fall out of love when you have a child and eleven years together? She grasped for some sense of control as her nuptial life dissolved in a mire of angst and unanswered questions.

As the example above portrays, many divorces occur in the depth of confusion with little communication or common resolve. There is no real template available for how to understand this complex and often ambiguous process. What exists is mainly practical advice such as a step-by-step manual for implementing and managing divorce. This book makes no pretensions to serving as a "how-to" guide. On the other hand, if it can create deeper understandings then it could well be helpful to professionals and the enquiring public combined.

Can there be such a thing as a "good divorce?" Given that sixty-two percent of premarital cohabitations and thirty-three percent of official marriages end in separation within ten years in the United States, we should hope so.[1] Since the 1980s in Canada, the divorce rate before the thirtieth wedding anniversary has fluctuated between thrity-five and forty-two percent.[2] Assuming sociological continuity between the countries, therefore, the majority of marriages fail before the ten-year juncture with approximately four of every ten official unions failing over the lifespan.

"Good divorce", though, should not be confused with the ethics of divorce.

This is not a polemic about the merits of ending marriages. I am sure the reader shares my concern for Sean and Sally but who knows what has occurred between them to bring Sean to this point. In any case, this is a personal decision and it is clear that Sean believes strongly in the merits of his resolve. He has no desire to remain united with Sally and is on his way out.

Having accepted the reality of divorce, it remains necessary to investigate the many challenges and issues created when unions dissolve. How can separation and divorce be implemented in a way that is as respectful, responsible, and protective to self and others as possible?

Divorce expresses so much at the core of the human condition. It begins with the need for attachment and its social expression. The married couple is reminiscent of the first couple—mother and baby—from which human life evolves and is nurtured. Intimate partnership establishes the elemental ingredients for starting a new family. The issues are the same whether the couple is straight or gay/lesbian. New technologies and the freeing of institutionalized love from the constraints of the one man/one woman paradigm have also created further avenues for divorce.

Divorce reflects the breakdown of this fundamental unit of intimate partnership. Failure in this realm is very personal and painful, often undermining identity in the short term. If the ultimate human catastrophe is to be alone, divorce exposes this fear once the coating of marriage is removed. Relationships are disrupted and social reinvention is required. Divorce, thus, creates multiple challenges: psychological, social, economic, family, and community. There is no simple divorce and no simple way to understand its implications for adults, children, and community.

Divorce also carries its weight of guilt and recrimination, a social stigma for many that brands them despite its frequency. By thirty years of age, three-quarters of North American women have been married. Of course, many will separate and effectively if not legally divorce.

The good divorce is an ethical divorce. It recognizes that whatever the fate of the union, there is a need to separate in a rational and considered way that best protects all concerned. This includes establishing a process that allows for reflection and working through of issues with the former spouse. Ethics implies that there is a way to navigate this often stormy and inevitably destabilizing life event to limit long-term damage and increase the odds of getting on with life in an adjusted way.

Psychologists are well trained to be helpful and I began my practice in 1974 with this goal in mind. Psychotherapy led eventually to training in psychoanalysis, which greatly deepened my understanding of human nature and the human condition. I have practiced as a psychoanalyst for the majority of my career. The reader will identify the psychoanalytic perspective at least in terms of a focus on inner experience. In this regard, my approach is psychodynamic rather than empirical.

In the late 1970s, joint custody emerged from trendsetting California as an option in divorce. A close friend had recently divorced and shared custody of her two children with her former partner. Together we wrote a short article on the subject and this initiated my particular involvement. Meanwhile, in my clinical practice, I was well aware of the depriving consequences of the usual anemic sole custody models in place at the time that reduced the non-residential parent to infrequent visitor status. Too many children were short changed particularly on the father side even when these dads were capable and willing to parent.

In the 1980s, a lawyer asked me to prepare an assessment for the court in a disputed custody case. General theorizing gave way to the clinical complexities of the particular case. Each was unique and had to be assessed on its own terms. More than thirty-five years later, there has been an unbroken chain of assessments, arbitrations, and clinical interventions involving divorcing couples and families in the mix.

This work on divorce does not presume to review the academic literature although it is informed by it. Clinical experience is a further source of knowledge and a major impetus for this book. Professionals and the educated public alike seeking a deeper insight into the divorce process should find this exploration useful. My goal is to provide the thinking, clinical basis and rationale for sound choices and informed decision-making as compared to simply identifying the mechanics of how to proceed. In my view, deeper understanding provides the seedbed for good decisions as well as offering guidance to those faced with the complex challenges routinely arising during the divorce process.

Among existential crises, divorce is a top tier event in terms of stress and consequences. It matters a great deal how it is managed. Superficial advice does little for people trapped in the maelstrom of divorce conflict. To be sure, there is no evidence that all the self-help books currently available make an appreciable difference in the turmoil associated with this event. Divorces are easier to get in this era but no less painful.

Meanwhile, society's way of understanding and configuring family life is changing at a rapid rate. It is important to ponder these issues in meaningful ways in the light of divorce and re-partnering. The formation of new social units with looser fixed ties to gender and biological filiation has revolutionized how we think about family. The old authority laden and linear model of mother-father-child is no longer the sole template by which society is measured. Some boundaries that we might have assumed in the past were permanent features dissolve and allow new opportunities for creating a family from combinations of individuals. With much increased freedom, there is less certainty and less standardization.

In the space of my career, therefore, the old linear certitudes of psychic and social life have been transformed. There is no going back, I suspect, and this could also be seen as progress. Yet, as much as society's values have shifted, there is ample room for pain and conflict. Relational breakdown and divorce are a study in human disillusionment and its social and emotional consequences. This has not changed mainly because the human need for trusting, intimate connection, and the corresponding fears of aloneness and abandonment continue to drive human behavior.

I have used the central idea of ethics to help articulate the thesis that destructivity in divorce is linked to conduct as much or more than the loss of the relationship itself. Without a simple morality based on cultural taboos, ethics assumes greater importance precisely because there are no clear fixed standard ways of operating or treating others. This is especially significant during times of greatest uncertainty and catastrophe such as often occurs in divorce. What is important for adults and children is to retain hope in both human relationships and the future. Ethical thinking and judgment arise from inside the person. We must touch base, therefore, with what really matters to sustain hope and prepare for a future in the face of many difficulties. I have thus written the book to help foster ethical thinking and to consider values within the realm of divorce. In my understanding, ethics emerge from insight, which requires a deeper exploration of experience.

CHAPTER ONE

The good divorce

Marriages are essentially voluntary relationships and the time honored phrase "till death do us part" no longer applies in at least forty percent of cases. The reasons for this are legion but certainly include the secularisation of society, liberal "no fault" divorce laws and an undermining of marriage as the only context in which to bear children. Enhanced independence of women and an ethos built on comfort and consumerism also emphasize change over stability. If "love" has become the sole reason to unite in matrimony, then the consequence has been a much inflated divorce rate.

Of course this does not mean that divorce is taken lightly. It is a source of anxiety and pain for many ex-couples, those with children but also those without. It is a curious paradox of our postmodern society that although we have made divorce more possible, we have not made it less painful. This is especially true when the break-up reflects the intent of only one of the parties while the other must absorb the impact often without notice or real warning. This amounts to a traumatic rupture and is often just as stressful as the unexpected and sudden death of a spouse.

Even when the divorce is not a particular surprise, the psychological rupture can be hard to bear. What does it mean to no longer love someone that you felt strongly enough about to marry? If anything, it represents the final demolition of the dream with that person at the center of a shared life. What is left then when so much hope is dashed? There is much to recover with no simple prescriptive path to follow.

Although a failed marriage is never easy to swallow, it helps when the couple has worked hard to make sure that separation is the right road to follow. Separation with respect and dignity is still painful but does not constitute an assault on the partner's rights and vulnerable position in the couple. When the union ends dramatically, however, blindsiding the other partner due to lack of warning or process, emotional damage can be extensive. It is less that the union was doomed than the undeniable fact that the initiating spouse acted unscrupulously or at least refused to treat them honorably. In this regard, the leaving spouse ignored or failed to acknowledge and abide by the ethics of divorce.

Hence, this is our first topic for discussion.

It is much easier to be the spouse who ends a union than to be the one who had no idea that this "final solution" was percolating in the partner's mind. It is probably wishful thinking to believe that divorces mainly occur in the context of mutually desired action. In many cases, this is simply not true. If couples could agree that they indeed had a bad marriage needing to end for the good of the two individuals, this would, I believe, put them in the minority and imply a capacity for common action not shared by many separating spouses.

More likely, one partner perceived the end of the marriage as a necessity without sharing with the other until it has been worked through and decided in the leaver's mind. The groundwork may, therefore, have already been laid before the issue is formally raised. This could involve having started a new relationship but this is not essential to the process I am describing. The initiator might have already met with a lawyer, ascertained their rights and how to achieve legal ends before the left partner even knows this is coming. The emotional side of divorce might not be given its due particularly when the leaving spouse is resolute in their intention to leave.

Breaking up a marriage can definitely be the right step even when it is foremost in the mind of only one partner. In this regard, we should take no stand on whether divorce is the appropriate solution. It happens and sometimes this is for the best and at other times solves little.

Generally, the leaving spouse has made a decision that terminating the union is in their own and perhaps the couple's best interests. Some assume that the spouse must, or at least should be, of the same mind. Often, however, this is far from the case. Even so called "bad" marriages might not lead everyone to conclude that a union should end. The soon to be left partner might never imagine taking such a step particularly if there are children involved. In this context, one partner takes the lead while the other is often playing catch up in the divorce process.

To be sure, such an imbalanced dynamic is a source for much of the unnecessary grief, hurt, fury, and retaliatory vengeance mental health professionals often see in these complicated divorce situations. This leads me then to offer a first principle of responsible or ethical divorce.

Every spouse deserves the opportunity to know they have a bad marriage before being left

So what does it mean to deserve to know about a bad marriage? The essence of this standard is that unhappy spouses need to communicate this state of the union to their partners in order to give them a real opportunity to address what is wrong. Simply announcing that one intends to leave and then taking the shortest path out does not amount to the due process expected.

As such, everyone deserves a heads-up about a bad marriage if only as an opportunity to either address what is wrong or be reconciled to the fact that the marriage should end. When spouses are forced to bear the impact of their partner's action in failing to consult them, it tends to put a lie (in the left partner's mind) to the belief that they were ever a couple in a committed relationship in the first place.

Therefore, it is one thing to have a relationship fail despite one's best intentions and efforts but it is another to be discarded, as if one is the last to know and there was never a treasured union to be safeguarded.

This might sound self-evident but is frequently observed not to be the case. Marital therapies where one spouse has already decided to leave are essentially faux treatments and are basically a waste of time. Equally fraudulent are those situations where the leaving spouse already has a new relationship but has failed to inform the one person who most deserves to know: the spouse.

I have been surprised over the years by how many cases feature a unilateral initiative taken by one partner who undertakes a solo initiative not shared with the spouse until the final stage of implementation. "He/she had to know", is the common refrain but, in fact, the left partner might have had no idea that the marriage was actually ending or at least was not ready to accept this conclusion. Of course, the leaving spouse proffers a decisive argument: "We haven't had sex for a year", or "We agree on nothing." The argument amounts to a rationalization for taking a unilateral action in what is, for better or worse, a partnership that deserves to be treated as such whether it fails or succeeds.

One factor to keep in mind is that people differ in their tolerance of relationships and what would be considered grounds for ending a marriage. For instance, insufficient sex might sound the death knell for some while others would view this as unfortunate but never a sufficient cause to actually end a marriage. The same could be true for lack of intimacy, support, kindness, or any dimension of marital life.

Divorce is a remedy provided by society to deal with a failed marriage. In its rightful place, divorce makes sense and couples should not need to be chained together where both could face years of unhappiness, turmoil, and conflict. Violence whether episodic or ingrained and systemic are valid reasons for divorce. No one should face the threat of injury or severe emotional damage at the hands of another person even if one agreed to marry this person.

It would be foolhardy, therefore, to ever suggest that divorce does not have its rightful place. Marriages are based on a balance of needs and mutuality. Intimacy is the dividend of a good marriage. It grows with time and evolves in a shared space that the couple happily and trustingly perceives and designate as their marriage. Sexuality remains a powerful current that touches all aspects mentioned above: mutuality, needs and intimacy. Over the years sexuality suffuses through the couple's togetherness even when it becomes less genitally focused. Nonetheless, it remains a wonderful part of life that greases the wheels.

What designates a bad from a good marriage is a vast subject and must be individually assessed or understood. In other words, it is hard to generalize. On the other hand, the kernel of truth that runs through the gamut of examples is that in bad marriages there is a failure to create or preserve the shared space called the marriage. It can only be mutually created and it is not reducible to either protagonist. Hence, the partner who feels entitled to exit the union without really consulting their spouse precisely exemplifies the absence of this shared space that is deemed worth preserving.

It is not surprising perhaps that couples seeking marital therapy, who have this fundamental shared space but who face relationship or family problems, have a good chance of succeeding in their efforts. In contrast, couples that expect the therapist to help them actually build a shared marriage with its dividend of intimacy and healthy mutuality will be disappointed. Of course, no marriage meets all needs but good marriages must meet emotionally fundamental needs and this positive synergy serves as the foundation for the shared space created together.

In today's world with later unions and second marriages common, women in their late thirties facing a biological limit often pair with men with family ambitions without taking into account that real relationships only evolve slowly and solely as a result of shared experience. They marry and multiply only to flounder when life demands require them to have an authentic union on which to draw strength and solve problems. In many cases, there is a child before there is a valid relationship and certainly not one that has had the chance to develop the shared space required to face life together.

Everyone has egg on their face when a marriage ends. In other words, it is a personal as much as a relational failure in our minds. It is no surprise therefore that marital break-ups create enormous guilt. This brings me to my second principle for an ethical divorce.

Avoid blame

Those professionals who work in the area of divorce are well aware of the scourge of blame that best characterizes high conflict divorce. Indeed, high conflict represents at its core the failure to divorce. In this instance, blame serves as toxic glue that holds the couple together while they flail at each other inside and outside of the courts.

Excessive blame undermines interpersonal relationships and erodes a capacity for empathy and collaboration. On the other hand, externalization can feel more tolerable than guilt: better to blame the other than accept the painful truth of personal failure and the damage caused someone we willingly married.

But why is guilt so prominent in divorce? There are not many decisions in life that carry such a social, emotional, and otherwise wide-ranging impact. Indeed, in marriage there is an emotional contract that precedes a legal one. We undertake to care for our partner and fundamentally to take responsibility for their welfare. Of course this does not mean that the other is absolved of self-responsibility but it does imply that the duty of care is high when it comes to marriage. Thus, even if society has made it easier to divorce, there has not been a concomitant lowering of the expectation placed on marriages. Marriage is no trifling matter.

As such, marriages are not merely friendships, which can come and go. They take their cue from our earliest most primal relationships with caregivers, which underscores why they do not simply end with a whimper but rupture, figuratively at least, with blood on the floor. The rip and tear of divorce that seems to be the norm more than the exception speaks to the elementary nature of marital unions and why divorce is so painful and heart wrenching over such a long period of time. Is it any wonder then that guilt is the primary emotion associated with divorce?

Nevertheless, we should be clear when describing the specific quality and kinds of guilt manifested in divorce. First, there is the guilt of wrongdoing. This is the case, for instance, when the initiating spouse covers up the existence of an extramarital liaison, which has shifted the balance towards leaving. Guilt in this instance is quite real and reflects the understanding that our actions were harmful to someone we were supposed to love and care for.

Some guilt for sure is inevitable in divorce because we cannot leave a partner without bearing some responsibility. This is healthy guilt. It is part of atoning for what failed and our personal role in that failure. Mixed with guilt though is often sadness and mourning. Even willingly ending a union does not necessarily mean that the partner is not missed or that parts of the relationship were gratifying and painful to lose.

There are some who instigated divorce only to experience a subsequent depression when they cannot bear the rebound of aloneness and emptiness that unexpectedly surfaces. This occurs most often when there is a history of prior psychic trauma usually in the leaver's childhood background. It is as if two parts of the person collide. The adult decides that it is best to end the marriage while the residue of a traumatized child is terrified to be alone and unprotected.

As an example, Ben had little positive to say about his wife. He was a gruff, almost disagreeable man who lacked respect or affection for his spouse. There was little time for exploration before Ben left his wife. Quickly, however, his mood and confidence collapsed. He felt abandoned even though he had pushed for the separation. Ben's mother had suffered repeated hospitalizations for depression when he was a child and a sister committed suicide as a young adult. Ben's father had been consistently unfaithful and openly devalued his "useless" wife. Hence, the lack of nurturing and the history of repeated and traumatic losses had scarred his psyche. He could neither be married nor leave his wife.

In terms of other complications, for some individuals guilt is particularly harsh. Admitting guilt would be (in their mind) accepting total blame for the failed union. They feel that guilt must be answered with severe punishment. Hence, in this context, the pressure of guilt is relieved through projection. Projected guilt is expressed as intense blame of the other and serves as a way to disavow guilt.

We can conclude that not everyone is equipped to handle guilt and this is especially true when it is of the punitive and severe kind. This is often the stuff of high conflict. For those in the thick of high conflict divorce, for example, blame is the weapon of choice. Conflict masks the incapacity for healthy atonement and taking real, ethical responsibility for what has occurred. There is no situation that I have seen that could be called high conflict where some form of professional assistance is not required.

Unfortunately, services aimed at managing conflict, such as provided by parent coordinators, might also serve as a forum for combat that only shifts the venue while not lessening the severity of aggression used to avoid guilt and self responsibility. I still view parent coordination as a useful and valuable addition to the tools available to assist divorced families. However, unless there is some parallel therapeutic process to deal with the mindset of extreme high conflict, ethical divorce will remain beyond the repertoire of such couples so long as even one of the partners is immersed in this toxic mindset.

Yet, for the majority of divorcing partners, being mindful of guilt helps avoid the pitfalls of blame no matter how appealing this route seems at the moment. There are specific advantages to being able to acknowledge self-responsibility for the impact of our actions:

- It allows both parties to be better aware of their impact on others including the spouse, the children, and extended families.
- It fosters the capacity to also remember better times and the features or qualities of the partner that attracted us in the first place.
- It underscores an important truth in divorce that the duty of care particularly where children are involved extends beyond the marriage itself.

- It facilitates mourning for what was lost by leaving space to acknowledge what was good and worth preserving. This is especially helpful to children who need a space to love the other parent.
- It serves as a counterbalance to the anger, injury, and disillusionment that can be so powerful in divorce.

The third principle of ethical divorce may appear to be straightforward but is very often observed in the breach.

Honesty and respect for due process is the best policy

It would be naive or at least unrealistic to state that married people should not engage in extramarital affairs or relationships. Statistics speak to their frequency and marriage counselors can certainly attest to the many occasions in which couples enter into therapy with a hidden elephant in the room that stymies any progress that could be made.

Marriages cannot tolerate the impact of relationship triangles for too long before they snap under the pressure. Whatever their longevity, marriages can only function as a shared space between two individuals whose mutuality takes precedence at key moments over the couple's individual needs and destinies. Hence, when one party steps out of this frame, the union inevitably suffers. This might not happen immediately but it is sure to follow.

Of course, people entering into extramarital liaisons are often oblivious to consequences. Excitement fuelled by rationalization and denial of repercussions creates a kind of blindness to what others might see clearly. It is simply too juicy for the individual to forfeit such pleasure and the potential price to pay is ignored or disavowed for the gratification of the moment.

Before proceeding further, however, it might be helpful to distinguish between affairs and actual relationships. We should also remember the role of perversions such as heavy reliance on pornography, prostitutes and strip joints as a further form of triangulation that can cut off the lifeblood of a marriage.

Although such obsessive preoccupations lack the personal dimension of the affair or relationship, they drain away desire and are extremely undermining of marital unions.

Affairs are extramarital liaisons that occur outside of any relational commitment. In this regard, the married person who engages in an affair is not looking to end their union necessarily but only to seek some private pleasure that does not have to be shared or acknowledged with their partner. Hence, the affair is the icing but not the cake. It is often tragic when these liaisons come to light (as they frequently do in this age of smart phones and email) because the offended spouse is at high risk of not forgiving their partner.

When the painful discovery occurs, the offending spouse might minimize the intent or importance of the affair while the offended partner will invariably grapple with themes of betrayal, lying, and sexual rejection. Some spouses faced with this discovery are able to overcome the impact as long as there is authentic accountability. In other cases, however, the offended partner might find it insurmountable precisely because marriages are at base contracts founded on trust and honesty. In my experience, it is hard to predict.

The ties that bind are also powerful. Loyalty, commitment, love and devotion to family are powerful bonds that can serve to restore harmony even after one partner has strayed and deeply hurt the other. At the same time, being lied to regarding something so fundamental as sexual relations with another person can be very hard to overcome. Hence, it is a toss up whether the union will survive the blow and not easy to predict.

Extramarital relationships are a different genre when it comes to triangulation of a marriage. First and foremost, these are relationships that have emotional significance and are cast in the same mold of "love" as the marriage itself. In this regard, they function as a hidden intimacy and are intended as an alternative or needed supplement to the marital union. Extramarital relationships are the purview of the lonely, frustrated and needy spouse who, for whatever reason, does not feel sufficiently held, understood or gratified in the existing marriage. These relationships are often profoundly emotional whether physical or not. They might arise when life events create added psychological stress or demand but can also arise from growing closeness.

Extramarital relationships could still be intended as a supplement in the mind of a spouse who lacks the will, courage or resourcefulness to leave an existing marriage. This could be due to paralyzing guilt, feelings of responsibility and/or fear of consequences including emotional, financial, and social, not to mention the impact on children. The repercussions of ending a marriage are huge and many spouses approach it with realistic and appropriate trepidation. The extramarital relationship, therefore, can be intended as a fall back position so that one does not have to leave or, alternatively, it can provide the rationale and impetus to finally take the step. When discovered, there is usually no going back. Marriages might survive a sexual competitor but they almost never survive an alternate or rival love.

If a partner does feel the pull of another, whether for sex or love, it would be best to bring this sense of lack to the other spouse in the proper forum. The idea, for instance, of dropping a bomb such as, "Oh, by the way, I felt really attracted to this man/woman at the office and thought how nice it would be to be with him/her", is not what I mean. Honesty occurs through the communication of lack or discontent in the right context as a starting point for a deeper discussion.

Naturally, conveying such sentiments as lack, loneliness, sadness, or frustration is never easy but at least the spouse can work with it. It might be upsetting but it does not amount to acting out and betrayal. In this context, what is essential is to create a forum, perhaps with professional help but not necessarily, to come to grips with what ails the marriage and what can be done to address it. It is no crime to be drawn to other people. Indeed, this is human nature and the pull of supposedly greener pastures can be powerful. The underlying principle is respect for due process and an honest confrontation in dialogue with the partner. The idea then is that the marriage needs to be addressed in its own terms and not be derailed by forces to which only one partner is privy.

But what if a partner has already become involved? Maybe it is an office romance between two co-workers who surrender to attraction and lust or, more poignantly, an intimacy evolves that deepens despite the better judgment of the participants. Here, the principle remains the same in terms of respect for due process and the welfare of the spouse. One cannot turn feelings off and on but it is possible to create an opening for communication with the spouse by first refraining from the full bore rush into the new relationship. The key is to deal with the marriage first in a sensitive and open way that sincerely attempts to tackle what is wrong and makes room for honest communication. No matter how much the new relationship feels unplanned and even an aberration, it signals that something was amiss in the marriage beforehand that set in motion a search. In other words, these relationships are not accidental.

Putting a hold on the slide into a new relationship is easier said that done in the often turbocharged passion and novelty of a new love. Moreover, no spouse can easily compete with a new lover and will almost certainly suffer by comparison. Equally, the initiating spouse has a vested interest in the apparent validity of the new encounter and will look for justifications to make it seem "right". Indeed, it might be an action that brings an unfavorable marriage to an end and this could be for the best. Yet, it could also be an escapist flight into fantasy that defies reality and courts disaster. The need to create a space for thinking is huge even in the face of passion and excitement. Being able to share what is happening with a trusted friend or professional who will not take sides can also be very valuable. When we speak to another, we also hear our self in a different way than when thinking and feeling. This provides a further point of reflection.

Many in this position become hopelessly mired in a parallel universe and do not manage to pull back and deal with their own self and existing union. They try living out both realities and become exhausted in the process. Discovery is inevitable and the lack of integrity at this point is so huge that recovery is next to impossible. For the offended spouse, they have been left without ever being informed and this adds insult to injury. Hate can be marshaled as the antidote to pain and rejection. The betraying spouse is cast as a rogue with bad character who threw their partner under the bus. This might not be the case but the end-of-marriage rupture will take its cue from the infidelity.

Hurt inspired wishes for revenge fuel litigation and feed the engine that drives court battles and endless controversy. The offended spouse could also feel they have cause to rethink the capacity of their (former) partner to impart proper values to children. In other words, the failure to pull back and deal with the marriage first in an authentic and credible way can have dire consequences that are felt over many years to follow.

Before closing this discussion, the issue of honesty itself should be addressed as it represents a core value in healthy divorce. Honesty is based in communication and the right of the marital partner to know how the spouse feels and what their intentions are. Whether this translates into open disclosure about affairs and relationships is another issue for which there is not always a straightforward answer.

Of course no partner should have the right to stray from the commitment of marriage simply to satisfy his or her ego or momentary desire in an affair. Even in societies where there is a liberal treatment of love and sexual relations such as France, hurt and pain are no less evident based on media reports. If infidelity has occurred and there is still some emotional room and motivation to address marital issues, then the argument could be made that informing the spouse right away could cause needless hurt and distress. This does not mean, though, that the spouse should not be told. The relevant factor appears to be the context in which a disclosure is made. If marriages require honesty as a fundamental value, it is likely impossible for real healing to occur if this truth remains hidden. Where a spouse has taken responsibility to address issues and be accountable, a couple can often handle acknowledging infidelity.

When a deeper emotional relationship has formed with another person, the first step would be to set this relationship aside in order to deal as openly and sincerely as one can with the marriage. The second step is to create a meaningful forum to begin addressing marital issues. Within this process of hopeful repair and reconciliation, disclosure would need to occur with the intent of taking responsibility for one's actions and acknowledging the hurt and betrayal this has caused.

Of course, if there is no wish to repair the damaged union and find a way to love and care for the partner, then disclosure would at least end a deception and has merit on this basis alone. Such truth can be painful but better to hear it from one's partner than to be told by a third party sometime in the future.

In many cases, people fall into extramarital liaisons and relationships more than making a conscious and deliberate choice to pursue them. They might not recognize or want to acknowledge their readiness and even implicit search for another love object. To be sure, of course, there is a subset of individuals who are serial and opportunistic pursuers or who partner or marry but never forfeit the right to have additional lovers. They marry tongue in cheek so to speak and ego needs routinely trump loyalties. Another group are inflated by life successes and feel they deserve not to be limited in terms of available lovers. Power and success fuel greed and entitlement rather than self-esteem in this group. Moreover, the forbidden fruit is invariably experienced as sweeter.

A large group of those who stray from marriage, however, are buffeted and strained by life's demands and turn to others for respite, distraction, or comfort. During the course of time, however, they might understand the depressive feelings that lurk below the emotional surface that led to flights of fantasy, as if someone new could deliver them from life's perceived misery. Even without outside intervention, however, these individuals might come to see the futility of this path. It could run its course or he/she might start to experience issues and complexities with the lover as well. When the bloom is off the rose, re-evaluation is possible and the lure of a loyal, supportive caring spouse at home can regain its luster. Such re-assessment and growing perspective re-energizes love and creates a strong desire to repair links with the partner.

Naturally, spouses in the predicament of having engaged in extramarital affairs and relationships would wish to avoid a painful and risky disclosure of what they have been doing behind their partner's back. Unfortunately, the price of non-disclosure is often a false harmony that erodes desire and places guilt and disappointment at the center of the couple's unspoken discourse. Although disclosure creates risk for both spouses and for the marriage, there can be no real marriage without honesty. Marriages built on lies are incompatible with loving unions no matter what rationalizations are marshaled.

Wary of not wanting to sound contradictory, I am also aware that no blanket statement can reasonably cover all human situations. Values exist in a tension between principles and actual context. In these pages, I have been discussing principle rather than every permutation or context of interpersonal encounter. Hence, I would not want the reader to assume that there is absolutely no choice but to disclose in every situation. On the other hand, I would expect these to be few and far between and only to characterize those uncommon situations where the individual being told would result in emotional damage and where the intent of the offender is to continue to repair and strengthen the union.

This could apply, for example, where the non-straying partner suffers from a mental disorder and could not bear the stress of such disclosure in the context of a continuing relationship. Nevertheless, this would not spare the offending partner from the obligation of working to stabilize the union and addressing the underlying fault lines that led to what occurred. There could also be no fudging of the boundary that brings the extramarital relationship or liaison to a close.

Finally, it is worth noting that all forms of triangulation create hurdles and obstacles for marriages. These include men who spend hours pursuing online pornography or women who become lost in Internet chat rooms indulging in a plethora of virtual relationships. Such activities drain marriages and are never innocuous in their impact. In many ways, our increasingly web based world has created apparently "safer" ways to dream about another life that omits any need for love and care for a real human being. How could a spouse fail to take this personally?

More sinister in its impact, however, is the influence of online indulgence on the psyche, which gradually loses the capacity to be drawn by a live person. Excitement takes a virtual turn and becomes bound up with fantasies that have little to do with real life or real relationships. The effect is crippling both on minds and marriages. This has less to do with ethical divorce, however, than with ethical marriage.

The final principle with regards to ethical divorce could be included under the heading.

Everyone left deserves an explanation

It might be surprising to learn that in many cases I have observed over the years, the rejected spouse does not really understand why they are being left. If the spouse is told, it is usually couched in blame: "You always had to have your way" or "It should be obvious." The common refrain that "we grew in separate ways" or "we lost what we once had in common" are often meant to convey some general effect or outcome rather than plumbing or acknowledging a cause. This could be offered as explanation to spare the feelings of the spouse but it is usually meant to avoid closer examination.

The post-mortem of why a marriage failed should be seen as essential information and a moral imperative of the duty of care. Why is it important? Mainly, it is important because few projects in life are as significant as whom we marry and what happens. Failure in marriage is a huge pill to swallow. Even if the two people can be said to have grown apart, this still begs the question. Why? What would have been needed in order to grow together? Did this mean that the essential contract was faulty and there was never actual love or commitment? Or did something happen to dislodge the union and create instability or drift? Who did what to whom and why was there not a bilateral effort to change the direction of tilt towards each other?

Without some real information and feedback, grieving is more difficult and complicated. In endless circles, blame and self-blame jostle for ascendancy. A healthy divorce, however, will more likely lead to greater capacity to provide care and better family life for children. This includes exit communication that replaces speculation and controversy.

There is a tendency in society to underestimate the impact of divorce and how long it can take to recover. Feelings of anger, depression, lower self-esteem, vulnerability as well as loneliness and fears of ageing and aloneness are often hard to overcome. Ex-spouses, particularly those dumped without preparation or explanation, often will long for the spouse despite the shabby even cruel way they have been treated in the aftermath of the union. The sense of being deserted and trashed adds to the pain and difficulty separating.

Hence, the benefits of a constructive divorce are legion. It is not only a moral imperative but also a sound strategy to preserve or salvage something of value. The grounds for a healthier break-up are established with communication, which does not have to be elegant but nonetheless needs to occur. When there is an honest attempt to discuss what happened and why the union is ending, the conversation can be upsetting but it will also clear the air and make way for smoother adjustment as well as improved relations in the future. Although I am describing this in the singular, more than one conversation might be required to constitute sufficient communication.

It is important to distinguish between a constructive, healthy retention of what was good about the ex-partner as compared to a paralyzing ambivalence in which love and hate create emotional havoc and inconsistent behavior. I can recall a case, for example, of an ex-couple trapped in agonizing litigation that, nonetheless, would get together sexually and cling to each other. Their children were understandably hopelessly confused and the divorce regressed into high conflict and dysfunction.

Ambivalence, when extreme, promotes clinging and non-acceptance. The individual is torn between love and hate, which creates interminable chaos. Such confused and confusing mental states will not help to resolve the complicated legal and socioeconomic consequences of break-up. Yet, this is often precisely the timeline in which divorces are negotiated, which only adds to their complexity. The need to separate in the right way is one piece that both parties can control. It pays dividends when it comes to dissolving a union that it has been done with integrity and soundness.

It would be unrealistic, though, to presume that communication at the end of a marriage would lead to unanimity and shared divorce. The goal is to deal responsibly with the "other" for whom we undertook to love and care. The purpose of the communication is not to engender change of heart but, rather, to demonstrate respect even in the context of the intention of leaving a union that feels so unfulfilling that it deserves to end. Again, I would emphasize that no partner would necessarily want to stay married or committed against the other partner's will. The issue then revolves around how the union ends *vs* whether it terminates or continues.

Conclusion

One cannot discuss divorce without bearing to some extent a heavy heart. It is not a happy subject or a life journey that people face easily or even well. Indeed, many of the problems that end up in the courts and rip families apart, in my view, are due in large part to how marriages end. Of course, this is a far-reaching statement and there are other factors that intervene. Nevertheless, it matters a lot how one partner leaves the other. It is an independent factor that exerts its own harmful influence when this phase has been botched. Partners who do not simply end their marriages with mutual sorrow but who rather, abandon, betray, lie, cheat, blame, replace, or any combination thereof, add a layer of injury that often fuels much of the tumult and bitter recriminations seen in far too many divorces.

Consequently, I am proposing that there is much to be said for ethical divorce as a goal or prescription for future dealings and to improve the climate for resolution and healing. If more attention were paid to how we exit marriages, much unnecessary angst and conflict would be avoided.

Although community based services and religious organisations offer prenuptial classes, post-nuptial counseling seems to be a rarity. It is a gap that should be filled. How many divorcing couples attempt to mediate the unpacking of their joint lives in the midst of suffering unbearable states of mind racked by complex and conflicting emotions? Such people would be better served if they took advantage of pre-mediation or pre-negotiation counseling in order to end their union on a note with which they both can live.

Some of the questions that would invariably come out:

What happened to us?
What could have been done differently?
Why did I fall out of love?
Did you ever really love me?
What did I do to deserve this?
How did this affair happen?
At what point did this begin?
Do you love this other person?
Do you hate me?

Only after these difficult questions are faced in an open, honest, and yet respectful way can the couple get on with the business of separating.

As much as society has made it easier to divorce, there has been no lessening of the many expectations placed on marriage. Among the possible major failures in life, divorce ranks in the top tier. Hence, it is understandable why repercussions are so significant and long lasting. It takes time to adjust even in the most rational, mutual, and ethical of divorces.

Two years is commonly indicated as an average readjustment period but this obviously depends on individual cases. The more complicated divorces, especially those turbocharged by a traumatic ending, can take much longer. The layering of hurts adds to the emotional complexity and works against mourning and re-engagement on autonomous terms.

Ethical divorce is one way to control the impact. Simply turning one's back on someone as important as a life partner or treating her or him shabbily or cruelly is the wrong approach. It will backfire every time. Acting ethically will not erase the pain of divorce or eliminate all conflict but it will set a tone of respect that should lower the many costs incurred as a matter of course. Mediation and other non-adversarial approaches will have a greater chance of succeeding. The spouse on the receiving end of a divorce might not be happy with the union ending but they will not necessarily feel abused or abandoned as if they never mattered in the first place.

By insisting on ethics as central to a healthy divorce process, I am also suggesting that ethical failure is a complex study in itself. When psychoanalysts speak of the early encounter between child and mother, there is awareness of a reciprocal interaction: what the baby wants from the breast and what the breast wants from the baby. Does the parent offer the breast as an opportunity to be willingly "chosen" by the baby or does the parent demand that the baby suck? Is the parent consistently or sporadically available, waiting for the baby's spontaneous gesture or is there a rigid timetable for feeding and burping? Children absorb these elemental messages and with it a sense of obligation, permission, and responsibility to the other. Fast-forward many years to a marriage rupture and the same themes present. Conflicts emerge over responsibilities and obligations to the other and these likely have deeper roots leading back to foundational relationships. Rage, shame, disgust, humiliation, and rejection fears fill the space as both parties disentangle what each wants from the other. How often in life are we obliged to return to the beginning to unravel the first dependencies and establish what we owe others and what we owe to our self?

CHAPTER TWO

Post-divorce adjustment

Going through divorce and adjusting to the new frontier of post-divorce life and relationships is never easy. Hopefully, though, marital break-up can offer the kind of stability that was not present beforehand while the couple was together or married. The key, in my view, is to have a successful divorce, which, perhaps counter-intuitively, is by no means inevitable. It is another of these major life hurdles for which there is no training or preparation. Nevertheless, it has to be done right and with its own particular thoroughness and integrity. A bungled divorce can extend misery long into the future. Moreover, many divorces are bungled.

To explain this concept better, it could help to view divorce as an intervention much like a surgery for a dysfunctional back. If the indications for the surgery are sound and the procedure is handled with skill, the result will be a more stable and functional back to support the person. Nevertheless, all operations create their own challenges and rehabilitation might be required. Hence, if the patient has reasonable expectations and understands the limits of the procedure then much can be accomplished.

Likewise, divorce is an intervention that at its best can finally allow for personal and even family stability and equilibrium. In this regard, it is a remedy to correct what ails a long-term committed romantic relationship that has failed. Yet, there is no guarantee that divorce will work in all cases. Sometimes the separating of lives simply shifts the field of battle, especially when the couple remains tied through children and/or through unhealthy connection. A failed divorce then becomes the seedbed for the chronic, high conflict scenarios that preoccupy family courts and require huge societal resources to handle.

In the absence of children, the process would seem to be easier but this is only relatively speaking. Continuing ties might be unnecessary and even relationships as close as marriage can fade with time. Yet, many people in this seemingly straightforward situation continue to struggle in their own way. The struggle can be with the former spouse due to legal entanglements but it can also be deeply personal. In this regard, issues and struggles are focused inward as the separated person attempts to make sense of what happened and anticipates a life after divorce.

No matter how meager the financial or property ties and even without children, broken marriages imply broken dreams. Hopes and dreams inspire marriage. It is an opportunity to build something very personal and special with someone we love. What could be better? In the aftermath, therefore, with hopes and dreams in shambles, it is common for self-doubts to take over. Trust becomes an issue and if the leaving spouse simply departs as if the relationship never existed or meant anything then the bad feelings are made even worse.

It is an injury at many levels: what was and what could have been. There is no easy way to walk away from such a catastrophe without taking the time to work through the feelings and come out the other side. Like a bad flu, it is risky, following divorce, to prematurely advance as if one is actually thinking straight. This takes time and is part of what makes the post-dissolution process unsettling and difficult.

Divorce with children, of course, adds hugely to the real life complexity of the situation. One must not only untangle a broken union but also make plans for how the children will be raised and shared in the future. The paradox of separation with children is that the broken union must continue to exist within a post-divorce family unit. The marriage ends but the family persists, although redefined, often expanding to include step-parent, step-siblings and step-grandparents. The complexity can be staggering in its demands on all family members although there can certainly be ample rewards.

When we think of separation and divorce, the prototypic couple in their early forties comes to mind. Let's explore a general example.

Dan and Laura have been married ten years or so and have school age children but they have not thrived together despite other life successes. Families are busy units and the duties and responsibilities can seemingly put the adult relationship in the back seat of life. This has gone on for a long time. Perhaps early life experiences, including divorce in their own families of origin, might be a factor in raising divorce as an option. Laura is particularly uninspired, feeling unfulfilled and contemplates growing old with a person she no longer treasures. There is growing conflict with complaints centered on lack of sexual intimacy and poor communication. Sometimes, though, there is little noise to accompany or herald a growing despair. A quiet catastrophe takes form with Laura leading the way. Dan feels likewise but would still seize any opportunity to make it better. Divorce is not as ready an option as for the initiator. When the call for divorce happens, it arrives like a huge slap.

There is another demographic, however, that is receiving increasing attention and this concerns the rising divorce rate among fifty and sixty year olds.[1] Divorce at this age can have particularly harsh implications that are economic, emotional, and social. This is often particularly hard on women who are more likely to face their older years alone. Two different scenarios come to mind. First, as people remain healthier well into midlife, they might have already been divorced. Remarriages are statistically less stable in all age groups for several reasons, one of which is simply that the remedy has already been used. In other words, they are vigorous enough to want to leave and start again despite age. Second, with longer lifespan, midlife expectations for marriage have been extended in time. This is especially true for individuals who fear ageing and for whom divorce creates a further opportunity for youthful romance and sexual gratification.

The prototype of this type of break-up might be as follows. Sally and Ron are in their early sixties. Sally is retired while Ron is a health professional who continues to practise. Their children are grown and they are grandparents. Sally understands the limits of her marriage but she identifies with Ron and she is very involved with her children and their children. They have a good life together in her view and there is much to preserve. Ron is an active, youthful person who feels anything but old. He loves to be relevant and although he takes pleasure in his children and grandchildren, he has not foreclosed on ambitions for himself. He fantasizes about other women and longs for romantic excitement. Settling and growing old are threatening to him. It feels like end-of-life rather than a period of stability and deepening of opportunities including relationships. He announces that he wants out. He acts coldly and this both shocks and deeply disturbs Sally. The break-up is tense and divisive. Both must make do on considerably less money. She is alone and misses her husband desperately. He has what he wants for better or worse.

Consequently, in considering post-divorce adjustment, we cannot think of one age group alone. Both have their challenges while the paths are different. In the first, hypothetical example of a couple in their early forties, we could surmise that the divorce might have been indicated even if it was not a joint project from the outset. The initiating spouse has reached a limit of tolerance for a situation that remained unfixed and unfixable in his or her mind. Hopefully, they tried to repair the union but it could have gone too far. The desire was no longer measurable at least in one of them.

In the second example, however, the indications are vague. Is this an aging crisis turned into a marital problem? Although no one should hold a spouse in a union against their will, does this not constitute a type of acting out with destructive consequences for both parties? Where does this leave the suffering wife who finds herself with few prospects? Her married friends, constituting the majority of her social network, look at her differently. He has his new life and quickly finds a girlfriend. She is more alone than she has ever been.

When divorce is the wrong solution, adjustment is made that much harder. Emotionally, the left spouse does not even have the comfort of knowing that a bad situation has come to an end. It is usually more traumatic in this case or at least more likely to be a trauma as well as a rupture. In this regard, sleep and concentration problems, mood and anxiety symptoms as well as obsessive preoccupation with the leaving spouse are common. Sometimes anger takes hold but not in all cases. Some ex-spouses in this category continue to love and even idealize the partner that left them for reasons they may or may not understand or accept. Depressed feelings are frequently observed. No one should underestimate the toll that divorce can take especially when there was no control or input into it happening.

Even when divorce is well indicated, adjustment is complicated by numerous factors. As there is a healthy way to leave a marriage, some appreciation for the trials and tribulations of post-divorce adjustment can help ease the way.

One step at a time

It is understandable that the topsy-turvy of divorce creates a strong motivation to pick up the pieces and move forward as quickly as possible. This is true for all parties—the one who initiated the break-up and the partner obliged to go along. The reasons for this are varied but certainly some people simply want to get on with their life whilst others seek to deny that anything major occurred, as if to acknowledge a loss would be more than the other deserves or more than one could bear. The major impetus, in this mindset, is to begin dating or, as is often the case, to re-partner quickly. It is not surprising, though, to learn that these turnaround relationships are at high risk of failing.

The idea that partners are replaceable, however, might be true when it comes to dependencies but it certainly does not apply to intimacies. The latter can only be developed slowly and in the right mental state. Dependencies are characterized by a wish to be looked after and to have security needs met. Intimacies, on the other hand, are love relationships that reflect a coming together in the co-creation of a shared life. Dependencies carry the implicit expectation that the other will be the answer while intimacies create opportunities to find answers on our own terms. Intimacies are founded in actual experiencing together, not simply words and promises. We can only come to know others through experiencing them over time rather than just listening to what they say or espouse as beliefs or values. In this regard, the worst gossip can lay claim to being a private person. Others attest to kindness until they actually have to be kind.

It is understandable that the severe disruption of divorce leads to the search for comfort and companionship. It is wrenching to be alone without another's company. The urge to replace the lost partner emerges from many levels: physical, social, and psychological. In any case, dating is cumbersome, risky, full of situations that could promise a lot and still deliver little. The urge to find someone compatible in short order to fill the hole can be hard to resist. In terms of "love", we can tell ourselves what we want to believe. Like shopping for food when hungry, the situation is not conducive to making good choices.

One step at a time represents an alternative perspective. Adjusting to divorce is a very real phase that requires particular attention. Divorce is not something simply to get over like recovery from an illness. Disruption in core relationships is always deeply unsettling and this certainly applies to marital unions. Could anyone avoid mourning the loss of a loved one, especially someone towards whom feelings were extremely complex and conflicted? We live in a society, however, where technology has revolutionized the meeting process. Online dating sites offer almost instant reprieve to the motivated with a credit card. There is no need to wait to create a space for reflection, consolidation, grieving, and new learning. "Self help" from this point of view is aimed at avoiding the painful past and moving forward. Short-term relief, however, carries high risks for the future.

As much as the unraveling and rupture of a union represents a major loss, perhaps the comparison between divorce and death is overdone. But to what else would we compare such a loss? True, no one actually dies but for many people something very precious dies. Human beings only mourn bit by bit through a process of gradual detachment from what and whom we loved. Broken marriages, thus, have to be mourned. The "who" that is lost is clearer than the "what" that is lost. It is the death of a dream and an expectation that somebody we loved enough to marry will not grow old with us and be our partner for life. Moreover, marriages are deeply personal encounters that leave an indelible trace on the self. The individual has to adjust to this change in circumstance and gradually regain her or his former shape and texture as a single person.

Much like the widow or widower although without universal sympathy, the transition between being situated in a committed, often legal and religiously sanctioned union to being a single person with a new frame of reference is emotionally complex. Of course, there is profound loss but served in a cocktail with other emotions and challenges such as anger, rejection, failure, trepidation, and hope. There are logistical changes and lifestyle alterations that come all at once. Children need special attention over this transitional period and the adult might be hard pressed to find much personal time to focus on him or her self, especially where childcare is a major responsibility. Clearly, at the outset, divorce causes important shifts and changes in lifestyle, economic status, and relationships with friends and community.

One step at a time reflects an appreciation that the first goal is to consolidate, find a new center of being, allowing for the severe disruption of separation to settle and accepting that now is not the time to make major decisions. How long is difficult to say. Mourning is both physical and psychological. Some people mourn memory by memory; others grieve less consciously under the surface of their life. There is no singular pattern although those who bypass mourning and who rebound into life's fast lane of new relationships take major emotional and life risks. Failure to grieve does not dispense with grief as if out of sight means out of mind. Rather, it seals grief within the body and mind where there is no chance of resolution. Risk of clinical depression or anxiety rises as well as psychosomatic dysfunction when the body must express what the mind won't feel.

Parenting becomes more of a challenge when marriages break up. Upset parents are often too much in the grip of their own feelings to effectively parent in the short term. There is a gap between what children need during the transition and what they often get. From the kids' perspective, life becomes unglued and the two people most important to their security and continuity are too upset to be available. This is most often a temporary phase but in an attempt to put up a brave front and cope for the sake of the children, personal mourning is more difficult and prolonged.

One way of bypassing or minimizing grief is to assume a simplistic and fault finding perspective that focuses on blame of the spouse. Part of grieving is to begin to accept responsibility and to appreciate our own role in the marital breakdown. This is a central tenet of ethical divorce. Attributing blame, however, sidesteps this stage and lays blame solely on the failings or actions of the partner or spouse.

Hence, we are likely to hear statements such as: "She cheated on me", or, "He was always angry and unhappy", or, "She was eager to fool around before she got pregnant and after there were only excuses." There is often a confusion of cause and effect. This leads to not really delving into the impact of one's behavior on the other person and the cycle of projections and misalignment ending in marital impasse.

Of course, it is true that unions take two to fail and the ex-partner does bear actual responsibility. Nonetheless, the major advantage of reflecting on our own role is that it opens a door for self-discovery and offers something concrete on which to focus inquiry. It is not about blame but rather self-understanding and insight. The ex-partner who can acknowledge failings and frailties has a big advantage when it comes to future encounters over the individual claiming victimhood.

Again, there is no cookie cutter approach when it comes to the human condition and there are boundaries that must not be crossed in any relationship. Physical violence, addictions and sexual acting out do victimize spouses. It would be ludicrous and deeply cynical for the victim of spousal assault, for example, to have to claim responsibility for being attacked. Yet, that individual might be helped a great deal by understanding why they accepted such a relationship or found themselves in it in the first place. In other words, there is always something important to understand that will promote self-development and can be deemed essential to future success. There is no greater teacher than learning from experience. This takes time, however, and in many cases can be aided by counseling or psychotherapy as well as speaking with close friends, siblings, clergy or wise, empathic family members.

Let's look at an example.

Beth married Glenn when they were in their early twenties. It was too young from her parents' perspective but they had confidence in their daughter and, although they expressed concern at the time, they went along. Glenn was a serious political science student. Smart, academically strong, and very motivated to conquer the world. He joined the civil service and promotions came quickly. Three children followed: two boys and then a girl. They bought a few increasingly larger and grander houses in quick succession.

Then, seemingly at the apex of their rapid success, it all fell apart. Glenn was drawn to Jenny who worked in the same building. She was certainly more adventurous than the stable, home-centered Beth. Jenny proved to be an elixir to Glenn. He evaded, lied, and went through all forms of machination to be with Jenny. Soon, of course, Beth found out. Glenn could not imagine continuing with Beth when he compared her to Jenny, he said. He wanted Jenny, his children half of the time, for Beth to begin working full-time and for a favorable financial settlement because it was his hard work that had produced their lifestyle in the first place. The marriage broke up amidst his demands and entitlements and Beth's despair and growing anger.

The children initially gravitated to Jenny partly out of fear that not accepting her would lead to the loss of their dad. Beth's life was turned upside down and Glenn blamed her for making the separation difficult. Tensions escalated dramatically as lawyers became involved.

Glenn's relationship with Jenny proved highly unstable while Beth shortly met a nice man, also separated, whom she dated until she realized that this was entirely premature. She had wanted comfort and to rediscover what she had enjoyed so much in her marriage.

Glenn criticized Beth for worrying more about the kids than him. She had been a reluctant social partner, he observed, and did not play her part to help him advance his career. He had little insight into the emotional factors that had sent him rocketing out of the union he once appeared to treasure.

In this snapshot, the telltale signs of a break-up without an appropriate space for reflection and consolidation is apparent. In his defense, Glenn related that there had been sterility during the last years of the marriage and he had emotionally drifted by the time Jenny came into his life. In any case, he might add, what example would it have been for his children if he simply settled? Beth might note that she missed adult company and found the humdrum of ferrying children to activities too limiting. She wanted some reprieve and to know that she could attract other men. In other words, neither felt the need to retract, take stock, think, feel, and figure out what it all means and who they are in this new version of self and life.

The impulse to act can be very strong. Action occurs at the level of the psyche that is close to the drives and passions. Consequences are immediate. Glenn is typical of people who prefer to act rather than ponder. His marital disenchantment did not lead to emotional distress as much as it took the form of action meant to address the source of distress, which was, in his mind, Beth. His solution was Jenny even before it was divorce. In turn, Beth turned to another quite quickly, less out of urgency and more because it met short-term needs and answered questions and self doubts. In the interim, this liaison helped her feel desirable as a woman again, which bolstered self-esteem.

The couple's young children accepted these new partners because they were not yet at the age where they might take their own stand or suffer loyalty conflicts. One can only speculate, however, at the deeper meaning conveyed by an adult world that sheds and replaces partners almost overnight.

Emphasising the far ranging effects of divorce, the late Dr. Judith Wallerstein followed 131 children of divorce for twenty-five years of longitudinal research. The findings were unexpected in their stark portrayal of difficulties, underscoring the problems children of divorce could face in achieving emotional and sexual intimacy, as well as commitment to marriage and parenthood.[2]

As much as recovery from divorce is routinely measured in years, many people in this situation do not take time to pull back and reflect on their lives. They underestimate the complexity of the life change and how difficult this can be. Coming to grips with one's part in the break-up can be painful and difficult. Many would prefer to accept simple rationalizations and excuses. There is an internal pressure to avoid grieving and reflection by seemingly replacing what is lost. The hazard, however, is that the whole project backfires as these new relationships prove to be more problematic than the one just left. Confusion consumes the family at this point and stability is undermined.

Even without children, the loss of a marriage is major and is often transformative. When these intimate and significant unions rupture, identity is strained. Relations are broken that extend beyond the two people involved. Lifestyle changes occur. Legal conflicts can erupt in people who have never experienced anything close to this before. It matters hugely when someone we believed in and loved enough to marry or call them our partner decides they want rid of us. Even for the partner initiating the separation, the process of killing a marriage carries deep emotional resonance. Guilt, shame, loss, turning our back on someone we promised to protect and love is never easy. Having others, close couple friends, neighbors, and family by marriage refusing to have anything to do with us can be hard to bear.

Further, the more the rationale for the break-up is justified with expedient phrases such as "drifting apart", the more risk is uploaded into the life and relationships that follow. These generalized and superficial justifications mask the deeper truths that are needed to become smarter and wiser. Without new learning and a deepening of insight, solutions are at significant risk of being inappropriate or unstable.

I am not implying that newly separated people hide in some back corner. Self-care is extremely important during this phase as it is often a period of angst and loss. On the other hand, retaining a private space where one can meaningfully work through what has occurred and why it happened is vital. This will pay dividends in the future. Sometimes this can only be done with the assistance of a counselor or therapist but not necessarily. Therapy is a personal choice and not always required as long as space for examination and reflection exists.

Others find writing or journaling to be particularly helpful. For example, one could narrate the history of the marriage from the perspective of the self without reference to the other's failings. It helps not to dwell exclusively on how the other failed or their misdeeds. This is not a legal document intended to marshal a defense. Instead, it helps to write about the experience of the relationship, motivations for entering into it, ways of relating, resolving conflicts, communicating, and feeling. Were there blind spots and, if so, why did we choose not to see? Did we mislead our self, believe the unbelievable, make excuses, take shortcuts, sell ourselves short, expect too little or too much? Was the chosen partner in the image of the father for a woman; in the image of the mother for a man; or, rather, the "unfather" or "unmother"? What could this say about the impact of origins on romantic choices?

Marriages are very powerful relationships that can accomplish a great deal but they are also limited in scope. In their proper place, they can meet many important needs. They need to be directed at meeting the right needs in the right couple. Needs for intimacy and sharing are the proper purview of marriage. Hence, marriages favor care over caretaking, romance over simple sexual excitement, and knowledge of the other over impression, and mutuality over self-interest. These are essentially "adult" progressive needs. Of course, everyone occasionally brings more regressive needs to the partner. This is inevitable in life. On the other hand, if too much of the overall relationship is dedicated to regressive needs, the marriage has a high probability of failing. For example, if the marriage is formed mainly to counter fears of being alone or to resolve a family of origin issue, the odds are strong that the union will falter.

Let's take an example. Edward was troubled if not haunted by images of himself as an awkward, unattractive adolescent who had trouble getting a date. He married Diane, a successful but emotionally brittle young woman in his circle whose early family life had been quite troubled. Edward was thrilled that such an accomplished woman would accept him. He felt better about himself in her presence although the insecurities never really abated. Two children followed in quick succession. Confronted with the heavy demand of two very young children, Diane turned into a micro-manager, finding fault with Edward and railing at him for perceived failings. At this juncture, Diane's success paled in value next to his fury about how he was being treated and his lack of real affection for her. Despite marital counseling, the union ended six years after it had begun.

Even failed marriages, however, might have met some important needs and not all sectors of the relationship necessarily fail. For instance, a couple struggling with how to make decisions without one or the other feeling bullied might have a great time together when they travel with none of the usual strains evident. Otherwise, there are many examples of couples that had a strong sexual connection despite a miserable relationship. It is doubtful though whether sex or travel would ever be enough to keep a couple together. Ultimately, as I have noted, marriages are only resilient when they are platforms for intimacy. Money, sex, security needs, and even children can carry weight but will on their own not usually prevent a bad union from ending.

In this same vein of unhealthy motives for marriage, dependency without intimacy tends to lead frequently to relationship breakdown. Relationships, which mainly prop up one or both partners in the face of life fears, also do not fare well. In addition, there are character traits that create specific and notable risks in a relationship: selfishness, selflessness, exploitative personalities, argumentativeness, and excessive self-preoccupation, among other traits, undermine a capacity for intimacy. Personality disorder in one or both partners can be extremely hard on a union or marriage because adaptive skills are limited and adjustment capacity suffers greatly as a result.

In summary, in the aftermath of the break-up, the two partners must redefine themselves and often their relationship. Events have to mean something personal and particular about both protagonists in the failed union. It cannot only be about others and who did what to whom. Reflecting on a failed marriage is a way to create meaning that gets beyond the dimension of supposed conduct. Finding meaning helps deepen self-understanding, which in turn bolsters growth and self-maturing. This paves the way for new learning and less pain in the future. Those who simply enact their lives without pausing and taking time to adjust and think through issues are often destined to repeat the same problems over and over. Pre-existing personality issues and maladaptive traits further complicate the process and make this reflective phase more difficult although no less necessary.

Rebuilding a life: getting it together

The implications of divorce go well beyond the relationship between the two participants. Indeed, the dislocation can be drastic and encompass family relations, friendships and community support mechanisms. A change in neighborhood as well as changes in economic circumstance is commonplace. Single parenting comes with its own major stresses, as does losing everyday contact with children and being forced into what can be perceived as an arbitrary and restrictive schedule. In other words, the rip and tear of divorce can make one feel that life is in tatters.

Where children are involved and custody disputes erupt, the loss of control can add substantially to the impact crater of divorce. Family law imposes its own template on parental disputes and, in the absence of parental agreement, the judiciary can make momentous decisions in the children's interests independent of parental wishes. This can be very stressful in its own right and occurs in addition to powerful emotions surrounding the loss of the marriage.

Mainly, the issue of disruption is more problematic for the one left and less for the leaver. Being in control of the loss and getting what one wants is a useful salve to the messiness of divorce. On the other hand, even when marriages end by mutual decision, the adjustment can be difficult and emotionally taxing. Divorce is not a single moment event that quickly passes. It is a long, drawn out process that can have implications well into the future. The more reason then why it has to be done right.

For instance, Beverly, aged sixty-two, was deeply involved with her in-laws over her long marriage. She had experienced a difficult relationship with her own late father and took special comfort in her close link with her father-in-law and husband's aunt. The couple had two children, a daughter married with children of her own and an unattached son with personality problems who lived in another city.

When Beverly's husband unilaterally ended the marriage, the connection with his family quickly eroded. Her father-in-law died shortly after the break-up and Beverly was relegated to the fringe of the funeral. The relationship with the son that had been tenuous in the past became distant as he sided with his father over his mother. Because her husband made an issue, his extended family members, with whom Beverly was especially close, withdrew completely.

To make matters worse, the relationship with Beverly's married friends changed, as she was no longer part of a couple. Beverly felt tarnished and blamed as if others believed that she must have done something terrible to have her husband leave her at this stage of life. Her daughter was supportive for sure but refused to discuss or even tell her when she was seeing her dad who quickly became involved in another relationship. Beverley experienced mounting losses in many sides of her life all seemingly based on her husband's desire to end their union.

Need I say more to illustrate how severe the dislocating losses can be in divorce? In the case of younger couples, the rupture can be equally disruptive and the changes immense. The matrimonial home might get sold and the individual has to adjust to divorce and a new neighborhood simultaneously. The loss of financial security or simply having to depend on an ex-partner who resents paying or who looks for ways to pay less can be scary and disturbing.

Apart from the host of problems facing newly minted single parents, there is the issue of becoming a single person once again. Marriage encourages people to define themselves through the couple, as so much of social life and identity is expressed through the couple dimension. Divorce eliminates this aspect of identity and lifestyle. Even in the case of conflictive or empty marriages, the couple element can still assume importance. When the couple life ends, identity has to be redefined in different terms.

My impression, as well, is that there is a fundamental difference between a single woman or man and a divorced person who is now single. By definition, being single opens the possibility of uniting with another as a couple. It is a developmental readiness for adult attachment whether the individual actualizes the potential or not.

Divorced/single is not an inevitable stage of readiness but an existential predicament. Some feel that they are "damaged goods", which is far too harsh a perspective but commonplace. Nevertheless, it is true that something has changed and this in turn changes the individual. Considering that remarriages are less successful statistically than first unions emphasizes the challenge faced by divorced/singles. The divorced/single knows first hand about the challenges of marriage or its equivalent but it is important not to identify with the failure, which is precisely what the "damaged goods" comment implies.

Divorce is a failure, personal as well as relational, but no one is spared failing in life. Mainly, it is how we handle failure that is more determining than failure itself. In this regard, divorce should not be treated as a brand or label but as an opportunity to learn and deepen one's personality and insights. Indeed, the issue is not whether there has been a divorce but whether the person can articulate what has been learned and, in particular, their specific contribution to the problem. Hence, getting it together following divorce requires that we do not treat the failure as a self-defining blemish or fate that can never be erased. It happened and there were likely problems and issues on both sides.

Unfortunately, many in this situation do not as much get it together as flee from the failure by leaping into new encounters or, the converse, hiding from the world. Neither strategy is good in the long run.

The first step in terms of rebuilding a life is to deliberately set out to reconstruct social and support networks. This includes informing relevant people and services that would be better able to respond in a helpful way because they know of this change in relationship status. Doctors, children's teachers, and important neighbors come to mind, as this is significant information for them to better and more sensitively meet the divorced person's needs.

Connections with old friends need to be remade. Perhaps these links were sidelined during the years of the marriage or contact was minimized. Which relationships will survive the break-up and which won't needs to be determined. Some will strengthen and others will go by the wayside. It may be impossible to continue friendships with someone who still associates with an ex-spouse who cheated, lied and betrayed us. There will likely be a significant shake up. Divorce creates social divides particularly when there are hard feelings and continuing conflict or controversy.

Some prior acquaintances, however, can be transformed into friendships over time. Other friendships, though, might not pass muster in the new reality. Either these friends will disappoint excessively or, in turn, they might withdraw from the now separated friend for their own reasons.

Take the situation where two women are friendly along with their husbands. One woman gets divorced and the other woman, her longstanding friend, cuts her off because the status of her friend has changed. She now views her divorced/ single friend as a potential rival and is uncomfortable socializing with her any longer.

In another example, two men are friendly and the couples also spend time together. When one marriage breaks up, the divorced man moves to an apartment and establishes a single life. The wife in the still married couple becomes uncomfortable and worries that her husband will envy his friend's new single circumstance. She becomes upset when he wants to hang out too much with the friend. The married man is concerned for his wife's distress and withdraws from his separated friend to appease his partner. The divorced/single man is very hurt by this action and cuts off his friend for being weak and lacking "balls".

In this life rebuilding phase, it is important to assess one's needs and know what is required. Babysitters, health professionals, social service support organisations and family members including grandparents on both sides are all important connections. Likewise, building in opportunities for leisure, fitness, and recreational activities from the outset are essential.

Much of the chronic stress of divorce occurs because the mudslide of emotions, changes and added responsibilities tend to swamp the individual. Conscientiously working on constructing a fabric of significant and supportive connections can make the difference between coping and sinking. For instance, family service centers and health teams often offer programs for newly divorced people, especially those with children and major family responsibilities. These programs open a door to other support services. The reason why these services exist is because early stage divorce is a huge stressor and known to be profoundly disruptive to life. What is critical is to make use of them.

It is important, however, not to "medicalize" the problem of divorce. Although often a shock and a blow especially if one is on the receiving end, it is natural to feel sad and anxious. There is no need to take antidepressant medication, for example, because one is upset for a specific and clear reason. In other words, sometimes feeling depressed is the appropriate emotion for the situation. Worry for the future, guilt, and even shame for what feels like a public failing are all typical feelings and thoughts. The presence of complicated feelings does not in itself constitute a mental disorder nor is it an indication for medication.

Being organized and following a reasonable sleep-wake cycle and diet can help the body and mind cope in the initial phase of divorce. Being active and in communication with friends and relatives can also assist. There is no need to advertise one's divorce as if this is all that is important but, at the same time, hiding it like a painful secret is not good for body or soul.

Of course, if psychological or physical symptoms persist and are so strong that adjustment is impaired then some intervention is certainly warranted. This could include medication, psychotherapy, or both. Part of the challenge is to assess one's needs accurately and put those services in place that will support healthy adjustment. Hence, seeing a counselor to promote the adjustment process might then preclude seeing a more specialized clinician later on or requiring medication to handle intrusive symptoms.

Holmes and Rahe in 1967 developed a life change scale that ranked various life changes according to rankings provided by 5,000 participants. Apart from the death of a spouse in this critical study, there was nothing more stressful than marital separation and divorce.[3] Researchers were able to demonstrate a positive correlation between a one year life change score and subsequent medical illness. The idea is not to suggest that marital break-ups make people sick but that the extent of life disruption should not be minimized either. The research underscores the importance of self-care when facing stressful life events and why establishing a solid support and lifestyle network from the outset can make a world of difference. Divorce is never a cakewalk.

Thus, we can identify two major factors in rebuilding a life: self-care and accountability. Self-care takes into account the enormity of life changes that often occur through divorce including economic, social, and psychological. Accountability is very different from self-blame and shares no common features. Indeed, blame whether towards the self or the other, can be a way of denying responsibility for our role in fateful life events such as major relationship breakdowns. Rather, accountability is the active process of self-reflection or examination in pursuit of deeper truths so that we can better know what has happened and how to avoid repetition and avert claiming this as a fate to be endlessly repeated.

What to do with toxic emotions

The ties that bind can be emotionally very strong in divorce even in defiance of logic and reason. Separation is both a physical and emotional process of disinvestment and this can be incredibly taxing and complicated. Marriages are forged at a very fundamental level combining desire with hopes, dreams, and attachments. Hence, we surrender these attachments slowly and, in some cases, the loss feels so great that identity is imperiled in the short term. Many freshly separated people are particularly vulnerable or brittle. Emotions run amok; behavior can be erratic and judgment faulty. It is the worst of times, only made worse perhaps because no one has really died.

Sadness, the wish to cling, fear, insecurity and loss mingle with more toxic emotions such as vengefulness, bitterness, and envy. These toxic emotions are more intense when one is on the receiving end of divorce or where the partner is perceived as betraying or going out of their way to make the process as painful as possible.

When a spouse busts the partner's world apart, the wish to retaliate is understandable. Hurt pride and the desire to inflict pain in kind are common feelings. This is not true of all separated spouses. Retaliation is meaningful to a subset of people who associate it with justice and regaining equilibrium. Perhaps this is truest when the leaver seems to suffer no consequences while the left spouse feels shattered. In this case, one act of retaliation is sometimes enough to let these feelings go. In other cases, fantasies persist and actual acts of vengeance and punishment remain an issue for some time.

Proportions vary but usually they are aimed at making life difficult and treating the other as one has been treated. For instance, spouses who pay support or alimony may make the other wait every month for a check rather than arrange direct deposit. Checks come late, arrangements are foiled by latent uncooperativeness meant to irritate and punish. Sharing children offers ample opportunity to withhold information, refuse to accommodate a request, being purposely unreasonable or simply communicating a dirty look or taking a verbal shot when it is cost free to do so. The problem is that toxic retaliatory actions can easily poison a post-divorce relationship and limit capacity to function for some wider cause such as children. Moreover, hatred might cover up emptiness but it won't solve it.

The chronically vengeful person is unforgiving and even ruthless in pursuit of getting even. They might view this as retributive justice but no matter how it is described the mindset is the same. Resisting the urge to punish can be hard for many ex-partners, adding fuel to the dysfunctional fire that characterizes many divorces.

The conscious aim of vengeance is to achieve peace of mind or satisfaction by extracting a pound of flesh. Beyond this one dimension, however, the vengeful spouse is struggling with his or her own sense of emotional damage. The need for the continuing love of the spouse is usually an important ingredient. At a deeper psychic level, the injuries of childhood that were also experienced as damaging to the self, still linger. The need for vengeance is particularly fostered when the individual feels injured beyond any capacity for healing. I have not usually encountered the chronic form of vengeance unless there are childhood antecedents that affected self-love and the capacity for self-care.

Faced with the rising tide of retaliatory emotions and fantasies, what can be done? Vengeance is almost always obsessive as if the individual cannot rest until they hurt the former partner as much as they have been hurt (although this is never reached). It is fostered by feelings of deprivation and a sense that part of the self did not survive the loss. Hence, only hatred can keep or recapture a connection that has been lost.

Countering this devastated feeling is essential. Of course, there is life after divorce but this is not obvious to the person in the throes of divorce vengeance. Having outlets to speak about deeper feelings of loss, sadness, failure, damage, and emptiness are essential to healing the vengeful state of mind. It is not just the act of filling a life. The challenge is to acknowledge how much the partner was needed, how difficult it is to detach and how hurt he or she feels. Problems with self-preservation and self-care need to be confronted as these are likely lacking. This must be done in an empathic space with another, often a psychotherapist, who knows about psychic trauma and its soul damaging consequences.

Indeed, the difference between a stress and a trauma is the presence of an empathic other to cut through the aloneness and give a sense of presence at a critical point of need. Certainly, persistent fantasies of revenge are a valid indication for psychotherapy in that the trauma is never experienced as in the past.

Perhaps the most malignant form of the revenge mentality concerns a divorced parent who works to turn the kids against the former partner. This is commonly called "parental alienation". In these cases, a smiling demeanor that keeps the malevolent rage in the background might mask the damage of divorce. There is no acknowledgement of revenge feelings or even hatred. The children are described as showing independent judgment, as if they have simply come to the same rational conclusion that the estranged parent is unworthy or harmful. Indirectly, the alienating parent feeds their bottomless emotional neediness by claiming all of the children's love and loyalty. The family climate is twisted to make it impossible for the children to love two parents at the same time. Loving the other parent is discredited and this fills the empty space left by divorce with the children's love and admiration. As a result, alienated children can see no wrong in the alienator and no good in the vilified or rejected parent. This is discussed in greater detail and depth in Chapter Seven.

At all levels from conscious vengeance to parental alienation, however, deprivation and the loss of needed love and support is behind the preoccupation with hateful retaliation. Only by articulating the sense of abandonment, despair and loss and making some real connection with another human being can the vengeful feelings recede. The therapist in this case has to help the individual find his or her way back to the continuum of time where there can be a past and therefore a future. Vengeful people like vengeful societies act outside of the dimension of time. Years can go by but the injuries and wounds are treated as freshly damaging and current.

Am I then saying that all vengeance or at least the wish for retaliation is inappropriate? I would make a distinction here between avenging and revenging. Avenging a wrong means to inflict punishment as a way of bringing justice to bear on a wrong that was done. Society avenges crimes through the criminal justice system. Sometimes an ex-spouse harbors a legitimate grievance about how they were treated. For instance, carrying on a prolonged affair and then when discovered blaming the unwitting partner for all problems. The left spouse might let others know what happened and refuse to protect the rejecting partner from the optics of their actions. There is justice to this approach that avenges a wrong by insisting on accountability.

Revenge, on the other hand, is focused on inflicting pain and punishment to even the score. It is aimed at hurting the other probably more than one has been hurt. In other words, the divorced person might be saying: "You ruined my life and now I will ruin yours." This would include the myriad of ex-spouses assessed over the years who claim that the former partner threatened to take the children away. Retribution can become a fixation, overwhelming the personality and placing hatred at the forefront of motivation.

Hence, we should provide some place for limited avenging actions that relate to the need for justice and distinguish these from revenging actions that seek the downfall and destruction of the other or of their wellbeing.

Examples of an avenging spouse that come to mind:

- Telling the rejecting spouse to "fuck off" when he abruptly acts civilly and is friendly in a social setting after months of shabby and cold treatment.
- Denying or failing to defend the former partner's misconduct when this is raised.
- Failing to do what the spouse had formerly expected and enjoyed as a dividend of the marriage.

In contrast, revenge knows no bounds. Examples of a revenging spouse that come to mind include:

- Submitting a false address change to the post office to divert mail.
- Informing the tax authorities about some irregularity to create as much trouble as possible for the ex-spouse.
- Making serious but unfounded allegations to child protection authorities or police as a way to discredit and punish the former partner.
- Slashing tires, writing to the ex-partner's employer to instigate job loss, forcing a spouse to waste thousands on legal bills, etc.

It is also common to observe runaway competitive impulses in divorced couples with children. This helps children play one parent off the other and adds to the challenge of family adjustment post-divorce. Occasionally, competition can become so flagrant that each parent goes to great lengths to win the approval of the children with one expensive toy matched by another. Generally, however, unwarranted competition is an irritant and does not reach toxic proportions. Envy, however, is more sinister in its repercussions.

It is important to distinguish between envy and competitive jealousy. Competitive strivings relate to rivalry. The origin of this word gives a clue to its meaning. It derives from the same Latin root as the word "river". Think of two tribes competing for who would get the land next to the river. Competition thus implies a contest for supremacy. Each wants to win over the other but there is no destructive intent implied.

Envy implies malice or ill will. It stems from the Latin signifying grudge and looking with hostile intent. One who envies sees the other as having what can never be obtained. Hence, envy inspires the wish to spoil it for the other. The envious person covets and hates the other for what they possess.

Paul left his wife, Lorna, after approximately ten years. It was a contentious and strife torn marriage. He was glad to escape and not too long after found bliss with a somewhat older woman who offered affection and serenity. He was grateful and happy. Lorna was full of envy for what Paul achieved. She had experienced a difficult relationship with her own father who had doubts about his daughter's capacity to get along with others. In her state of spite, she tried hard to ruin Paul's happiness mainly through manipulating the loyalties of their daughter. This adolescent child eventually found the situation unbearable and after cutting her father off for a year reversed position and cut off her mother. Lorna then came for treatment but found it incredibly hard not to focus on Paul's failings and how abusive and allegedly assaultive he had been in their union. She struggled to acknowledge her envy of Paul's capacity to love and be loved. She greedily demanded all the love that Paul or the daughter could offer. Underneath, she did not think that she could love anyone.

The role of counseling and psychotherapy

Counseling can be extremely helpful for people who are undergoing separation and divorce. It is perhaps not for everyone but the abundance of counselors available in many communities speaks to the demand for these services. Indeed, talented and experienced counselors often make a big difference.

Counselors can be graduates of social work, educational psychology programs or pastoral counseling studies. They are not traditional health professionals but neither do they need to be. The aim of counseling is to help foster stability and growth. In this regard, such services can be extremely useful especially in the maelstrom of divorce. Specifically, counseling can help grieve the loss, think through the issues and decisions that have to be made, counter the emergence of toxic emotions and set a course for life after divorce. Counselors in this category can also have specific knowledge and expertise in relationship problems within couples and families. Hence, they are well placed to provide the type and level of assistance needed.

One caveat, however, concerns counselors who would steer the focus almost entirely to the failings and poor character of the former spouse. In my view, this is based on a gross misunderstanding of what comprises "support" for someone trying to come to grips with a broken union. In its original meaning, support meant the support of the ego or self in its relations with drives and conscience. In other words, a self under siege needs support to adapt to the difficult and complex circumstances it is facing.

Reducing the concept of support to the idea that the counselor should stand behind the aggrieved client and point out all the faults and failings of the ex-partner might be appealing in the short term. In the end, however, it leads nowhere. Without a focus on the client's contribution to the break-up, struggles with guilt, shame, anger, and fear, among the plethora of possible emotions, will stymie real personal progress. It is at minimum a lost opportunity and at worse an abuse of process that will set back the process of adjustment.

Counselors who work in this model of simplistic advocacy are inclined to support the virtues and victim status of the client. Examples include:

- Writing letters of support to be used in court often praising the client as an excellent parent even though the counselor has never observed this aspect of the client's life.
- Spending hours focusing on the apparent diagnosis of the ex-spouse often elaborating on particularly negative descriptions such as "narcissistic" or "sociopathic" to emphasize the extent of the disorder.
- Assuming that the subjective perceptions or version of truth espoused by the client are objectively valid.
- Criticizing the ex-spouse and validating the stance of the client to support their cause.

I am not suggesting that counselors should disbelieve their clients or that some discussion of the ex-partner is not necessary and inevitable. Of course it is. Moreover, there are situations where the spouse is a severely disordered individual, which needs to be understood and put in context. On the other hand, it is low hanging fruit to take on the ex-partner not present to defend him or her self. Further, the majority of marriages and committed unions fail with joint participation. It is not a solo enterprise even when it doesn't work.

There can be much to discuss that can be extremely helpful to ease adjustment and learning from experience. Expectations, problems handling conflict, difficulties with trust, emotional dependence or problems achieving or feeling safe within an intimacy, among many other possibilities, could be relevant. If there is no process and opportunity for new learning then the counseling has failed no less than the marriage.

Where symptoms or repetitive failure in relationships are dominant features then psychotherapy as compared to counseling is likely indicated. Symptoms could include anxiety, insomnia, excessive weight loss or gain, deep insecurity, despair, suicidal feelings, among other issues and preoccupations. Sometimes symptoms have more to do with behavior or personality features such as perversions, chronic involvement in unlikely scenarios that defy common sense or are self-defeating, lack of control over anger or other impulses, withdrawal, and self-isolation. Those who have a history of failed unions would be better off taking the opportunity to examine their life and see what threads, assumptions or life themes predict what has occurred.

Psychotherapy is a treatment and is best administered by a health professional or equivalent with the required training. Examining one's life under the guidance of a therapist is not necessary for everyone but for many it is essential. Such a calamitous event as a divorce can be the precipitant that brings underlying problems to the foreground. In this sense, it represents a catastrophe but also an opportunity to come to grips with what ails and to acquire the new learning to make a difference in the future. Psychotherapy does not change who and what we are. It does however create freedom of choice where none existed previously. It also expands awareness. These can make a major difference.

The role of mediation

Mediated settlements short-circuit what can be a potentially protracted, emotionally costly, and financially depleting divorce process. The process is inherently ethical in that it is based on a collaborative, symmetrical system of negotiations guided by a neutral, skilled professional mediator. In the best of cases, the two partners sit with the mediator and are assisted through the decision-making steps needed to finalize an agreement. At the end, a shared text is produced that comprises the terms of the agreement. Each party then seeks independent legal advice to insure that their rights have been protected and nothing has been missed.

There are a number of prerequisites for this optimal mediation process to occur:

- Ability to sit in the same room
- Mutual desire and authenticity to conclude an agreement
- Sufficient capacity to understand the issues and to discuss views in depth

- Sufficient trust to engage the other and believe that the terms of the agreement will be honored
- Some capacity to resolve conflict in both parties
- No couple history of systemic violence, major power imbalance, or widespread use of intimidation.

Not all couples of course have this capability. At times, therefore, lawyers will attend mediation and assist the parties. Some incapacity can be overcome in this lawyer-assisted form of mediation. For instance, the parties and their legal counsel can work from separate rooms with the mediator going back and forth. While not as efficient, it can overcome obstacles such as one party's inability at that stage to handle the pain of the other's presence.

Unless the above criteria are met, in my view, separated couples should not attempt mediation. Doubts about motivation aside, there has to be sufficient collaborative and conflict resolution potential remaining in the couple to handle the demands of the mediation process. If the conditions for mediation are not met then the ex-couple could choose to go directly to a form of arbitration in which the arbitrator makes a decision that is binding on the parties. The idea is to find an efficient and cost effective means of alternate dispute resolution whether this is achieved through consensus (mediation) or third party resolution (arbitration).

Sometimes resolving the business of the divorce must wait for the parties first to share essential feelings and perceptions concerning what happened between them. There could be too much controversy to process or collaborate on such a pragmatic level despite the urgency of settling these issues. A leaving spouse might need to be honest with their former partner in a way that they have not been previously. If betrayal, lying or cheating occurred, there can be much that needs to be said on both sides. The optimal scenario for ending a marriage is when there was a long process of trying with both parties calling it quits on reasonable grounds. This is often, however, not the case, which adds a measure of unresolved tension and loss rather than relief.

Whatever the roadblocks, pre-mediation sessions with a counselor or therapist might be necessary before the minimal conditions can be met. In the absence of meeting the core conditions, the hazards are manifold. We should note that all pain, including emotional pain, if extreme, immobilizes progress. The very essence of mediation requires an acceptance on the part of both that something is over and something else is needed to move forward. The problem with pain is that it has no "past" and always occurs in the current now. Thus, a surfeit of pain inhibits and can even stymie mediation.

Specifically, there are many permutations that signal failed mediation. One party might highjack the process to lash out at the other and retaliate for past wrongs. They might actually conclude an accord and then refuse to sign it. Why would this occur? Mainly because "giving" the other what they want could feel unjust next to the pain and misery that the other spouse went through. In other words, it is folly to assume that only rational forces prevail and that divorcing spouses want to resolve differences and actually separate. Even if this is partly true, other more primary emotions and reactions can be easily triggered with a capacity to completely derail the process.

Of course, each situation is different but the principle is that both participants must come to the table with an open mindset in which to accomplish the business of divorce. They must be in the "après coup" of the painful experience of divorce and beyond the blunt force trauma of the "coup". If the minimal conditions are not present then a pre-mediation series of sessions is needed to reduce tensions and make success more likely. Only then can the couple constitute a past as past and turn to a new chapter.

Are there some cases that should not settle through negotiations or mediation? Perhaps. I am thinking of situations where there is unlikely to be enough respect for a mediated agreement involving the care of children to the degree that it would not be followed. Family law and the courts work within a legal structure where adherence to agreements is taken for granted. Occasionally, this might be beyond a couple's capacity to implement due to character problems, addictions or both.

Some family law lawyers, however, will push hard for clients to settle no matter what the situation is on the ground. Sometimes, though, only the court can impose the types of safeguards needed to cope with this type of situation. These are rare, however, and are usually restricted to a subset of cases referred for court assessment.

Conclusion

We are all born into relationships and this is often how we feel most alive and connected. We conceive of mother and child as foundational but this quickly extends from parents, close relatives, best friends, first loves and finally to a life partner. It forms a chain of "otherness" that supports, nurtures, and defines identity.

No wonder, then, marital rupture and divorce can leave us feeling that we have lost the thread of life. It is disconnecting and fracturing. How can we remain steady in the midst of such turbulence and destabilization? How to self-right, focus on what is essential and find the inner strength and direction to persevere and get through the journey ahead?

The word "adjustment" seems so banal to describe this journey. Yet, survivors and experts have written much about the post-divorce period. It is clearly a huge challenge for many people.

In terms of this journey, it is probably more apt to speak of the need for transformation. This implies that when long-term unions end, what is required amounts to a fundamental shift or change in how we see our lives and ourselves. This is based of course on the experience of loss, its impact on identity, but also on the very personal processing of this loss. Such a transformation augments self-knowledge, self-appreciation and offers a better sense of relationship needs for the future.

Unfortunately, many who separate avoid this unique transformation that takes effort, time and space to accomplish. Denial, rationalization and flights into romantic fancy are easier paths and might look adaptive but avoidance almost certainly raises the risk of failure in the future. Divorce requires work to remedy. There is no way around it.

CHAPTER THREE

Telling the children

Parents are universally very protective of their children and the idea of exposing kids to emotional pain, worry, and distress runs counter to every parental impulse. Yet, there is no way out when it comes to telling the children that the parents are separating. Likely, their particular situation will not be the first on the block or in the classroom. Nevertheless, it is with a heavy heart that parents make this announcement and hope for the best.

There are so many family permutations and variables that it is hard to offer a primer that would apply to every situation. The age of the child, personality, degree of emotional resilience, presence of siblings, capacity of the adults to co-parent, degree of post separation changes, among many other factors shape how the child will receive and handle the news. Hence, I would ask that the reader use this section as a general resource and guide but not as a specific prescription for managing this important communication.

On the other hand, no matter what the child's age, several broad factors apply generally:

- Be honest in the information you impart
- Gauge how much is conveyed to the age and maturity of the child
- Tell the child together and both parents should speak
- Consider telling the children separately if there is a marked difference in age
- Listen to the child as much as you tell them what is happening
- Reinforce both parents' love for the child
- Answer the child's questions but otherwise stick to the general outline of the changes to be faced
- Avoid conflict when the child is told.

Divorce is never a one step process and this includes the narrative that conveys the parents' intentions to the child. Children of all ages will resonate with the news. In some cases, there is little apparent noise and almost an under or muted reaction is observed. In other cases, children can react strongly expressing devastation and even pleading for it not to happen. They can take the event personally and erupt in anxiety, grief or hostility, which can then spill over into parent–child relationships. Much will depend on the child's emotional health and the state of the family at the time of break-up.

Hence, the initial conversation opens the process to the child and, in this regard, the "telling" can be controlled although not the reaction. The child's process and the parents' process are separate although, of course, they interact. What is at stake is an essential communication from the parents that although life will change, the parents' love and capacity to hold, protect, and nurture their children will not suffer as a result. In this regard, the parents are establishing for the child that they will continue in their parental role despite the sad fate of their union.

Consequently, telling the children is an exercise in listening but also "holding" by which I mean the capacity to contain the child's anxieties, fears, and insecurities in order to offset the feeling of catastrophe. It is a key element of the good divorce when kids are involved.

One general but important finding is that the reaction of children to the news of divorce is very much age related. Of course, other factors are also important such as culture, temperament, and how resilient and emotionally healthy the child is when the break-up occurs.

Divorces are profound events that cut a huge swathe through the family's life field. It isn't just an announcement but a cataclysmic pronouncement that life as the child has known it is about to change drastically. For the child, it is humbling in as much as all children want to be "enough" to keep their parents together. Feelings of failure, rejection, worry, sadness, and aloneness are common.

Parents who lament how much open fighting and conflict the children have witnessed might expect that the children will be relieved. In my experience, this is not usually the case. Children want their families to stay together through thick and thin, as this is the only context they have known. Divorce is an unknown and the news is rarely received with calmness or equanimity. Nevertheless, children will take their cue from their parents and they definitely respond to supportive efforts. On the other hand, the unknown of parental separation is scary for children and can raise fears of aloneness and abandonment.

Ten-year-old Jonah's parents had been separated for four years when I interviewed him. His parents shared custody and care but were frequently in a logjam when it came to making important decisions. Jonah related that he had a complete life in each home with his own room, toys, and electronics. Both parents had good jobs and were able to provide materially. Jonah stressed that he would be happy if his parents reconciled although he believed that he had mainly adjusted to the break-up. When not at school, however, he often found himself dwelling on his parents' break-up and this perplexed him. He admitted that it represented a "disaster" and still makes him sad. He acknowledged dreaming about playing family games together such as hide and seek in which his parents are together. Jonah found it reassuring to see each parent often and he did not mind frequent transitions during the week.

Jonah's experience is typical. Parental divorce is a major event in children's lives and represents one of those indelible events that are recalled with detail and context. Where were you when President Kennedy was shot? How did you learn of 9/11? When did you first learn that your parents intended to divorce?

Young children: preschool years

Young children are inherently adaptable and take their cue from the security of their attachments to their parents. Continuity of care, consistency, emotional availability, routine, and attunement to developmental needs are important ingredients to getting though the initial break-up experience.

Infants and toddlers are not as much told about the impending separation as experience a change in routine including, at least temporarily, the diminished emotional availability and responsiveness of their parents. Of course, early preschool children should be told but they will not necessarily understand until the event actually occurs. This has to do with cognitive immaturity in which they cannot as yet project new experience into the future.

It is best to tell young children closer to the leaving date in order to remain within their range of capacity to handle it. If, for instance, the child is told two to three weeks before that one parent will be moving out of the family home then both parents can refer to it and set the stage. Preparation is important. The parents should answer questions but not elaborate beyond what is asked. Ideally, the parent leaving the family home could show the child where he or she will be living.

Even young children will have questions and concerns although reaction, when it occurs, tends to happen after the break-up and not usually before. Mainly, younger children respond to the family climate of the moment. Hence, rising tensions, preoccupied parents and open fighting will cause more distress than any anticipated future leaving. The goal is of course to avoid open conflict and emotional volatility in front of the child. Overwrought parents cannot help their child contain or process feelings, making it harder for the child to understand what is occurring in their terms. Emotions that spill over in raw and turbulent form will inundate the young preschooler and create distress.

Children in the three to five year age range are old enough to feel fear, sadness, and above all, confusion. Regression is commonplace and can be quite dramatic. The three year old, for instance, might cling to a stuffed animal, wet the bed, hit a sibling and demand increased attention and soothing. The objective in telling an older preschool child is to give sufficient detail to create understanding, leave room for the child to express feelings, and reinforce love and continuity of care.

Telling a young child could take the following form:

MOMMY: Do you remember the house we showed you today; daddy will be living there in a few weeks. Mommy and daddy are not going to live together but you will be seeing daddy often and staying with him sometimes in the new house.

CHILD: But what if I miss you mommy?

MOMMY: Mommy and Daddy will be close by and you can always speak to us whenever you want.

DADDY: Mommy's here and Daddy's here and this won't change. We love you and we're both going to spend wonderful times with you.

The father might have been tempted to add details such as that the child will have a second bedroom or other details about the new home. This would be going too far in the initial telling and would only be confusing and potentially anxiety provoking. It is never what children want.

It is a bewildering communication for sure any way it is conveyed but, above all, children need to be told. Having events such as family ruptures occur without warning or explanation is entirely traumatic and would severely undermine any sense of control a child could feel over their world.

The main points to be conveyed are that mother and father are separating; one parent will be living in another house, and the child needs not fear being unloved or alone. The news is still shocking and this is unavoidable but the very act of reaching out, making connection and communicating is precisely the first step in helping a child "contain" what is transpiring entirely out of their control and desire. It might matter less precisely what is said than the fact that the parents are framing the experience for the child and this, in itself, signals a degree of control that would be reassuring.

It is hard to ask too much of a couple at the edge of marriage rupture when children are involved. Nevertheless, making efforts to spend quality one-on-one time with kids despite the situation can pay dividends in terms of child adjustment. Young children, in particular, need to know that their parents can still keep them in mind, devote time to them and allow them to feel held in the emotional sense of the word. Much as articulated in fairy tales, fears of being lost or abandoned are universal and speak to the core of early childhood anxieties. Hence, it is imperative that parents try to stay attuned to their children even while they walk this difficult and tumultuous personal path of separation and divorce.

When I have seen young children, whose parents have separated and are disputing custody and access, there are a number of general findings that could be helpful to share as much as they reflect the experience of preschool and primary school age children:

- Family drawings and play often revolve around the intact family where mommy and daddy live together happily
- Young children can readily attach to new partners without serious loyalty concerns
- They are most attached to their parents although "mother" and "father" are also role categories especially for the youngest in this segment
- Aloneness, rejection, and abandonment take on new meaning for the child, as the durability of human relatedness has to be questioned.

Primary school aged children

If there were ever a sweet spot in terms of divorce, it would be children in the five to eight year range when they are still very much dependent and accepting of their parents' decisions.

This is the age when peer friendships arise and children gravitate to new situations and caring adults such as teachers and even new partners. Loyalty conflicts are still not that common unless parental pressure comes to bear on a child's neutrality.

Of course, individual differences will always prevail but, in general, the younger primary school child is emotionally flexible and adaptable, as long as her/his emotional needs are not ignored. This appears to be true whether the primary caregiver is the mother or the father. Children are forward gazing in this phase, having usually relinquished the pull of infancy they are acquiring skills and proficiencies at a rapid pace. It is a time of relative calm developmentally and it is great time for parents. Primary school kids in the early grades are wonderful companions and seem so open and willing to explore and learn.

Parents of course are well aware of how much they enjoy their children at this phase especially after the travails of infancy and early childhood, which were so physically demanding. Now it is easy street in comparison. Thus, the fear that divorce will throw a huge wrench into the mix nags at parents at the cusp of separation.

Primary school children can be surprisingly capable but this does not mean that we should expect too much from them. Yet, telling the child can be challenging because they are old enough to understand the essential message. Mostly, they resist and might beg the parents to reconsider. They almost certainly will cry or experience upset and distress. It is a disorienting and confusing message that threatens to turn life upside down.

Children in this age range are generally more reality oriented and require facts and concrete answers to help solidify their coping. Fears become quite real and take on new meaning, including loss and abandonment. Young children need help to mourn but will grieve if their parents give them a space and help to do so.

They can also feel responsible for the break-up even if their parents tell them otherwise but this is only one possible reaction. This corresponds to a developing ethical sense apart from parental demands for obedience to rules.

Telling the primary school child should depend still on age and maturity level. But if we take the middle range and think of a seven or eight-year-old, it will help to orient the discussion.

DADDY: Mommy and I love you very much but we have not been very loving to each other. Sometimes this happens between adults like it sometimes happens with friends. Mommy and daddy are sad about it but we have decided to live in separate houses. Daddy will be staying with you in our house and mommy will be moving to a new house. It's only about ten minutes away. You will have two houses to live in.

CHILD: But how will I get to school when I am with you mommy?

MOMMY: I will take you just like now before I go to work and when daddy is taking care of you he will drive you to school.

CHILD: Daddy, do you hate mommy? I don't want two houses! I don't want Mommy to leave.

DADDY: I know you don't want this and mommy and daddy would like it to be different. I don't hate mommy. I love that mommy and I had you and thank mommy every day for you. But sometimes it doesn't work out for adults. We will always be your parents though.

MOMMY: Yes, even when daddy is caring for you, I will always call you to say goodnight. Mommy loves you very much.

Children in this age group are old enough to be concerned about their own situation and how the impending break-up will affect their lives. It could upset them, for instance, if they do not have friends on the new street or if the family home has to be sold. They will sense that changes are inevitable but they should also be assured that their parents intend to do their best to keep the rhythm of life in place.

In this regard, there is burgeoning independence at this age. School life, extracurricular activities, and peer relations are important anchors of continuity during the initial upheaval of divorce. Both parents should undertake to continue activities no matter which parent is providing residential care at the time. This helps enormously to get over the hump of the wrenching changes and stresses that children bear when their parents separate.

If children of this age appear to be struggling then it is important to respond to their comments and pick up the threads they introduce. In other words, the parent should take his or her cue from the child and not oblige the child to talk or insist on certain topics. Reassurance, expressions of love, and taking concerns seriously are important guideposts.

A child might be more sensitive than usual, more combative with siblings or fighting with friends (actually an identification with the feuding parents). Anxiety or sadness is also common. On the other hand, sometimes concerns are more practical: "Daddy doesn't know how to brush my hair or help me with my pony tail." Fears of loss can extend to favorite toys and activities.

Other times, the child will share an impression: "Mommy is always so angry and it's really annoying." Of course, it is critical not to use the opportunity to devalue the other parent. It will come back to bite us for sure, as the child will lose respect for the very people on whom he or she depends for security.

Sometimes a child will tell a parent something that should be shared with the other parent. This can be a delicate situation particularly if the child's comment mirrors or aggravates an existing wound or point of controversy. For instance, an eight-year-old boy, Billy, complained to his mother that his busy executive father was always on his cellphone. Let's imagine that the wife in this case knows perfectly well how deprived and lonely she felt in the marriage when her husband's love affair seemed to be with his work and not her. Now one of the children is mirroring the same complaint!

One can imagine the email from wife to husband: "Now you are doing to your kids what you did to me. I will not let you hurt them so you'd better change or else you could lose them." The husband responds that the son is grossly exaggerating and blames the wife for stirring up problems to punish him. We can appreciate the vicious circle and wasted energy, not to mention that the son's comment is important and should somehow be addressed.

The option is to communicate solely in a factual way without any editorial or emotional inflection. Thus, the message to the husband could be: "Billy commented at breakfast out of the blue that he feels you are too involved with your phone when you are with him. I thought you would want to know." The husband would still not like the message but he would be less likely to attack the messenger and get his back up.

Children in the five to eight-year-old range often harbor fantasies that the parents will reconcile and all will be well. These can be very pronounced and last for years. They might advocate for such an outcome. Although anger and blame tend to arise in the slightly older child, it is possible particularly if one parent is designated as the one who broke up the family. Again depending on personality, not all children will be overtly or even consciously angry.

What has startled me over the years is how many children of divorce can be amazingly adaptable and conscientious even when their parents are regressed and dysfunctional. In part the family chaos encourages these children to grow up quickly. They simply cannot afford to let go of their emotions. Thus, these kids are socially precocious and get rave reviews from teachers for how cooperative and mature they are in the classroom.

A particularly undermining factor, however, is when children become embroiled in their parents' conflict. Whatever composure they could otherwise muster goes out the window as they are drawn into the fracas. Anger at one or the other parent and taking sides severely undermines the needed zone of neutrality that allows the kids to go back and forth without excessive conflict.

This particularly applies to the older primary school years from approximately nine to twelve. Children are not simply blank slates though ready to be indoctrinated by manipulative parents eager for allies. They have their own judgments, feelings, and impressions concerning their parents and the parents' actions. In the context where they take sides, this can be extremely difficult to control.

Moreover, this is precisely the age when children can be most turned to serve as advocates and allies. Loyalty conflicts are common in the nine to twelve year age range and the older child is capable of considerable righteous anger and blame. Moral reasoning is in place by this age although it can tend to be harshly applied. If a child feels that one parent is solely to blame for the divorce then, depending on personality and context, some will blame with ferocity like a righteous judge.

We should keep in mind that many marriages end with bitterness and even betrayal, adding salt to the wound when a new partner shows up in the leaving parent's life. The situation is then ripe for a firestorm if the older child identifies with the rejected parent as victim and seeks retribution on behalf of the injured party. In this case, the child will share the victim identity and perceive the initiating parent as ruining their lives.

Of course, not all variables can be tallied to predict how a family will react. Children of divorce do not process these life-changing events in one moment in time. They return over and over to the family rupture and work it through, as they gain more insight and perspective into what occurred. The reworking, however, can start to include distorted messages that draw the child into the conflict. Yet, in calmer waters, children can form attachments to step-parents and find their equilibrium when the family environment keeps them and their needs in mind.

Both parents must react against any tendency for a child to take sides, not just the parent directly affected. Empowering children to discipline or judge parents is a bad precedent that will affect the entire family in the end. Family meetings with or without professional intervention must demonstrate that the parents can pull together and show a common front. If it happens then the children have to be told that it is not their role and neither parent accepts it. The pulling together is hugely reparative in these situations and will usually bring this polarization to a halt. Where an aggrieved parent signals implicit approval or at least passive agreement to the point of complicity then there is often no end to it.

Older children need careful handling. Thus, the parents must resist embroiling the kids in adult conflicts or expecting the children to serve as confidante or support. Some ten or eleven-year-old children are extremely capable and they can be quite independent, articulate, and skilled. Moreover, they are acutely sensitive to their parents on whom they have depended entirely since infancy. Ever more reason to be particularly prudent not to burden them. Struggling parents need to turn to family and professional resources for help rather than turning to their children. No matter how angry, resentful, or furious the parent is with their former mate, using a child to avenge a wrong will only hurt the child.

When the late Judith Wallerstein, social worker and psychoanalyst, re-interviewed a large sample of children of divorce she first studied as children twenty-five years earlier, these young adults were still struggling with what had occurred.[1] It is a lesson in the magnitude of divorce in the life of an individual and how important the ethical dimension of divorce can be to overall life adjustment.

Pubescent and adolescent years

Whether children, including pubescent and adolescent children from thirteen to eighteen years, dwell on the moment they were told of the impending divorce or not, it is a watershed event for sure. Nonetheless, it is what comes after that really gets their attention. Big changes could be in store including the sale of the family home, relocation, change of schools, less disposable family income, and parents who struggle in their own lives and with each other. This is what really matters to them and for good reason.

Teenagers have enough on their plate working on their own identity, peer and sexual relationships to welcome the intrusion of their parents' divorce. The one exception, however, in my experience, is when the parental relationship has been so chaotic or dysfunctional that there is a consensus that it should end. In this regard, acceptance of the divorce is usually related to how comprehensible or reasonable it is to the teen.

Divorces that come out of nowhere, however, and seem very selfish and wayward can be hard to take for this age group. Trust can be shaken at the very time in development when the child is least in self-control and the world becomes rapidly more complex on many levels. It can lead adolescents to see their parents differently and this can include a loss of respect.

Teenagers will tend to resent when their parents steal the limelight and mess up their lives. Hence, they can be judgmental, take sides or react angrily. They might feel that they have to support one parent due to the actions of the other and they won't necessarily want access arrangements made without their input.

If some react with anger and non-compliance, others react with great sadness and feel the loss of childhood in one massive blow. The demand of school and peer relations now pales in comparison to the challenges at home. It is deeply unsettling for adolescents whose own developmental tasks are already so demanding.

Frankly, this is the age range where reactions can be most intense. This is not intended to be a pessimistic view but only to stress that the process has to be handled with care and tact. If there is sustained emotional reaction in this age group, it can be directed inwards in terms of sadness and insecurity or outwards as in anger and acting out.

In terms of telling adolescents, all the same principles apply. They will want to know details and specifically how this change will affect them. If parenting has already suffered due to preoccupied, depressed, avoidant or quarreling adults, the adolescent could have already factored in that the family was not going to hold up much longer. Nevertheless, this comes with its own risk precisely because adolescent adjustment is already complicated even without divorce.

Specifically, the risk amounts to a type of fracturing of childhood as if childhood ends at the point of parental break-up and the teen needs to face a harsher less protective world. Some teenagers feel that they have to look after their parents especially if a parent is obviously suffering. The child could conclude that they must be self-reliant and not ask more of their parents.

One of the major impacts of divorce is that children, including adolescents, do not take their parents for granted as much as kids from intact families. Divorce is a lesson in fallibility as the last strand of the ideal and magical parent of early childhood withers.

To the adolescent who optimally acquires independence slowly, divorce can open the floodgates. No need to divide and conquer the parents, they have done it themselves! Parent–child relations can be strained in part due to disillusionment but also when the adolescent no longer feels the same parental availability as before. Further, if the adolescent is already struggling with powerful drives and passions then divorce could add to the maelstrom rather than providing a useful container.

In my experience, therefore, a cluster of issues need to be addressed with teens in particular when they are told. These include:

- The parents take this separation seriously and have tried to overcome the issues that divide them (including some details)
- The parents love their child and will do all in their power to help him or her through this adjustment
- The parents recognize this is not a welcome change but they will consult the child whenever possible over specific decisions that directly affect them
- The parents will tell the child what they both need in terms of cooperation and attention to duties
- The parents will assure the child that they will explain how decisions will be made concerning them.

Hence, the appropriate message is one that stresses the frame or parenting container. The danger of free-for-all is handled by stressing continuity, parental communication, continuing expectations, and respect for the child through a promise of consultation where appropriate. In this regard, it is the solidity and continuity of the container or frame that supports stability through parental divorce.

The breakdown of the parental container can create chaos for teenagers, especially those who depend on structure and oversight.

Cindy, a somewhat strident fifteen-year-old accustomed to pushing limits, is struggling with her newly separated mother who shares care and custody with her former husband. Her mother is trying to keep a tight frame for Cindy and maintain a sense of discipline and if necessary consequences. In a fit of temper related to her anger over her parents splitting up, Cindy tells her mother to "fuck off" and storms out. The mother takes away computer privileges for two days. Complications arise due to a school project and Cindy's second day extends into the dad's time. He blows up when the mother asks that Cindy not be allowed computer access for the one evening to complete the punishment. He accuses the mother of interfering with his time, tells her it has nothing to do with him, and refuses her request.

Sometimes the parental system appears to dissolve following separation and this can lead adolescents to feel that they have to fill in the gap vacated by their troubled parents. As if parental divorce marks the end of childhood, some teenagers report having to grow up instantly.

John, sixteen and in the eleventh grade broke down in tears over the desolation that describes his current family experience. His mother is a "basket case" and can't stop crying and railing about his "son-of-a-bitch dad". His father is so excited about his new life with his girlfriend that he has effectively disappeared. His parents' marriage didn't end as much as exploded over his dad's affair. Neither parent has actually spoken to John about the situation. He feels completely alone and overwhelmed. He worries about his twelve-year-old sister who retreats to her room after school and is immersed in texting her friends. John is finding it hard to concentrate at school although he finds it helpful to talk to his friends. He feels cheated by his parents, especially his dad and is really disappointed in him. This is not the same dad that John adored, he believes. He wants to see his dad more, though, and misses him. His mother opposes more visits and sees his dad in very negative terms. John states that he is afraid of his mother's emotions, especially her need for comfort. He worries that he has to fill the gap left by his dad and he finds this "weird".

One can see in the example how the parents' own experience and agenda dominated the field leaving John and his sister to fend for themselves. This is the opposite of the good or ethical divorce. There is no holding back, no communication with the children and no process of making sure that the parental structure or frame survives the break-up. The husband is in full action mode, euphoric in his flight to the new woman. The wife is crumbling along with her marriage, reeling from the bomb that has gone off in her life and trying to hold on to her own stability and functioning. The sixteen-year-old boy has to confront his father's fervent sexuality directly, which is never comfortable for children. At the same time, he feels unprepared and even unwilling to be the "man" on whom his mother depends. Moreover, his mother and sister both feel dumped for some new flame and John feels guilty even wanting to see this man who has hurt his family so much.

John is unlikely, however, to be drawn directly into the parental conflict. He feels more burdened by the whole situation and there is an underlying emotional retreat. This is true of the majority of children and adolescents even when there is prevalence of high conflict with parents bad-mouthing each other. It is not typical for children to become protagonists in a wider family struggle.

Some children, however, are drawn directly into the field of parental conflict and adolescents are more likely to be aligned with one parent than their younger siblings. Indeed, these adolescents embrace the role of avenging advocate for one parent or the other to the point of rejecting the other parent. There is no simple description or constellation to identify those at risk. Moreover, refusal to visit can be directly associated with actual abuse or, the converse, a conscious or unconscious strategy by one parent to alienate a child from a previously loved and loving parent. The dynamic is always complicated and must be understood in depth on a case-by-case basis.

Aligned children are not necessarily alienated. To earn the label "parental alienation", the parent must be urging the rejection and waging a campaign to possess the totality of the child's love at the expense of the irrationally despised parent.[2]

Sandy was fourteen when her parents' marriage ended. It had been stormy for a long time and, as the eldest of three children, she was immersed in her parents' every disagreement and inevitably took her mother's side. Sandy was unruly after the break-up and seemed empowered by her role as mother's avenger and family powerhouse in her own right. The mother's weak identity and underlying hunger to be mothered derived from her own difficult family history marked by her mother's untimely death from cancer when she was a teen. She had been ill prepared for marriage with unresolved dependency overshadowing more mature needs. Sandy's father was well meaning but overwhelmed and prone to depression. His involved parents and close friends bolstered him personally but he was not able to effectively handle his ex-wife or oldest child. The rising crescendo of litigation worsened the family climate. Sandy refused treatment, refused to visit her dad, and the situation settled into chronic stalemate.

Was this alienation or a refusal to visit founded in alignment with a preferred parent? Some teens will respond to power vacuums, garner unwarranted force and act in an entitled and harsh way. This can be extremely hurtful to parents on the receiving end of their adolescent child's rebukes and rejections. The aligned child will often lack empathy and blame can be intense. The "good" parent might have little motivation to dissuade the child even if they do not actively promote the child's rejecting behavior.

The more severe cases can be hard to change, as there is often a vested interest in justifying rejecting behavior. These families invariably require social, legal, and psychological help to address underlying problems. Moreover, the issues are usually not reducible to black-and-white judgments. For instance, the disfavored parent might be awkward, not as involved before the break-up or lack sufficient effective parenting skills. An objective observer, however, might still not perceive sufficient cause to end a child–parent relationship. Where cause for the refusal is deemed sufficient, the label of "realistic estrangement" applies.

The apparent cause or trigger of resistance or refusal can be attributed to historical factors (e.g., "He was never interested in me since I was little") or might be linked with the break-up itself or what occurs after. Hence, for example, if an older child or adolescent blamed the rejected parent for the separation, then this could tip the scale towards alignment with the preferred parent. Psychopathology in a child or parent can complicate matters and add to the problem of differentiating what is the source of the refusal.

Twelve-year-old Sarah was hospitalized for depression and suicidal ideation in the midst of her parents' divorce. Her fifteen-year-old brother John, became very protective. Initially, Sarah refused to have either parent involved in her in-patient treatment but this gradually eased when Sarah was discharged. The parents' union continued to disintegrate and ended in an explosive crisis with the husband accusing the wife of being violent. Father and children left the family home together and soon cut off contact with the mother while relocating to another residence. He appeared relatively passive but was clearly pleased to be standing up for Sarah and John and bonding with them at this critical time.

Confused and close to psychosis, Sarah accused her mother of numerous assaults. The image of a "bad mother" dominated her psyche and was interpreted literally by Sarah, her brother and presumably her father based on the eruptive episode that ended the marriage. The mother lamented that she had been their one reliable caretaker during their childhood as her husband was often absent from the marriage and the family. There seemed to be some truth to this observation but it also appeared that Sarah in particular had no natural path to emotionally separate from her mother. John, however, had no difficulties separating and seemed fundamentally healthy. Hence, the divorce created an opportunity for separation although it came with the violence of estrangement and much pain for the mother. John supported Sarah and refused to link with his mother as long as Sarah struggled to maintain her sanity.

Resistance to visiting and outright rejection fortunately only describes the minority of separating families but are still encountered frequently enough when it comes to adolescents and parental divorce. Is it any wonder then that divorce exacts such a toll on these children and families? My impression is that some of the collateral damage of divorce on children's psyche can be traced to how these break-ups unfold and not simply that marriages end. In Sandy's case, the marriage ended with shrill accusations of blame and negligence followed by years of legal and psychological mayhem. In Sarah's case, her father had ended the union, which destabilized her vulnerable mother who continued to yearn for some positive resolution despite the obvious disintegration and rupture occurring in the shadow of Sarah's difficulties.

This brings us full circle to emphasize the inherent value of an ethical divorce and the precious lives it can better protect and support despite the circumstances.

Conclusion

Telling children about an impending divorce should be geared to the appropriate developmental stage as well as the particular needs of that child or teenager. The conversation that introduces the separation is never the last word but it sets the stage and conveys a tone for how the process will unfold. Successful communication in which both parents address the break-up serves as an example of joint parenting that signals to the children and parents alike that containment and cooperation are possible. In this regard, it represents a success in the midst of a failed marriage.

Children need to know that a broken marriage does not mean a broken family. As much as children have their own experience of divorce and lessons to learn about human relationships, they very much need to feel that something essential will survive the rupture of their parents' union and that this will sustain them.

CHAPTER FOUR

Caring for children post-divorce

From one home to the other: the exchange or transition

Divorce tests the flexibility and resourcefulness of an ex-couple and their children to remain a family despite the chasm that now divides them. There are three main spatial elements in the system:

- Household one
- Inter-parental space
- Household two.

The households actually don't touch. They relate to each other for sure but primarily through the inter-parental space, which serves as a conduit through which the children and anything concerning the children pass. The inter-parental space includes communication, mediation if this is occurring, and the actual physical transition when the children must be dropped off at one home and received by the other. This transition is an important exception to the notion that households in divorce fundamentally don't touch.

During transition, the parents must administer a process for the children to exit one care structure and enter the other. This point of transition serves as a bellwether that in many ways predicts the health of the whole parenting system.

Thus, in situations where there is neither flexibility nor resources to maintain stability, the coming together during transitions can be fraught with risk and tension. In this case, parents must use a neutral community location or a third party to achieve the transfer as, although the family system can still hold together, it is often precarious. For example, I have seen parents who leave the child outside the door and retreat behind it when they see the other parent arrive. Often, however, the problems are less flagrant but no less significant. Staring, glaring, provoking, ignoring, raging, baiting, and swearing are not infrequent signs of the bad divorce during transitions. Even in moderate cases, the parents are strained with each other and the kids know it. Unresolved issues from the marriage or its breakdown might be behind the tension. Sometimes this is worsened by recent conflict but it almost always has antecedents.

The transition tests the parenting couple by putting them precisely in the situation where they have to actually practice putting the best interests of the children first. The approach can be filled with trepidation. Perhaps the leaving spouse insists on being accompanied by the new partner and, as it were, rubbing salt in the wound. Of course, there is no need for the new partner to be present. From the leaver's perspective, though, this is the new reality and everyone better get used to it. From the position of the spouse left, the insensitivity is a huge and painful reminder of an emotional wound. Note that in this hypothetical but not uncommon scenario, the position of the child has been usurped by an adult agenda. There is no actual need for the new partner to be present and if there was reason, the new other could stay somewhere out of line of sight.

Transitions test the basic parameters of divorce and assess the degree of collaboration possible. There can be all sorts of permutations when it comes to parents' fears and limitations. They might do any of the following:

- Come to the door but not inside
- Refuse to come to the door
- Refuse to park in the driveway
- Refuse to cross the property line
- Stay in the car and let the child do the walking
- Refuse to speak.

They might say any of the following:

- Speak to me so that our child sees that we can address each other
- Careful, I record every exchange
- You have to do all the driving
- I have a camera affixed to my car and it is always turned on during exchanges
- You cannot come to the house, only McDonald's will do
- We can only exchange the children at a police station.

Even the North and South Koreans can depend on a Demilitarized Zone (DMZ) between them to facilitate exchange and communication! This does not apply to all divorces. In part, I view this as a failure to comprehend the true nature of the exchange and what a child expects or needs. Instead, the family field is under siege usually by the same pressures or forces that plagued the failed union. For instance, safety and boundary issues or lack of communication, over the top aggression or anger, unspeakable tension, subtle devaluation and contempt, etc. will all find their re-expression in the exchange ritual.

In this regard, an empty marriage with unfulfilled partners who finally divorce does not typically lead to stormy or dysfunctional transitions. When exchanges are dominated by unresolved parental tensions, the failure of containment is obvious.

Under the surface, of course, the adults have agreed to import the problem to the exchange situation. They do so for their own reasons and this never has to do with the welfare of the child. On the other hand, it is easy to judge and moralize; much harder for some ex-couples to get control of the situation. It is particularly difficult because even if they were to try and act differently, there is no guarantee that the other will follow suit. In other words, how can one change a couple dynamic without some venue or opportunity for communication?

There is no good divorce with children involved without a good process of child exchange and transfer of care. Imagine the situation from the child's perspective with two glowering parents in a stare down as she or he moves between them. Existentially, it is a lonely, isolated moment for the child, as there is a certain subtle realisation of being usurped or ignored. Children often experience the moment as a type of no-man's land in which they are utterly alone. Naturally, the parents are satisfied that the mechanics are working and take comfort that the basic aim is met. As such, whatever the limitations faced, the child still moves from one household to the other.

Nevertheless, there is an important point missed. Children are psychologically held in three important ways: first, by the mother and her desire, then by the second other (often the father) and his love and desire, and finally by the image of the original parental union that directly or indirectly created the child. In other words, a scene of creation that made the child and continues to foster identity. It is precisely this third component of the parental crucible that is under threat during transitions.

I can only extrapolate from adult reconstructions during therapy but my impression is that the central trauma concerns the aloneness experienced when the child loses the idea that he or she was conceived out of love. This brings us back to the essential challenge of divorce with children, which is to preserve some aspect of the family in the absence of the union or marriage. When the core fantasy of original love is destroyed, the child is left as it were in empty space where the very notion of family takes a major pummeling.

Children need to know that they were created out of love and that this love survives the adult break-up and will determine the ambience of exchanges. When the opposite occurs and hatred or contempt fills the space, this essential pillar of identity is attacked. It damages the individual's capacity to trust and believe in love or the durability of relationships.

Simply giving advice about best practices in divorce often fails with couples whose conflicts are ingrained and unresolved. In my experience, however, it helps to keep in mind that no matter what has transpired, how much water under the bridge, two people got together out of love and/or desire and created a baby. This is exactly what is at stake during transitions. The parents, whose own union stumbled and ended, must remember a time when they came together and made a baby. Whether this is a heterosexual, gay or lesbian, adopted, in vitro or whatever does not matter. The fact is that they came together and made this child. Exchanges are the one moment post-divorce when this is recalled. In this regard, transitions are a form of remembrance.

Hence, when exchanges are highly dysfunctional, antagonistic, threatening, scary, volatile or risky, it represents to the child an attack on his or her origins. There was a baby but no love, no coming together with hopes, dreams and ambitions for a child-to-be. Of course, divorced parents enacting the hateful exchange are not conscious of any of this. Someone might suggest a code of conduct or other checklist solution of how to behave. Undoubtedly, this won't work. Such unhealthy circuitous interactions are hard to untangle and it is a challenge to act differently.

What can help is that beyond the hard feelings, grief, anger, disillusionment and other disturbing emotions that often linger for many years, there can still be a memory of what was good once upon a time: a love or desire for the other that gave life to a child. If the parent could see in the exchange from one household to the other, a mini-coming together replicating the original promise and embrace, then this could make a huge difference from the child's perspective. Consequently, when parents hurl abuse, stare angrily, mock or devalue each other at the exchange, they are either trying to deny that this was someone once (or still) loved or are denying that there ever was love. In the majority of cases, love was in the air and with it came hopes and dreams.

As an example, Steven and Beverly had a baby boy but no stable relationship. They never lived together. When Steven drops off their three-year-old after a visit, he is careful not to look at Beverly for fear that she will argue with him. He feels belittled by Beverly and denied a proper place in their child's life. Hence, in this case, there was never any actual coming together or union apart from sexual relations at a crucial biological point. Steven says there was no decision to have a baby and he thought Beverly was taking the pill. Beverly states that she thought she had fertility problems and was at low risk of pregnancy. Beverly dreads the exchanges because they are so fraught with tension. She could receive several texts after he departs full of accusation and vitriol.

One can imagine the transition from the child's point of view. He definitely has two parents but there is no concept of their linkage as a loving couple wanting to forge a family that was more than the two of them. In this regard, the son likely exists in two solitudes that must not touch out of fear of attack. As mentioned above, the transition serves as the bellwether for the divorce relationship. It tells a lot.

On the other hand, we can envision a much more positive scenario. Jerry and Diane's marriage ended painfully but it was almost certainly for the best. He had returned to university and became a lawyer. She had her own career but had made room for Jerry to study and achieve his dream. Yet, the marriage failed. They had two school age daughters. The couple was able to find homes within several blocks of each other. Transitions were uneventful. The parents used the occasion to review future events involving the girls. They were welcome in each other's homes although each remained at the entrance. The parents and children lingered. The girls had a chance to experience the collaboration of their parents and they could perceive that something remained that represented the family their parents had built together even though both mom and dad had new partners and new lives.

My sense is that some of the more pessimistic research on the impact of divorce on children fails to take into account that it might not be simply divorce in a global sense that is the determining factor but how well the parents are able to preserve something that continues to nurture, contain, and define the children long after the union has ended.

Of course, there are situations where the inter-parental space collapses and with it the pathway from one house to the other. Children can also refuse for one reason or another to pass through the corridor particularly if there is high conflict or where they have been mistreated or influenced. Refusal to visit can be an extremely difficult problem. Some older children and teenagers will balk if transitioning from one parent to the other becomes too conflictive. In the case of high conflict, any neutral or demilitarized zone between the parents may be squeezed to the point that it becomes too perilous for travel.

Children who are influenced and then refuse to visit the other parent represent a serious problem for the family law system. It is tragic to see actual brainwashing particularly when the offending parent has no insight or awareness of what they are doing. The concept of "gatekeeping" seems apt in the case of divorce. Both parents operate a gate, which opens to the inter-parental space between them. Naturally, in the case of a primary caregiver, this gate is the more influential. In co-parenting situations, we have two keepers of the gate that optimally maintain a mutually supportive, facilitating, and communicative stance to one another whether they continue to like each other or not.

We can easily visualize a continuum in how the gate is operated from facilitative to restrictive to shut. The determination of factors involved is never simple and one has to keep in mind that, in some instances, refusal to visit is partially or completely understandable. In general, however, there are numerous factors or variables, not to mention the personality, temperament, and contribution of the child. In other words, each situation is different. Nevertheless, an ethical divorce requires that whoever operates the gate at whatever moment shows compassion, respect, and support for the other parent.

In cases where children are being influenced, the undermining and restrictive gatekeeping can be subtle. For example, in divorce or at vulnerable moments during the separation period, there can be lapses in parenting. Even the best parent can falter at times for many reasons. How the other parent treats the slip up or moment of negligence can be a powerful influence. The facilitative gatekeeper knows that they too have been there and that everyone is human. In the long run, it is in everyone's best interest to support the other parent. The restrictive gatekeeper, however, pounces on the slip to devalue the other parent and convey negative messages to the children. When the children complain ("dad was really late picking us up after school; it was so frustrating!"), the restrictive gatekeeper says nothing supportive or softening. "Well, you know your father, he was never involved", she might say, instead of something like, "I am sure he felt awful. Dad and I hate it when we let you kids down."

The rejecting parent who most wants to slam the gate shut will play up the faults of the other parent, present starkly negative assessments of situations, stereotype and even caricature the rejected parent in the children's eyes. The subversive influence is chronically undermining of the relationship between the children and the other parent. These "alienating" influences might not affect all children alike nor do all children collude in a mutual effort to poison the well. It is a complex dance when it occurs and hard to separate the specific roles of the dancers from the dance. Further, it is not always a matter of one innocent and one guilty party but a mixture of influences. The main point is that weaknesses and faults of the target parent are used without perspective to justify blame and promote estrangement.

Children unequivocally do best when they have two mutually supportive parents, albeit divorced, who support their right to go back and forth and still experience a respectful family system aimed at promoting their best interests. Of course, there are situations that are plainly problematic and not everyone fits the mold of being a typical parent. On the other hand, for the broad majority, the back and forth describes a channel or gate through which the children pass from one household to the other. Viewing this pathway as a remnant of the original parental union or coming together that gave birth to a baby, provides ample rationale for giving these moments of transition importance.

Of course, parents might find it more efficient to use the school setting as a point of exchange. Hence, they do not need to see and deal with each other. Whoever is caring for the children after school is then responsible for pick up. Notwithstanding, there are still times or occasions where the parents will come together. It could be at a doctor's office, sports or school event. Whatever the context, these are important moments that convey as much about origins as they do about present conflicts and rapport. Even when children have no memory of their parents living together, they will continue to fantasize about the union that made them. It is very difficult for children to imagine a loving couple if the only evidence they have is of poisonous mistrust.

The care system

Caring for children after divorce is a vast subject that has many components to it. Let's start with the most general ingredients or minimal conditions for any care system to work. I would suggest the following:

- Two parents who are competent and available to provide the care stipulated in their parenting agreement
- An implicitly shared assumption that the parents and children still constitute a family
- An inviolable, neutral space between the parents through which the children can pass
- A workable arrangement in place for essential communication between the parents regarding the children
- An effective procedure for making decisions regarding the children
- An ability to give preference to the children's interests over either parent's interests when required.

When these conditions are met, there is no explicit obligation or requirement for the parents to get along famously or to enjoy an optimal and totally amicable rapport post separation.

Parents must be reasonably competent, which means that they have an essential understanding of their children and what the children need, including in relation to the other parent. In this regard, competence incorporates the emotional capacity to represent the child's need for the other parent and to function in the service of the co-parenting, no matter what the specifics of the schedule in place. Hence, divorced parents who are so competitive as to take comfort when the other lapses, lack this basic competence precisely because they relish the other's failings. If this is the dominant attitude or ethos, then each is pitted against the other for ascendancy in the children's eyes. The result is a skewed system that preferences competition over care. Children naturally internalize this family culture, which then interferes with psychological development.

Parental capacity and motivation is only formally assessed in extreme situations that have come to the attention of child welfare authorities or the courts. In most scenarios, essential capacity is taken for granted. On the other hand, all divorces have drawbacks and it is surprisingly easy to give in to baser instincts. One surefire sign of trouble is when the children's affections become the prize in a post-divorce family culture. The parent who pushes to outdo the other, buy loyalty and affection or win a popularity contest undermines and distorts the care system. The impact on children is predictable. They pick up on the theme, milk its capacity to divide and conquer their parents and further undermine their own best interests. Such competitiveness almost always leads to polarization and heightened conflict. Values are corrupted and children learn to manipulate in self-interest rather than to deal honorably and respectfully with the world.

Likely the best predictor of post-divorce parenting is what was happening before the break-up. Involved parents tend to remain involved and stay an integral part of their children's lives. Nevertheless, divorce can dramatically alter the socio-economic equation of the family and reduce parental availability. Even when parents are involved, work, psychological, and financial pressures as well as personal tumult are limiting factors. One very positive benefit of supporting the other parent is that it helps both weather the storm of re-adjustment post separation and creates a normal parenting space, which can be comforting, reassuring, and an extremely helpful identity anchor during rougher times. This has direct benefits for children and adults alike.

Of course, not all divorces end up with two parents pulling an equal load. At the same time, in many cases, one parent, often a father, who was less directly involved in childcare before the separation, becomes significantly more involved and active after. The lesser contribution pre-divorce would not necessarily be a measure of prior disinterest but could indicate division of labor along traditional lines with father as "provider" and mother as "caregiver". This is especially relevant when young children are involved.

In cases of contested custody, the wife might declare that the dad was never interested or took such a back seat that she felt like a single parent even while married. A couple without children is mainly carefree as compared to the moment a child arrives. Choices and freedoms decline dramatically. A woman never needs her partner more than when she has a baby. It greatly accelerates the emotional and life demands she places on her partner. Ideally, the new mother sustains the baby while the partner sustains the wife. They become a team and a family. It is not that the partner, usually the father, is not involved or does not love the baby. Rather, their synergy provides continuity of care in the service of a new baby.

If, however, the father fails in this role or feels cut off or isolated, the mother could develop the notion, justifiably or not, that he never cared and was never involved. The elemental "pulling together", therefore, must begin here. It is a juncture where weak alliances often fail and the most fragile unions begin to unravel.

Hence, the failure of the fundamental unit of father→mother→baby is a common theme in divorces involving young children. For fathers or partners in this situation, the route to validating their authentic interest post-separation can be a long and arduous one. The mother grows the baby and sustains the infant's life with her own body. Her bona fides are unassailable. The dad in this scenario seems loosely connected. His former wife rails at his poor track record and how alone she felt. He contends that he was excluded as if, after the baby was born, she did not need him. He feels used and discarded; she feels abandoned and cannot believe that his interest in their child is sincere.

There can be truths in both narratives and it is no wonder that fathers often feel that the system is biased towards motherhood. The likely truth is that the family law system is conservative. Judgments are aimed at mitigating risks.

If there is no way of knowing precisely what mixture of truth and myth defines a particular scenario, the court will support what seems solid and predictable over what could or should be in an ideal setup. In other words, the courts cannot undo the original failure of the fundamental family unit despite the pleas of either party. In most instances, the failure is a joint one.

In any case, we should note that the parenting formula in place before the break-up does not always predict how it should work after the divorce. Understandably, this can become a source of conflict when the "primary" parent insists that the other continues to play a secondary role because this is how it has always been. Roles and responsibilities are dynamic concepts. What was acceptable and workable in one context does not necessarily apply when the context changes. This is why the focus should be on the children's interests and what they need *vs.* whatever role the parents feel they deserve to play in the new reality.

In extreme cases, the core framework of "family" fails to survive the end of the marriage. These are always heartbreaking and extremely hard on children's identity. As such, it is one thing for the marriage to fail but quite another for the family unit to seemingly dissolve with it.

As an example, Martin married Marion with the shared vision of starting a family. Initial infertility problems led to the adoption of a daughter. They were an apparently healthy and active two-career family raising their daughter when Martin became increasingly withdrawn. His despondency grew and Marion could get nowhere when inquiring about his changing mood. Within six months, however, Martin had moved out after informing Marion that he did not think that he was suited to the life they were living. He denied any extramarital involvement. Marion was desolate as was their child. The daughter acted out repeatedly at the outset. Martin saw the daughter in the short term but then drifted away. Eventually, he remarried and had biological kids of his own. The daughter spent years reeling from the collapse of the family and saw her father off and on but eventually accepted estrangement.

Mainly, though, divorced families stretch and bend to fit various configurations but manage still to function as a family. Whether they do so effectively or not is another matter. If there was no end-of-marriage process to handle hard feelings, then adverse emotions could persist in the family system and limit communication and family effectiveness. In some cases, decades pass and the ex-couple remain tense, hurt, and unresolved in respect to each other. This usually impacts on children even in their adult years.

Formerly married adults might not get along very well by the time the union ends but they still need to come together as parents in respect to their children. To the extent that they can do this effectively serves as a precise measure of their potential as co-parents.

If the parties cannot come together as co-parents for whatever reason, help is required. Ethical divorce does not always mean that one has the "right" feelings or the most appropriate reactions. This is often uncontrollable despite good intentions. It is what is done with impasses and unhealthy feelings or motivations that is the determining factor. As I have already stressed, society has made divorce easier but no less difficult or painful. It can seem unnatural to keep contact with a person who broke such a fundamental promise as the commitment to spend life together or made it impossible to fulfill the obligation.

As neighboring nations are joined through geography, divorced couples are joined through children. It is an inescapable fate that creates a very real challenge. Unfortunately, there is no United Nations for divorce as there are for countries. There is only the courts and this route is complicated and expensive and should be avoided unless absolutely necessary. Alternative dispute resolution mechanisms such as mediation and arbitration have made a significant difference and are clearly the preferred option.

Ideally, however, both former partners connect to an intermediate space where a remnant persists of what once was. This is the space where children can comfortably go back and forth, where the notion of family lives on, and where children can still glimpse an echo of the original parental love.

Post-divorce family system

Families are systems composed of people who relate through roles, relationships, boundaries, and rules that govern how the various family members interact. This family system splits in the case of divorce but, nonetheless, a family system remains, although a divided one. Hence, divorce does not end the requirement to function as a family although it can make it more complicated.

Functioning as a family is a very different perspective from functioning as individuals. There is a tendency in divorce to insist on an iron curtain between the two households. What happens in one home is opaque in respect to the other. Children are often uncomfortable discussing what happens in the other home unless they are in some kind of unhealthy alliance with a parent or are facing major stresses and have no choice but to talk. The adults for their part insist on privacy. To be sure, they are no longer married or its equivalent and question why any part of their life should be open to the other. They could view the children as the one point of interchange but experience this sharing as entirely circumstantial. Personal reference to the other parent is mainly detached if not a little menacing: "your mother" or "your father". The formal or gruff style suggests a need for distance and, more specifically, a disavowal of the family unit of which they are still a part.

Of course, it is understandable that former couples frequently do not part on the best of terms and they might want no more ties than absolutely necessary. Nevertheless, in the insistence on rigid boundaries, solitudes that never touch along with growling encounters, the ex-couple denies being part of a parenting couple within a specific family field.

Because it is a family system, when one person is affected by a life experience, the impact is felt throughout the family including in the other home. When there is a refusal to acknowledge the total family system, children can be deeply affected. In this respect, it is consequential.

As an example, let us look at the situation where one parent leaps into a new relationship only to have it end abruptly to everyone's surprise. The children might well have been introduced to this person and, hence, could feel the loss in their own terms. The event is destabilizing to the parent affected and the children become confused. Is there any permanence in adult relationships or is all up for grabs, they ask? The non-involved parent might need to comfort the children and address their anxieties even though she or he might well suspect that this liaison began before the marriage ended. This situation could also impact how the children react when the other parent begins to date. In other words, the children carry their worries and fears from one household to the other and the fallout is felt within the entire family system.

Optimally, the parents continue to accept that they constitute a family system and they are both equally active with their children. There is a respect for boundaries between the households, between the parents and between the generations. In other words, the children accept their position in the family and respect the authority of both of their parents in the two households. Boundaries are viewed as protective and containing rather than being part of an exclusionary process or impenetrable wall. There is an awareness of the interdependence of the two households and a need to coordinate efforts to best care for the offspring. They continue to refer to the other parent in personal and respectful terms that do not embroil the children in their parents' history or differences.

The parents communicate when necessary; call upon each other when required and both attend school and recreational activities without tension or rancor. They aren't likely friends but they will greet each other and not ask their children to carry the full load of bridging the two households. The children feel free to contact the other parent and there is permeability between households but not at the expense of structure, privacy or schedule. The parents resolve differences through mediation if they are not able to solve issues informally. They follow their Parenting Agreement and do not use their children as go-betweens.

This is the ideal setup and model divorce although it does describe many divorced families who make it work well. All divorces, however, are known or characterized by their limitations; what is possible *vs.* what is not possible in the particular family system. As such, limitations exist on a continuum from minor to major but are always present.

For instance, in many split situations, the parents might not be equally active or involved. The left spouse could be a great parent but too hurt and angry to easily cooperate with the former spouse. Or, the couple might not be able to resolve differences without a third party mediator. One parent might be more powerful and influential than the other in the family system. Sometimes both could be active but one might be more attuned and sensitive to the children's needs. Conversely, a child could be more difficult to handle for one of the parents. Each "negative" element creates a specific limitation in the divorce and will add to the challenges faced by the family system.

Power sharing

Extreme power imbalances between the parents are another example of family system stresses that are unfavorable to children's welfare. The problem, for instance, of a highly active residential mother and a much less involved father can create the type of power imbalance that is likely to have long-term developmental implications for children. The awakening of fathers' rights and the post-feminist breakdown of gender specific roles is a welcome trend in modern divorces. Research underscores the positive impact of fathering on children including less aggression and more emotional security in both boys and girls. Unfortunately, this can create conflict and power struggles when fathers feel diminished by a system that appears to favor mothers or when his time with the children is treated as "visitation" rather than equivalent and meaningful parenting.

When "power" is the language of struggle in a divorced family, everything can be looked upon through this one lens. Power can be interpreted as encompassing time with the children, the right to make decisions, or the power of gender politics where mothers have a head start over fathers by approximately nine months and can sustain the infant's life with their bodies. Of course, money still talks but it generally pales next to biology and maternal nurturing roles in the case of babies and young children. Nevertheless, finances are often an issue post-divorce and here fathers might have the lead simply because their work life is less likely to be seriously interrupted by pregnancy, birth, and infant care. In this case, money can be used in a struggle over support or more likely ancillary expenses that are not as clear-cut as court ordered monthly payments.

Power struggles are ubiquitous in bad divorces where they run amok. What leads to power struggles? It is hard to generalize but perhaps the leading cause is a pre-existing lack of any real history of engaging collaboratively together. In other words, power struggles fill vacuums. If there is no meaningful way for a couple to pull together due to personal, historical, and systemic limitations then the use and even abuse of power is one way to try and decide matters.

It is common for one angry ex-spouse to accuse the other of being controlling or even "a control freak". Divorce undermines the sense of personal control and this easily extends to children. Power struggles are thus more likely to occur when one parent has more access time and care-taking duties. This structural asymmetry aggravates personality and relationship factors to create a seedbed for power struggles to evolve.

How to address this issue then is an important challenge facing couples and professionals alike. Power generally circulates around three vectors in divorce: childcare time, money, and decision-making.

Time and power

When both parents equate time with involvement then power struggles tend to follow. Not all family situations suit the equal sharing of time. This does not mean that the parent with more time is more involved. Time does not equate with the quality of parent–child relationships. There are many other ways to be involved: coaching and attending recreational activities, daily contact by phone or device, involvement with school projects and homework, shared activities, communication with the other parent, holiday experiences, facilitating the child's relationships, and involvement with peers and activities, among others. In other words, involvement is a measure of the parent's capacity to fit into the child's life and support their everyday progression not simply how much time is involved in actual full-time care-taking.

Of course, this explanation does not usually wash with those who resent every extra minute the ex-spouse spends with the children and who view this as an unfair subjugation of their parental status. Yet, it has no meaning for children really in that their capacity for love and involvement is not linked to time. This does not mean of course that time is irrelevant. Too little time and there is not sufficient opportunity for natural parent–child interactions. Moreover, limited time per visit no matter how frequent also stifles parent–child relationships.

For example, one dad saw his son for four hours three times per week. In a way, he saw his child regularly but besides the limited hours, the time distribution was locked into after school visits and lacked the natural continuity of living that is so essential to family life. There was a comment from a professional involved in this case that overnights represent time sleeping and so, perhaps, it was a good arrangement. This missed the point. What is required is for the child and parent to experience living together in a natural way and this includes being put to bed at night and waking up in the morning. Sleep, in this regard, should never be equated with unconsciousness. To sleep, to dream, to awake occurs within the emotional sphere of the loving parent and this is vital.

Within reasonable limits, however, quantity does not equate with quality of relationship. So when quantity is obsessively targeted as the only criterion that matters, power struggles are common. The parent's focus is the other parent in this case and there is little appreciation for the child's view or needs. Hence, power struggles have a nasty habit of entrapping children in a strained family impasse that often becomes litigious.

Money and power

Money traditionally equates with potency and power in general. Hence, the parent with more money is seen as having the power to buy the children's love and loyalty and to afford a more attractive lifestyle. This is particularly evident when the children reach middle childhood. In these power struggles, the occasional child might be seduced by the allure of the newest gizmo but most kids inherently want to love both parents equally and would suffer if they felt undermined by the corruption of money. A parent trying to buy a child could create excessive guilt, shame or encourage a somewhat perverse approach to relationships in which the pursuit of material wants assumes a special status.

Beyond the exploitation of money to win favor is the exploitation of the children's affections to triumph over the ex-partner in a power struggle. Here the children's interests are trumped by the parent's need to control the children's love, loyalty, and involvement. In this scenario, the other parent's contribution and presence in the children's lives is constantly undermined in obvious and subtle ways. The children are in effect pawns despite the claim that the controlling parent is acting to protect them and their welfare. In this context, decision-making in particular is used as a tool for the exercise of power. If there is no check on this power then the imbalance can be startling in its impact. The child takes in a model of human relating that is void of all the safeguards and skills needed to succeed in relationships: communication, sharing, respect, and consensus-building.

As an example, Susan complained bitterly about her ex-husband, Brian, who had moved in relatively quickly with his girlfriend although he contended she had only been in his life since the union with Susan ended. The new partner had an excellent job while Susan, a teacher, was still working part-time as was the couple's plan before the break-up. Flush with a robust second income, Brian was showering their nine and eleven year olds with expensive weekend getaways, Disney cruises and the newest play systems. Susan feared that her kids would favor their father somehow over her and she was horrified when they actually willingly accepted his girlfriend. Susan could not stop herself from muttering sarcastically to the children about their dad when she felt so upstaged. The more Brian exclaimed about all the new adventures he was planning, the more Susan sneered about him in earshot of the kids. The children became distressed, which brought Susan into treatment. She came to understand that it was a useless power struggle that she could refuse to join. It helped her appreciate better her own history with Brian and what had occurred during their union.

Decision-making and power

The most durable trend in child custody in many countries has been shared decision-making. This has followed the equally strong tendency of the courts to favor a more gender-neutral approach to custody determination without preference either to mothers or fathers on some *a priori basis*. Mainly, this mirrors the societal trend towards both parents joining the workforce with neither having claim to domestic or family primacy. The underlying assumption, however, is that joint decision-making does not lead to family system paralysis, confusion, heightened conflict or increased risks of psychological harm to children.

Decision-making can only be shared when the two parents agree to come to an accord about any single decision that has to be made. In other words, it implies a system that supports decision-making as compared to impasse. Whether or not there is disagreement or the occasional requirement for third party mediation, the underlying assumption is that a decision will be reached. The parents place priority on the value of making a decision in support of their child's interest over the merits of any one issue or decision. They are likely to interact in pursuit of consensus and focus on issues rather than dispute the conduct, failings or motivation of the other parent. The parents are unlikely to involve the children in co-parenting disputes. They deal with issues in a compartmentalized way and keep this very separate from any residual feelings about each other that stem from the broken marriage or union.

In the case of a power struggle focusing on decision-making, achieving a specific decision or getting one's way is deemed more important than the value of arriving at an accord. There are often doubts about the other parent's value to the child and interaction between the parents is often minimal and conflictive with little specific focus on the actual parenting issue. In some of these cases, the struggle continues over who is to blame for the marital demise and, hence, the past is never the past. There is certainly a tendency in this group to involve the children in disputes. In fact, the problem of boundaries can be a more general one with little distinction between prior marital struggles, the post-separation relationship and children's needs. Without effective boundaries, the couple is often enmeshed and co-parenting remains unreachable.

In my experience, the core difference between parenting couples who can make decisions and those who use decision-making as a forum for power struggles is not the degree of conflict. Co-parenting and conflict can certainly co-exist as long as the ultimate aim of the couple is to arrive at consensus. In the healthy situation, consensus is the mark of success whereas in power struggles, having one's way is the mark of success. The former is child-centered while the latter remains fixated on the adults.

It follows that in the good divorce, power imbalances are not a source of struggle even when they potentially exist. Domination and victory over the other is the goal of power struggles whereas collaboration is the objective of the ethical divorce. Each party accepts the moral responsibility to support the other parent's position in the family system and when there are conflicts, these are handled through specific channels and mechanisms rather than left to reverberate in the family system like a ricocheting shell. Children are supported as they move between homes with the understanding that they are moving from one wholesome, accountable environment to another. The good divorce includes the understanding that although there are two households, they remain branches of a common family system even when step-parents and step-siblings enter the mix.

Boundaries

Boundaries are also essential to any family system whether intact or divorced. There can be no success in family life without secure boundaries. As noted above, these include boundaries between individuals but also between the generations and households in the case of divorce. The essence of a "boundary" is that it demarcates where one individual stops and the other begins. It is a prerequisite of autonomy and healthy self-development. Moreover, there cannot be intimacy without boundaries. Indeed, in the absence of boundaries, intimacy regresses into fusion: an intermingling of selves, bodies, generations or even psyches.

Hence, what psychologists designate as "parental alienation" is at heart a disorder of boundaries. The alienating parent cannot separate their psyche from the child's. It is a fusion of destinies leading the child to divorce the target parent. At the same time, the child surrenders autonomy to the alienating parent, which coincides with an appropriation of the child's mind.

Alienated children and adolescents stand by the reasonableness of their rejection. Yet, their minds are closed to negative evidence and they have no sense of being co-opted by one parent against the other. Their rejection is offered as proof of the other parent's unworthiness and in this regard the child assumes a powerful role in the family. Criticisms are harsh and often shrill, lacking in balance or any shred of love. They purport a history that cannot be confirmed and usually feature severe emotional, physical or sexual abuse by the rejected parent that makes the parent unworthy of any status in the child's affections or life. The alienating parent almost always lacks insight into her or his role but presents as a victim of the former spouse. The children are seen as secondary victims, reacting solely to their own experience rather than to any influence.

Healthy boundaries suggest a respect for the autonomy of mind. Between parent and child, for example, there is a core acceptance that the views and feelings of the child are distinct from the parent's. The parent aims to facilitate thinking in the child, not just influence what the child thinks. Children are not simply blank slates to be filled but are fully capable of their own thoughts and reactions. They have their own minds. In healthy families, this is accepted, viewed positively and is consistently nurtured. In families with poor boundaries between parent and child, however, the need for alliance and common cause is much greater than the need to develop the child's thinking on independent terms. Of course, this is not acknowledged in such cases. Nevertheless, in severe cases, the child and parent behave as one being in lockstep. Careful inspection, though, will reveal a very compliant child who has forfeited autonomy of mind for emotional safety and connection.

Generational boundaries are also an important ingredient of healthy family relations. The children are content to be in the child role while the parents accept their position of being responsibly in charge. This is a form of loving and not an exercise in power. When divorce destabilizes one or both of the parents, older children and teenagers sometimes feel thrust into a caretaking role. It is as if the generational boundary breaks down and the child must soothe, support, and even side with the beleaguered parent in conflicts with the other parent. This can be very hard to reverse once it becomes established.

Transient loss of self-control and functioning is common in the immediate fallout period of a marriage breakdown. Naturally, it affects the left spouse more than the leaver who is presumably getting what he or she wants. This period of destabilization can be short-lived or last for some time. It will affect the family system in both households. As much as the destabilized parent tries to keep the children out of the turmoil, they will resonate with the emotional state of the parent. Children tend to worry about the parent when not with them and, paradoxically, become irritable and even harsh when they are.

Communication is extremely important in addressing this situation, as the goal is to affirm the family structure and reestablish the essential generational boundary. The purpose then is not for the parent to deny problems or understate current difficulties but to appropriately acknowledge the issue while insisting that they remain a family unit and firmly in their roles. The parent can indicate what steps they are taking personally to solve the crisis or what the parents are doing together. In other words, there should be enough information to clearly communicate while not involving the children in the adult's world.

This raises another important quality of boundaries. They should not be rigid and impermeable. Rather, they should allow for close contact and separateness at the same time. Rigid and aggressively maintained boundaries are not protective. They shut people out and create injury and alienation. Perhaps an example would help clarify what I mean.

Dana had not had a happy or stable childhood. Her parents' troubled marriage led to her father leaning on her more than was appropriate when she was a teen. His need for comfort and the emotional demands he placed on his daughter crossed a line in terms of what was healthy. In this regard, it was a boundary violation that burdened Dana and subsequently caused conflict with her mother who apparently failed to protect Dana and, in Dana's eyes, blamed her for what occurred with her father.

Fast forward then to when Dana's marriage fell apart resulting in the shared care of the couple's pre-adolescent son and teenage daughter. Dana did not necessarily regret the union ending. She had wanted out for some time. Hence, it was surprising to her when she felt awash in self-pity and dragged herself around in the gloom of sadness. Dana's daughter experienced her mother's regression and did everything to support and comfort her. Dana found herself waiting anxiously for her daughter to return from school each day and she felt emotionally dependent and at a loss. Through the haze of her despair, however, she saw a repetition of her own childhood in the making.

Dana sought therapeutic help and worked through the childhood issues that were controlling her reactions despite her better judgment. When she felt more in control and could better understand the sequence of events and their impact on her, Dana spoke to her daughter. She told her daughter in general terms about what had happened with her own parents and the toll it had taken on her as an adolescent. She emphasized how grateful and moved she was by her daughter's love and support but that it was important not to repeat her own experience. Dana revealed that she was getting professional help and making progress and that her daughter should not feel responsible for her mother's welfare. Dana reported that her daughter seemed nonchalant when the discussion took place but subsequently observed a definite lightness in her daughter's demeanor.

On another track, I am sure that the reader will understand how interlocked partners can be in a disturbed or dysfunctional union or marriage. Their engagement with each other can seem inescapably powerful and collusive. There are really few or no boundaries between them: what they say, how they act, and how they treat each other can appear as a free-for-all with no holds barred. Indeed, such couples lack the flexible interdependence of an emotionally healthy couple that might become disenchanted or disillusioned enough to divorce but when separated naturally expect that meaningful boundaries will remain operative.

Communication patterns

Boundaries include the right to parent without interference, the right to privacy and the obligation to respect the privacy and autonomy of the other parent. Communications between parent and child are circumscribed in place and time not to interfere or appropriate the child's time and space with the other parent. In contrast, the legacy of disturbed marriages is often post-divorce in families where boundaries are uncertain or not respected in the main.

The boundaries between households have been made more complicated by texting and virtual communication in general. Older children and teens equipped with their own smart phone devices can stay in contact with the non-residential parent with ease. In most instances this is a good thing but not when used to appropriate the child's time and focus away from the other parent. This is especially troublesome when the parent cannot emotionally separate from the child and, particularly, where the parent treats the child as an extension and not a separate being with allegiances and needs for two parents.

Here is an example. Barry was unwise in love more than unlucky. He had two children by two ex-wives, a boy from the first and a daughter from the second. It is the latter union that concerns us. Barry's youngest child (a daughter) was then eight years old. Her mother was profoundly possessive of the child's time and cultivated a duo mentality that linked mother and daughter in a tight almost exclusive bond. The eight-year-old had a phone and the mother texted constantly. Barry had to put limits on phone availability and this led to tensions between the parents. He expressed that his ex-wife believed that she owned him and their child despite the separation. She had spoken of reconciliation but it felt like subjugation to him. The child was doing well, however, and did not seem particularly influenced or fazed by her mother's demands. Barry's response was to enforce limits without drawing particular attention to it.

There are certainly other situations that become invasive and harmful when communications are involved. In several situations that I have encountered, it was a needy stepmother who encroached repeatedly on a young child's space when the child was residing with his or her mother. The language of the stepmother's communications in these cases bordered on the romantic, which understandably raised alarm in the mother's home as the child became increasingly hard to handle.

Mainly, most parents accept the need for communication etiquette that provides an optimal balance between continuity of connection and respect for the boundary that separates the two homes. Communication between parents and children is important in divorce. Often, a thirty-minute window to receive calls works well, with calls kept brief and non-intrusive. This usually works well with younger children who do not have their own phone as long as there is also an opportunity for the child to spontaneously reach the parent with the residential parent's consent. In this regard, the parent providing care can determine if the call is appropriate and not intended to split the parents to avoid bedtime, discipline or some other similar unsuitable motivation.

New technologies are creating other useful formats for communication and this is a positive step as long as each parent appreciates the need for structure and scheduling at the home where the child is resident. Again, boundaries are essential but should never be interpreted as license to exclude the nonresidential parent. There needs to be some reliable window of contact to create the necessary bridge between children and both parents. When this occurs properly, which means ethically, the family identity is reinforced. In contrast, parents who refuse to answer the phone or who create an iron curtain between households allowing no contact, attack the links that are essential to that child. It can be viewed as an act of violence, which is internalised as such by the child.

Ideally, connections between the child and the extended families on both sides should be fostered. Integrating grandparents, for example, into the communication cycle can be very positive for children. Of course, it might not be very comfortable for the adults but it makes a lot of sense for children who profit enormously from the love and affection they receive from important non-parental figures. The system of communication then is built to meet the children's needs and the adults should adjust accordingly to what is adaptive for the child and not necessarily what is easiest.

Broader context of family

This raises the issue that too often in divorce children lose contact with the broader context of family, especially in respect to the non-residential parent in an asymmetric situation. Aunts, uncles, cousins, and grandparents are important figures in a child's life as they support identity and situate the child in a larger family context. At the same time, this can be tricky to arrange mainly because time with children becomes more limited in divorce even when there is an actual sharing of the time. In the most imbalanced of schedules, it is extremely difficult to sustain meaningful links to the broader family of the secondary parent, which adds to the stresses and losses inherent to these arrangements even if they do address other legitimate concerns.

When we look at the family as a system, we transcend a view that focuses solely on the individual as all determining. A family, even one split by divorce, is more than a collective of individuals or even of two-person relationships. For instance, for a divorced parent to insist that all that matters is their relationship with the child is to ignore that there is always the wider identity of the family; a composite of relations that for the child must bridge the divide of divorce in order to keep some idea of unity or shared family reality. When a parent refuses to acknowledge the bridging notion of family, the child will have no choice but to internalize the parent's negation in the form of a broken image of family. This will certainly have implications for psychological development.

In other words, it is not divorce per se that creates the internal perception of something damaged or broken but, instead, parental refusal to maintain any link with the former spouse or partner, including the vitriol and venom in the service of this negation. In the healthy context, the child will readily modify the sense of family to accommodate divorce and even remarriage. This flexible and encompassing mentality comes naturally to most children. In the problematic context, however, the child's basic need to maintain a sense of family is sacrificed to support the parent's emotional limitations. This is where the designation "broken family" is apt. As such it best describes a child's internalization of a fractured family caused less by divorce itself than by the parents' inability or refusal to maintain a residual of the unity intended at the outset.

The divorced family is always a divided one although it certainly does not necessarily have to be split or fragmented. Divorcing parents should seek to preserve as much as possible what they did together as an intact family unit. Hence, if they feel that they can both attend their child's birthday party together then this would be something to preserve. It is a small example but matters a lot to children who, as I have indicated, are likely to want to maintain a sense of family identity.

It is hardest for children to maintain this sense of overall family when one parent is seemingly expelled from the family unit and effectively lost to the child. This can occur, for instance, when a parenting arrangement fails to enfranchise a capable and involved parent or keep that parent sufficiently in the loop of the child's life. It can also happen when a parent moves away or chooses to become uninvolved. In other words, to the extent possible, custody arrangements need to respond to a child's need to revise the sense of family rather than to lose it. This should also include efforts by the parents to work on nurturing and supporting their children's lives with some degree of synchrony and coordination.

There is one sure exception to this rule, which is when the family unit was saturated with violence or the threat of violence during the union. In this case, it is often better to allow the divide to widen rather than to ask the child to sustain a family concept in what was clearly a danger zone. As such, when we speak of family we are speaking of preserving something good and identity defining.

How adults look back on these childhood experiences is an interesting topic in its own right. Here is an example that illustrates the potential complexity of the post-divorce family reality.

Manny was the oldest of three siblings when his parents finally separated during his teen years. His father, a heavy drinker at the time, was often away on business. There were episodes of explosiveness at home in which property was destroyed during parental altercations. His mother's neediness only increased as the union imploded in acrimony. Manny tried to fill the shoes of the missing father with his siblings, which led to conflict with them. He also feared physical closeness to his mother due to its incestuous overtones. The relationship to his father was feeble at best and never really recovered. Manny felt that his father had abandoned his children and there was little sense that any family unity had survived or that it should survive.

Even as an adult, Manny loathed the idea of his parents being in the same room together. He went to great lengths to avoid any milieu or event where this could occur. In his mind, they had chosen divorce and this split had to be honored. He was sure that they despised each other and found the idea of them sharing any space as repugnant if not dangerous.

The issues are complicated. Manny's father was weakly connected to his children during Manny's childhood. This preexisting factor likely meant that the sense of family was damaged even before the union ended. Second, in his fantasy life, Manny was the de facto father and, hence, he viewed his father as a counterfeit figure and emotionally expelled him from the family framework. Third, it was an angry divorce that followed a potentially explosive, unstable marriage. Manny saw his parents as dynamite and match, which should never come into contact with each other.

In conclusion, when marriages end, the frame or envelope that contains the family has to be revised to conform to new circumstances. It should be an envelope with two compartments but still one envelope. In theory this might sound rational and expected. In practice, however, it constitutes a major challenge for many. As much as boundaries are reassuring and framing, they can feel oppressive and limiting. Of course, this represents a distortion and the post-divorce family configuration is no less in need of boundaries than its intact counterpart. Understanding boundaries as protective and defining helps to see that children, parents and extended families need avenues of contact to retain a family identity. In this regard, boundaries are essential to sustaining contact much more than they are intended as aggressive "keep out" signs.

Step-parent role

One final element particular to the divorced family situation merits discussion. This concerns the role of step-parents and the realities of the blended family. There is already much written about the challenges of grafting non-related parental figures and siblings to an existing divorced family. Blended families come in many shapes and sizes, each with a unique mix of characteristics and challenges. Moreover, they come together as a result of death or divorce. Hence, there is a pre-existing loss in which the shadow of the former partner is superimposed on the family structure.

Parent–child relations in stepfamily contexts precede the relationship between the two partnering adults and can create loyalty issues for the adults as well as the children. There is no guarantee that values, habits or rhythms will easily mesh in the new family unit. Further, the blended family in divorce is usually juxtaposed to another household to which the children also belong. Thus, the stepfamily is not a stand alone entity but part of a wider family system. Finally, I would highlight that the step-parent–stepchild relationship must be created by the two participants and is not amenable to pre-definition.

There is no preset model to say what this relationship should be. It is a relationship of happenstance although it can be very significant in the life of a child.

The broad majority of children do well in the stepfamily circumstance while a small minority have increased problems as a result. In my experience, much falls to the attitude of the step-parent and the perceptiveness of the child's natural parent. If the parent insists on the step-parent as a fully authorized parental figure from the start then there could be trouble accepting this new order. In the ethical divorce, the adult allows the children to shape what role they would like the step-parent to play as well as the pace of the evolving relationship. Some children welcome the presence of another caring adult into their lives and immediately see it as value added. Others, however, are tepid in their acceptance, cautious, or need to warm up over time or even on each new encounter. Still another subgroup of children of divorce suffers loyalty conflicts, assumes an advocacy role on behalf of the other parent, and essentially resists the relationship.

Of course, not all variation in the "step" situation arises from the side of the child. Some new partners might not aspire to the parental role although they might be content to play the role of friend. This is very easy for children to handle. We should also leave room for the adult who is unenthusiastic or unprepared to function as a step-parent and mainly avoids an active role. The latter scenario is most likely to arise in asymmetric care arrangements where the parent has mainly alternate weekend access.

Whatever the disposition and aspirations of the new partner, problems often arise in the context of discipline. In the eyes of children, only parents have the authority to set and implement discipline. Hence, the litmus test occurs if and when the step-parent assumes this mantle and attempts to discipline a child.

My suggestion to step-parents is to distinguish clearly between a behavioral issue in general and one that arises specifically between the child and the step-parent. In the former case, the natural parent should handle the situation, while in the latter the step-parent should handle it. To take an example, if the child neglects to do their homework or provokes a sibling with no cause, it would fall to the parent to handle. If the child directly defies the step-parent or acts rudely and dismissively, the step-parent would need to handle it. As a general rule, however, step-parents should tread lightly in the discipline area other than assuming a supportive role vis-à-vis the natural parent. Hence, it is always a question of tact and sensitivity when serving as a step-parent.

Nevertheless, step-parents can be very important adult figures who represent positive role models and can provide a calm harbor in a storm. What the natural parent achieves through love, encouragement, and discipline, a step-parent can achieve through helpfulness, support, and rapport. In other words, discipline is not usually a major factor in child/step-parent relations. It is always special when someone who does not officially "have to" love us still demonstrates a caring, supportive attitude. Aunts, uncles, grandparents, and step-parents are all examples of this genre of caring adult.

There are many possible permutations to what is called the blended family. Consider, for example, two adults each with one child who get together. Thus, they are each the natural parent to one child while serving as the step-parent to the other. One can imagine the difficulties blending this new family configuration. The natural order in this case would amount to two pairs on parallel tracks with each child relating to a natural parent. They could live in harmony with positive bridges forming to the non-related adult. Of course, there is no guarantee that the two children will get along. This is not peculiar to the "step" situation but it can add to the complexity of blending.

Perhaps they are both single children and have no real precedent for the sibling experience. When each resides with their other natural parent, perhaps not re-partnered, they would regain their "only child" status. Consequently, the adjustment to a wider family context would occur in one family setting only. This might work well or it could create comparisons that make adjustment more difficult.

Let's assume that it is the mom who has re-partnered while the dad remains single but shares the care of the child. Mom works hard to create a new family identity that incorporates her new husband and stepchild. The dad, however, could become threatened by his ex-wife's eager embrace of her new reality. He worries about being delegitimized as a valid family unit. Hence, he subtly discourages his child from viewing the other child as a sibling. Now we have two different mindsets in collision depending on context. It could well lead to confusion and emotional conflict for the child who might feel disloyal for embracing this new brother or sister.

The basic point is that each blended situation is different with particular challenges and dynamics that are almost impossible to predict. Re-partnered parents and their new partners must retain a flexible approach that is child centered. What this means is that adults take their cue from the child and do not attempt to impose a preconceived template that is force-fed as a fait accompli. Parents, for instance, who insist that the child spend half of Mother's Day or Father's Day with the respective step-parent, demonstrate this form of tyranny in spades.

In actuality, children are pleased to honor and celebrate positive step-parent relationships. They do this naturally without devaluing their natural parents or asking them to share the stage with a step-parent in any official way. When parents insist on a step-parent being acknowledged on the same plane as the parents, it brews trouble, trapping children in the middle and subjecting them to guilt and conflict.

Sometimes the problems of blending might stem from unresolved conflicts and power struggles from prior unions. Jonathan and Beth were both divorced when they found each other. They each had one child. Beth's daughter Daniella, was ten years of age. Jonathan's son, David, was thirteen. Beth had been the primary caretaker of Daniella while Jonathan shared care of David with his former spouse. They melded well as individuals although both children attended school in different areas of the city.

Beth and Jonathan wanted to unite their lives and move to a nearby family friendly neighborhood. Both children would change schools and this would require a longer drive for Daniella's father in the morning. Thus, Beth's ex-husband fiercely resisted Daniella moving schools while Jonathan's ex-wife accepted as long as David could continue his athletic interests in the old neighborhood. Beth's ex-husband refused to relent and Beth felt unfairly controlled and prevented from getting on with her life.

No amount of mediation sufficed and it took a court order before it could happen. This is a good example of the potential impact of a power struggle and its capacity to create huge frustration and impasse.

Conclusion

As much as divorce ends a partnership between two once committed adults, it need not spell the end of the family. A divided world results for sure but this does not necessarily imply a broken sense of family. How this family is constituted, however, is rendered more complex by divorce while still being understood as a functioning system. These include dimensions such as power sharing and decision-making, boundaries, communication patterns, rules, roles, and responsibilities.

The goal in divorce is to preserve the remainder when the marriage is ended, which is the sense of family. Of course, all divorces include limitations and not every parent is optimally involved, attached, capable or committed. Nonetheless, to the extent possible, there is a need to keep the family entity alive even as the marriage succumbs. The direct beneficiary of these efforts is the child.

The increased incidence of divorce involving children in society has meant much greater diversity when it comes to stepfamily configurations. Each one is unique and they are all very challenging. The melding of unrelated children and adults in a post-divorce family unit takes tact and sensitivity. Parents need to have reasonable expectations and be prepared to follow the lead of each child in shaping the step-parent relationship. Tact and sensitivity communicates respect for the child's emotional adjustment process. The step-parent not only verbalizes that he or she is not the child's parent but waits for the child to find a comfort zone and establish rapport on their terms.

There is no rulebook that tells children and adults how to behave or even what roles to assume in a stepfamily. Each new family amalgam must discover what works in their case. It is a discovery process and should not be imposed or assumed.

I have seen numerous examples of children that developed very positive, nurturing relationships with step-parents that continued into adulthood. I have also seen children who steamed with resentment and felt forced to live in units that they outright rejected and despised. Sometimes this appears unavoidable but it can also have much to do with the attitudes and assumptions of the adults, including the non-resident parent in the other home.

CHAPTER FIVE

Custody and access

Of all the hot button issues in divorce, none is as consistently controversial as custody. Whoever has custody is deemed to exert family control. Custody, thus, has an inclination to pit one parent against the other, fathering against mothering and feminism against father's rights. There seems to be no end to the wrangling possible over what is supposed to be a question of the best interests of children of divorce.

Linking social theory with survey data, Canadian academic Paul Millar demonstrated why struggles could be so intense. Between 1986 and 2002 in Canada, women gained some type of custody eighty-nine percent of the time while men lost custody sixty-seven percent of the time.[1] In the United States, men have sole custody with primary residence in approximately fifteen percent of cases.[2] In other words, women are more likely to serve as custodians, which can also be described as the primary parent role. This includes exercising either sole or joint custody of their children. Men are more likely to lose custody whenever there is a court-mediated custody dispute.

These statistics, however, fail to do justice to the profound societal changes in play that have seen a less gender-based view of nurturing and parenting. One legacy of the joint custody phenomenon, beginning in California in the 1970s, has been the increased recognition that neither gender has a monopoly on good parenting when determining the children's best interests.

For sure, today's fathers are much more involved in everyday care, which is as much a byproduct of feminism as the far greater participation of women in the workplace. Research demonstrates that men can be as nurturing as women with infants even if their care styles overall are somewhat different. Yet, mothers still provide most of the childcare in western society especially in the younger years.

As to styles, mothers tend to provide attuned, connected "close" care with evolving separateness while fathers have a tendency to provide a protective presence, encouraging exploration into the world. In practice, there are particular parent–child relationships woven into gender narratives but pursuing the same goal, which is the healthy development of the child. Of course, a girl will learn about being a modern woman through her mother but her father's glint in the eye and way of responding to her will contribute much to her sense of herself including her femininity. Boys need the paternal relationship or its equivalent to find their way to manhood but their mother's experience with men, including her father in her own childhood, will impart influential messages about the kind of man she wants her son to be.

Divorce and custody considerations are superimposed on normal developmental family relationships. In the eyes of the court, the only question becomes what model of care will bring stability and minimization of conflict to the family in question. In this regard, high stability at the cost of parental involvement would be as negative for the child as high parental involvement at the cost of stability. The court's task is to find a balance between the two.

Custody and access are the primary tools or mechanisms by which the court can achieve this aim. These are the levers it can pull. Unfortunately, when one examines the factors that most contribute to outcome, custody and care arrangements matter for sure but less than the quality of parent–child relationships and the emotional climate between the parents. There is no legal antidote for incessant inter-parental conflict and hostility.

Custody refers to the legal authorization of an adult to make major decisions on a child's behalf. Generally, it is understood as a right more than a responsibility but it does include the duty to consult and work with the other parent. It is not a license for self-centered parenting. Both custodial and non-custodial parents share in the duty of care. Nevertheless, custody denotes legal authority and this carries weight in divorce.

Custody is not the same as residence, which designates where the child lives. Theoretically, one parent could have legal custody while the other shared in the care. Alternately, both parents could share in the custody with the preponderance of care in one home designated as the primary residence. Custody and the overall care arrangement are two different dimensions.

When one parent has legal or sole custody, the other does not. Of course, non-custodial parents are still valid parental figures whose relationship with the children is sanctioned and protected by the courts. On the other hand, custody is readily perceived as an empowering factor associated with decision-making status in the care system. Historically, during most of the twentieth century, the broad majority of divorced fathers were non-custodial parents. Effectively, this left women in charge of decision-making in divorced families with fathers exercising visitation or access. In more recent years, this trend has been softened as more men have insisted on equity in post-separation family care. Looking from the adult's perspective, therefore, custody is what matters most.

If we alter the perspective and look through a child's eyes, however, custody is much less significant. The custodial parent is not loved more than the other, nor does custody have much of an association with attachment. Custody might still be important in the younger years when many key decisions have yet to be made. It does not affect everyday decisions, which comprise the majority of choices impacting on the daily life of a child. "Can I watch TV?" is not a custody issue nor is the right to take the child to a doctor when circumstances require it under either parent's care. Moreover, as children evolve, they have more input into decisions affecting them and, in any case, most major decisions such as schooling are usually made in the early years. Thus, as children age, big decisions are less an issue.

So from this standpoint custody is also overrated as an issue and source of struggle between parents. From the child's perspective, it matters little who has legal authority as long as decisions are made with a minimum of fuss and conflict. A child's interest is served by ease of decision-making and low conflict, not whether parents share legal control or whether it resides with one parent or the other. Again, it might matter a great deal to the adults but this should not be confused with anything that really touches on the best interests of children at least from the child's perspective. To be sure, joint custody with interminable wrangling amounts to "no custody" and impasse. How can this possibly serve the interests of offspring even if the parents can declare a legal draw? Yet, the fear of losing custody is often its own motivation independent of other considerations. Hence, alternative dispute resolution services have become an increasingly important component of post-divorce care systems.

Joint custody in which two invested divorced parents work out what is best in a collaborative low conflict environment describes the best practices of both intact and separated families. In this regard, not all intact families actually follow a joint custody model, even if on paper they automatically share legal care and control of their children as presumed when parents live together. Sometimes one parent characteristically defers to the other and in other cases they struggle to reach consensus until one submits more than agrees.

Problems are most likely to arise when one parent more or less deferred to the other while together but has no intention of deferring once they are apart. Some advocates would say that divorce is no time to rethink parenting models and it is best to stay with what was effectively in place during the union. Women who undertook the mainstay of child care duties and responsibilities during a union most often make this argument. They resent or question the seemingly new found interest and involvement of their former male partner post break-up.

What worked when a couple was together, however, might not necessarily apply when it has ended. Involvement is a negotiated variable of family life and does not always reflect the level of actual interest. A man might feel that he had no choice but to defer simply to avoid interminable marital conflict. He would not want that held against him as if it mirrored his degree of interest and engagement. On the other hand, perhaps it is simply a convenience to blame the ex-partner as if this is entirely her fault?

Hence, there are diverse motives around the need to be authorized as a child's custodian, only some of which have to do with children. Here are some possibilities of extraneous and supplementary reasons that parents seek custody:

- Custody is a status symbol. "Non-custodial" is associated with not being deemed a "real" parent.
- Custody can be used to control the other parent.
- Custody can be interpreted as a measure of worth as a parent. Non-custodial, in this mindset, means inadequate or deficient.
- Custody usually means more time with the child and this can translate into money that one receives or doesn't have to pay.
- Custody is a means to salvage self-esteem and repair an identity that feels damaged by the failure and guilt of divorce.
- Custody is power whether it is solely or jointly held.
- Having custody can represent a victory in respect to the other parent.
- Having custody serves as a reason to stay involved with a child.

Of course, there are some excellent reasons to serve as custodian of a child and the sharing of custody in many non-contested divorces is much more common today. In this regard, shared care and control most matches the optimal arrangement in any family, together or divorced, and hence it represents the gold standard. Custody, however, has one objective only which is to create a mechanism to make effective decisions efficiently to serve a child's real time needs.

There is no ignoring, however, that custody is related to voice and authority in a post-separation care system. It might serve as essential leverage to keep both parents active in the family system. As an example, consider that one parent was the dominant caretaker when the couple was together. Now separated, this parent devalues the contribution and even the attachment that the child has or ever had to the other parent. The risk is that the secondary parent could be lost to the child simply by being overpowered and undermined in the child's eyes. In this context, shared custody might serve as a corrective to require an especially dominant primary parent to keep the other present and relevant in the family system.

Yet, there is no easy answer simply because assigning joint custody would not necessarily change the dynamic between the parenting couple. In the worst case scenario, it could spark conflict particularly if the secondary parent suddenly stood ground and refused to be pushed around as occurred previously. In other words, there is no guarantee that the court would completely solve the problem by giving the secondary parent the means to fight back if the outcome is strife and impasse. This is where clear mechanisms for conflict resolution are so important. Having some means to reduce pressure and solve conflicts is an essential component.

Perhaps the most momentous advance in the divorce field has been the advent of dispute resolution services including mediation and, more recently, parent coordinators. The latter are appropriately trained mental health professionals who serve essentially as arbitrators for divorced couples needing quick resolution of disagreements or disputes concerning major issues. The couple signs a contract that empowers the parent coordinator to make decisions on their children's behalf after hearing the views of both parties. In my view, custody should not be considered without equal reference to how conflicts are to be resolved. The two issues are inseparable.

Sole custody

Sole custody is associated with primary residence. The parent who has sole custody is then authorized to make decisions in the child's best interests although the duty of care also includes consultation with the other parent. Custody does not signify license to ignore the input of the other parent or to act in a despotic manner. Nevertheless, the sole custodian is legally responsible for the child and this responsibility comes with the authority to make all the important decisions concerning a child's education, health care, and general wellbeing.

Hence, sole custody is an efficient model and fits numerous scenarios such as when the other parent is not very involved, lives in another jurisdiction, is medically ill and not always available or is so personally dysfunctional that sharing care and control would adversely affect the child. It also can apply when the parents are uncommitted and the alliance is too weak between them to support sharing custody.

All custody determinations are essentially a form of risk analysis. What combinations of care and control will best protect the child and provide the best chance of achieving a healthy development? Although parents tend to reduce this question to a matter of custodial status and time with the child, psychological research does not actually support such a narrow viewpoint.

Let's take the situation in respect to grandparents as an example. Children might see grandparents periodically if they do not live in the same community although these relationships are ongoing. Yet, grandparents are often important figures whose affection and interest means a lot to children. In this regard, relationships that are built on regular contact and multilayered involvement often become significant attachments. In this same vein, remaining a non-custodial parent does not mean being unimportant as long as contact is regular and functional for the child.

The notion of the "visiting" and "fun" dad, for instance, would not meet the test for meaningful parenting. On the other hand, a parent who spends somewhat less than equal time caring for a child, with or without some form of official custody, could still be a very significant parental figure. The key is that the care experience should be functional for the child and not simply leisure oriented. To be functional, it must combine positive discipline, bedtimes, homework, and other markers of real life.

Custody often carries additional meaning, however, for both parents and this can add to the burden of post-separation adjustment. In particular, the one without custody has parental but not specific legal rights and this can be interpreted as devaluing or even denigrating. To be sure, the role is defined in the negative—non-custodial—and the power imbalance is hard to miss. This can have unintended consequences such as the non-custodial parent's drifting away or feeling less committed. Irrespective of custody, therefore, continuity of visits in a predictable pattern of caretaking supports the need of children and parents alike to remain connected.

Besides detachment, another unwelcome consequence of sole custody could be ongoing conflict if the non-custodial parent perceives this as a major slight or defeat. The custodial parent could then be constantly chastised for making decisions unilaterally and without consultation. Sometimes there is truth to this allegation especially with custodial parents who find it too stressful to deal with the other parent or who interpret custody as license to ignore the other parent's input. Of course, this is not what is intended by custody, which should represent simply an efficient model for consultation and decision-making to benefit children of divorce.

Although sole custody is deemed an outdated format, not in keeping with the mutuality and blending of roles of modern parenting, it still has its place. Separated couples might agree to this model or the court could impose it. The court's reasoning would include that building a care system around one parent with optimal contact to the other would more likely serve the needs of the child in the future.

For instance, there is no merit to applying the values of joint custody to individuals who cannot use it. As such, there is nothing inherently wrong with sole custody as long as the non-residential parent has sufficient, regular, meaningful, and continuous contact with the children. It is asymmetric for sure and one parent must take a less commanding position in the care system, but the real test is whether rational and timely decisions get made and whether there is room and opportunity for sharing of views and discussion.

As a rule of thumb, therefore, the care arrangement should not exceed the parenting couple's capacity to work within it. This does not mean that simple resistance to shared custody by one parent should ever be sufficient grounds to sink the idea. Here I am speaking of capacity not simply willingness, which is more superficial and sometimes tactical or transitory.

In the final analysis, what is essential is that both parents have a meaningful opportunity to know and relate to their child. As long as this criterion is met then whether one serves as custodian or non-custodian has to be kept in perspective. The main problem, as I see it, is when sole custody is applied when not necessary or reflective of the mutual capacities and engagement of the two parents. Consequently, it is the misapplication of sole custody that has been harmful over the years, not simply the model itself. This includes parents who create a false furor around the other parent in order to make it appear that shared parenting would simply be impossible.

Joint custody

Joint custody is considered the optimal arrangement in divorce for raising children essentially because it most simulates the intact family situation. Joint custody means shared decision-making and, as the term implies, it carries the intonation of being cooperative in a conjoint agreement based parenting system. It is the unmistakable expression of the notion that when the union ends there is still a remainder called "family" that binds or unites the two adults in collaborative parenting.

Shared custody is the option most worth considering as long as the two former life partners can "walk the walk" when it comes to the cooperative mindset just described. As one can imagine, when former partners agree to joint custody only to work against each other, children suffer. At the same time, parents who respect each other's roles and parent–child relationships and who work together on their children's behalf can reduce much of the harm or risk that arises in divorce.

It is likely that the families choosing this option do so willingly and are already predisposed to honor its values. In other words, they are more respectful of each other and their children, experience less conflict, and cooperate and communicate better than a comparable group of higher conflict ex-couples. What is consequential to the outcome for the children then is not specifically the form of custody but underlying variables such as healthy parent–child relationships, low conflict, and low socioeconomic stresses.

As long as we are clear that there is no absolute value to joint custody on its own to support the welfare of children post separation, then we can join others in the past thirty years in praising its merits. From a child's perspective, the important element is that decisions get made smoothly and without excessive parental strain. There is the added benefit that the child can experience the "remainder", which is the proof that the family entity has survived the divorce or break-up. Moreover, the parents communicate, refer to each other respectfully, collaborate when necessary and can be easily and comfortably with each other at a soccer game or school event. It is not the intact family but it approximates what any child would want to experience in a family of origin.

When speaking of joint custody, we are strictly referring to the joint authorization of the parents to make major decisions regarding the wellbeing of the child. Joint custody does not automatically mean shared or equal access.

Gina and Richard's marriage lasted fifteen years. Gina struggled with her values and guilt to end the union. She did not have the support of her parents to terminate a marriage she found lacking in happiness and devoid of emotion. Richard was an active father but immature in his view of intimacy and sexuality. She felt increasingly turned off. Her mind often drifted back to university and she chided herself for not ending the relationship immediately when her instincts told her that he was sure to disappoint. Consequently, Gina worked through her feelings and eventually ended the union.

The couple agreed on joint legal custody and shared parenting of their two children. They both had good jobs and were able to afford two smaller homes in the same neighborhood. The children went back and forth on an alternate week basis.

Gina respected Richard's participation and investment as a parent. He respected hers. There were no serious conflicts and when one child suffered a significant sports injury they were able to pull together and meet the challenge. It is not that all dealings went smoothly. Gina still found Richard's behavior adolescent at times but she approached it with goodwill now that she was no longer looking to him as a husband. The children managed the transition well and there was a flexibility of arrangement without absence of structure that suited their lives.

Let's compare Gina and Richard to another example.

George and Mary had been divorced four years when tensions spilled over and court action ensued. They had agreed to joint custody but were unable to cooperate in meaningful ways. Mary was exasperated and George remained perplexed as to why the arrangement wasn't working. He felt that Mary was always building walls to exclude him from the children while she found that he was impossible to deal with and kept pushing and manipulating to get his way.

The couple's two school aged children were stressed by their parents' inability to make decisions. Where would they be going to school and in what activities would they be allowed to participate? A daughter developed anxiety symptoms and this was noted at school. She could not cope with the chronic uncertainty that her parents' impasse created.

Mary offered many examples of George's conduct. He made the children feel guilty when he didn't get his way. Phone calls were impossible, according to Mary. When she called, the children were always busy. When he called, everything had to stop in order to accommodate his demand and he found countless ways to prolong phone calls. From his side, George viewed his requests as reasonable. He was an involved, caring parent, he stated, who put his children first. She felt psychologically battered. Decisions were made when one side or the other conceded in exhaustion. Until then, the children had no idea what would be decided and the stresses proved interminable.

There did not seem to be issues with basic care. Nevertheless, joint custody had created a war of attrition.

Mary and George illustrate well the problem when there is no capacity within the couple to make joint custody work. Shared custody might have given neither a legal defeat, if they chose to see it this way, but it did not lead to family functioning post-divorce either. Indeed, from the children's perspective, their parents' overestimation of what they could accomplish as co-parents created the worst of circumstances.

My impression is that joint custody tends to work when there is no history pre-separation of conflicts being channeled through the children. There has to be a capacity to maintain the childcare area conflict free or outside the bounds of any relational conflict. This implicit agreement then provides the intellectual and psychological base for joint decision-making. It does not mean that there has to be automatic accord on what decision to make.

There is an ethical dimension to successful joint parenting. Put succinctly, both parents must agree to act in the service of the joint custody. The joint custody must retain primacy as a value worth protecting. Its importance exceeds any right that one or the other parent might claim in the system.

Let's look at a further example. A father is camping with the children and one of the kids becomes ill with a high fever on the Sunday morning before they depart for home. The schedule requires that the children reside with their mother after 7pm that day. He is concerned enough to take the child to the nearest hospital to be checked. The child is prescribed an antibiotic because there is some concern of a bacterial infection from the lake in which they swam. The other child is fine. As they sit in the waiting room, the dad calls the mother and lets her know the situation. He then calls after they have seen the doctor and started the medication.

There was no requirement for him to call his ex-wife. She could be told at the drop off later that day. On the other hand, he understood that she would want to know immediately, as would he. He also implicitly realized that there was a higher value than his own autonomy at stake and this related to acting in the service of the joint custody. Hence, when he got home and the transition was made, there were no surprises for the mom and no bad feelings that she had been in the dark while one of their children was ill and at a hospital.

Here is an example that illustrates the opposite.

Mom and dad share custody of their one daughter who is now eight years of age. Dad has regular and substantial access but not equal time. It so happens that the daughter comes home with a notice pertaining to a school outing in which the school is looking for parent volunteers. The mother, with whom the daughter is residing at the time, retrieves the note. The dad is already anxious about his place in the parenting system. He feels that his ex-wife downplays his place in his daughter's life by assuming a joined-at-the-hip closeness with their daughter that shuts him out. The mom knows that the dad would welcome the opportunity to volunteer. Nevertheless, she decides that this is simply the luck of the draw and signs up to volunteer without telling the dad. It is only after the fact when it comes out during a conversation with his daughter that he realizes what occurred. He is very upset while the mom accuses him of overreacting. She advises him to work more on his relationship with their child rather than blaming her for what is wrong.

In this latter case, the mother might tolerate the joint custody on paper but she expects to dominate and does not really adhere to the spirit of the joint arrangement. She is actually competitive with the father and manipulates the child to embrace a mother–daughter duo that is mutually exclusive. In terms of family system theory, joint custody is unlikely to work effectively when power and boundary issues prevail and there is lack of capacity to act in the service of the shared custody arrangement.

Does this mean that the father should accept a non-custodial role in this case simply because the mother is unable or unwilling to grasp the spirit and advantage of joint custody? Perhaps the father should apply for custody in the court based on the premise that the mother devalues the importance of his link to their daughter. He could argue that he needs custody to offset this trend. Trials, though, are very expensive not to mention costly emotionally. They are depleting and uncertain in their outcome. Litigation polarizes couples to the extreme and children often become the losers. Even if the father succeeded legally in this example, the daughter might not be better off nor would the dynamic change.

Certainly, the father should not need to lose custody simply because the mother is poorly suited to a joint custody framework. Here is where the mechanisms for resolving issues and conflicts between the parents are as important as the parenting arrangement itself. For instance, up to two sessions of mediation could be mandatory for each issue. This would give the father a forum to confront the mother and secure a framework for moving forward. In some other instances, depending on jurisdiction, they might use a court appointed or voluntarily chosen parent coordinator who could impose a solution. In both cases, the involvement of a "third" can help bring issues clearly to light towards finding solutions. Apart from dispute resolution, a better strategy for the father could be to call for family therapy to address the troubling dynamic undermining his role.

For those separating couples that have the wherewithal to make joint custody work, the optimal approach in my view is to create a framework beforehand that leaves as little as possible to be decided on the spot. Here are key areas for consideration:

- Name the child's health care practitioners in the Final Agreement and only use these professionals unless in the case of emergency.
- Be clear on how conflicts over decisions will be handled. Make the system efficient and compact because many decisions are time sensitive.
- Outline a clear system for communication that is respectful of each parent's autonomy but provides a forum for transmitting information pertinent to the children.
- Always act in the service of the joint custody. Hence, never use the communication format as a forum for complaints or criticisms of the other parent.
- Remain especially attuned to any plans or decisions that could impact on the other parent's time with the children.

- Communicate well before a decision is made and seek the other parent's consent.
- Work out as many of the logistical issues as possible in advance. Who will register the children for extracurricular activities? How many activities per season? How to handle Halloween? Birthdays (including the parents') and birthday parties, among other special events?
- Keep in mind parental sensitivity to knowing where their children are while under the other parent's care. This applies particularly if a pattern changes or there is an unusual journey or event. The rule of thumb is that if you would like to know then the other parent would as well. As an example, "Suzy has a sleepover tonight at Meghan's." It's not necessary but is comforting and respectful.
- Create a precedent for dealing with unanticipated issues in the future and add them to the general rules when they arise.

The true value of joint custody emerges when the parents are able to retain as much of the original family matrix as possible without sacrificing integrity or autonomy. Children appreciate when their parents can collaborate. They feel properly contained and learn not to fear the insecurities and abandonment anxieties of divorce. This means that they can invest their coping resources where these energies are most needed, which is their own school, peer, and extracurricular life.

When children must divert too many emotional resources to their home life, having to contend with the strain of poorly separated or divorced parents, they can become depleted. My impression is that this further fuels much of the hyperactivity, excessive vigilance, attention deficits, and anxiety states that one regularly observes in children from chronically strained divorced families. Growing up is the job of children. In the good divorce, they are still contained and remain part of a functioning family. Their parents do not stop working together even if their personal relationship disintegrated. Of course, there is still the possibility of clinical problems but likely not much different from the intact family.[3]

Other types of custody

There are variations on the theme of custody that arise to meet specific circumstances. These are not frequently applied but they can be usefully employed in some families and in some contexts. On other occasions, they make little sense and offer no real advantages.

For instance, a separated couple live in different cities and they share a school aged child. Rather than argue about primary residence, they decide that the child will attend school for half the year in one city and then move to the other city and complete the academic year. The parents then share the summer. Instead of having joint custody, they agree to a split or divided custody model in which each has sole custody for the period in which the child is with them. They enroll the child in a private education system such as Montessori, available in both communities, and arrange for the two schools to coordinate the child's studies to facilitate continuity. They also alternate holidays during the school year so that the child can keep up with peer relations in both locales.

Could it work? Yes, as long as one is blessed with an adaptive child without academic or social difficulties who can help make it work. It would be incumbent on the parents to keep each other informed and to visit back and forth so that there is some form of family melding. It would not work if the parents were not respectful and supportive of each other and the child.

Nevertheless, there would be some risks even in the best of situations. One is that the child would skirt the surface of peer interactions and not learn to deepen friendships. The converse possibility is that the child would get quite close to friends and would then be exposed to incessant disruption and loss. How would extracurricular skill development work? Many activities are seasonal and this might be bridgeable in this case. Would it matter of there were two gymnastic programs? Perhaps, but it would make it difficult for the child to do an activity in depth. For instance, recreational gymnastics would be very possible whereas competitive gymnastics would likely be problematic. In this regard, all accommodations extract some price even when they solve other problems.

In this instance, we have two parents who are prepared to let their child go for long stretches and a child who is willing to live parallel lives. In other words, they would not be typical nor would their situation be one that was regularly faced. Yet, if they were flexible and supportive of their child, prepared to make concessions and aware that there would be some price to pay, then maybe it could work and the child might do well. It is likely that the formula would hold until the child reached a point in development, probably in early to mid-adolescence, when such a shifting life no longer made sense to the child. In other words, it would be time limited with the child putting an end to it before the parents would.

Although joint custody is usually reserved for those separated parents who have the capacity to work together, there are some who make the argument for a form of divided or split custody in which there is no overlap of duties or functions. In this regard, the parents might readily admit to having no capacity to cooperate or collaborate. To be sure, they can't be civil when they meet and any attempt at communication is usually a disaster. On the other hand, there is a begrudging acceptance that both have an equal place in the lives of their children. So what's to be done?

In this context, the designation of custody would seem less important than who does what in respect to the children. The challenge for the parenting couple is to specify every possible situation and divvy up the duties. One parent takes the children to the dentist and the other to the medical doctor. They alternate taking the child to the psychologist. One does soccer and the other does baseball. If they need to discuss anything or make a decision, they don't end up with mediation; they begin with it. If mediation fails then a parent coordinator makes the decision on their behalf. In these situations, there is no permeability between the homes. They are two sharply divided universes with the children going back and forth with little interchange between the parents.

Potentially this type of arrangement, custody as apartheid, could work as long as there was no malignancy in the parents' attitude towards each other that spilled over and contaminated the children's life space. The problem with many vitriolic separations is that they are dominated by turmoil and this is profoundly unsettling to children. There is no buffer to help the child absorb the emotional toxicity.

Split custody also includes the option of each parent having sole custody of one or more of the parents' children. There would again have to be reciprocal respect for the custodial rights of each while still maintaining access links with the non-custodial child or children. The risk in this situation is that the family splits and loses connection with the non-custodial parent and sibling(s).

Consider, for example, a gay ex-couple who had adopted a daughter and son from a foreign country. Even before the break-up, a schism had evolved in which each parent had a special rapport with one of the children. When they separated, they chose homes in opposite ends of the city. Each assumed sole custody of one of the children. Although the son was eager to keep a connection with his sister, the daughter and her parent withdrew much to the chagrin of the other parent. Despite legal efforts, there was no easy way to recover the lost unity particularly as the children reached teen years.

Such a fracture is not inevitable of course in the best of circumstances and there are likely situations where the split custody system has worked.

It is common to observe surprisingly well-behaved children in these high conflict post-union families. The children's normalcy, however, often occurs out of necessity and represents a survival tactic. The parents are usually too invested in the conflict to be attuned to their kids. The children fill the gap as if their well-behaved maturity will somehow undo the worst aspects of their parents' conduct.

Whether such an arrangement, if it worked, could be labeled a variant of joint custody is mainly academic. I prefer to describe it as a split custody in which overall responsibility is replaced by a micro apportioning of duties and responsibilities. The goal is to minimize future wrangling about who does what and when. The downside is the constant risk that what is not decided beforehand becomes a new source of conflict and defeats the purpose of the apartheid model.

In my experience, these arrangements are generally unstable although there might be cases that work and do not attract further attention. One would need to consider, as well, the experience of children growing up in a split universe in which each home exists as its own solitude. It is certainly a long way from simulating a normal home environment but could still be preferable to living in a war zone with its cumulative emotional risks.

Further comments on custody

Parents go to the wall over the issue of custody. Having custody is a badge of honor for many and not having custody is perceived as a major defeat or rejection. In truth, however, custody is mainly about decision-making as well as creating a clear anchoring point in a child's life.

The question becomes how to know what is best in a particular situation. When parents begin with the premise that custody is a direct measurement of their involvement, participation, or importance then the discussion quickly becomes one of parent's rights. The parent will make the argument that they need custody to attain a meaningful place in their child's life. This ignores the fact that children derive meaning from relationships that are consistent, ongoing, and supportive of their developmental needs. They do not accord meaning or significance based on how decisions are made.

Hence, if separated parents could begin with the idea that all that must be decided is how decisions should get made then the process becomes clearer. Parents might reflect on a specific important decision made during the union. This could include baby naming, choice of preschool or daycare, secular or religious education, this activity or another, among the many possibilities. How did this work out? Was there a cooperative spirit or was it stressful to come to a consensus? The best predictor of future functioning is what happened in the past.

There is, however, a distinct difference between deferring to the other parent who has the background knowledge to make a certain decision and an overall negligent passing the buck, which is a sign of disinterest, surrender or disregard.

If a former couple involves two parents who have both invested cooperatively in raising their children and have traditionally made decisions together then there can be no better choice that joint custody. The guiding principle is to maintain as much of the intact family situation as possible. If, however, there is little history of alliance, meager examples of cooperative and constructive problem solving and poor communication, then joint legal custody is likely not appropriate. Again, custody is only about decision-making.

There can be no ethical divorce if the parenting arrangement in place is permanently in an uproar needing third party intervention before any decision can be made. In this regard, joint legal custody with some clear and efficient means of conflict or dispute resolution included can provide the right balance between shared participation in decision-making and functional efficiency.

For involved and committed non-custodial parents, the emphasis should be on an optimized, regular, and meaningful access arrangement to facilitate having a full relationship with the child. This is what matters to children in the long run.

Note that the "right" in this case is not the parent's right to custody but the child's right to have decisions made in a timely and fluid fashion to meet developmental needs. Too often this basic ethic is ignored or rationalized so that the parent's own interest is equated with the child's.

As a final note, occasionally shared custody is used to bolster or provide assurance when one parent is especially wary of being ignored or disqualified by the other. In other words, although the conditions for successful joint custody are not really met, the hope is that with alternative dispute arrangements in place, the system might be more stable than if sole custody is imposed and the more tenuous parent feels cut loose or devalued.

From experience, I would say that this is a gamble and will only succeed if the remedy settles the core conflict between the parties. This can be hard to predict. One further accommodation to the mechanism would be that the primary caretaker has final decision-making with the non-residential or second parent having the option of quick arbitration in the case of disagreement over major issues. In other words, there would be a built-in capacity for efficient decision-making as well as an opportunity for recourse to prevent impasse. In addition, the parent initiating the submission would assume costs unless the arbitrator decided otherwise.

I can think of two situations in which I recommended this option. In one case it worked well because the second parent had confidence that the first would make good decisions and took comfort that there was a reserved path for arbitration if ever needed. In the second instance, it failed because both parties were too reactive and mistrusting to share decision-making even in this most conditional sense. By recommending a custody model that was beyond their mutual capacity to implement, I probably did them no favor despite my hope that the gamble would work.

Access arrangements

As much as psychological science can help explain child development and family systems theory, each case brings its own idiosyncrasies, its own challenging blend of strengths, limitations, and risk factors. There is no easy categorizing or "one size fits all" determinations. Every parenting couple must find the optimal balance in a post separation care schedule that supports parent–child relationships while not chaining a child to the parents' needs, sense of entitlement or agenda.

Besides developmental factors, there are other circumstances that present unique challenges and variables to consider when designing a care system. These include, for example, mobility questions with parents proposing for reasons of necessity or opportunity to move to another city or even another part of the world. Each situation has to be examined in its own context.

There are specific features, demands, challenges, and requirements that arise with children of different ages and stages of development. What would suit a young child in terms of frequency of access would create instability in an adolescent. Parent–child relationships cannot be removed from the needs and capacities of the child and this has much to do with age and developmental level. Consequently, what follows is a review of different stages of development and what are common attributes and principles to help determine appropriate access arrangements.[4]

Infancy

The first two years are foundational for the development of trust and attachment, which will endure for the lifetime. This is a crucial period for the infant to have a stable and reliable holding relationship with at least one parent, an attachment figure, from whom the infant seeks comfort and soothing. Infants can certainly have more than one attachment figure. Stability of caregivers and routines during this stage are the source of a secure sense of self and of later relationships. In the traditional family configuration, the mother is the first "other" and the father is the "second". Yet, he has also always been present so the overlap between first and second is substantial. Nevertheless, developmentally, there is a difference and this has nothing to do with gender politics nor does it imply that fathers are second order parents. The maternal relationship is primal in the human psyche.

When I used to consult many years ago at a chronic care hospital, confused elderly patients would often call for their mothers. At the base of identity are mother and baby. They form an inseparable unit that is foundational to psychic life. This does not preclude the father from being a part of the system that sustains the mother and provides care to the baby. In fact, the baby quickly recognizes the separateness of the two parents and can in good circumstances bond with both. Mother and baby, however, form a bio-psychological unit that evolves from fetus to infant to child. At the same time, the father's protective presence allows the mother to focus entirely on her baby. She relies on her partner to sustain her.[5]

Understandably, then, divorce and infancy mesh poorly as it is a time of primal bonding. Break-ups cut across these natural lines and currents, which is a major part of the stress when infants are involved.

Nonetheless, some guidelines to apply in constructing a care arrangement for an infant are:

- Keep daytime visits brief and more frequent, lessening gaps.

- Provide optimal stability, continuity of care, and routine while allowing bonds with parental figures to take hold.
- Organise access for infants around physiological needs—feeding and sleep/wake cycles—so that natural rhythms are maintained.
- Maintain consistency of care on overnight visits with the non-residential parent. Overnight access promotes involvement and strengthens bonds yet is neither obligatory nor out of the question. The psychological literature, though, is not completely clear on this issue when it comes to infants.
- Expect separation anxiety between eighteen months and three years of age on a diminishing scale. Healthy infants will begin to show some anxiety within twenty-four hours of being away from a primary attachment figure.
- Be aware that attachment (or bonding) is not restricted to one parent only.
- Optimize consistency and reliable scheduling for infants although many can tolerate care in multiple settings.
- Research confirms that fathers can be as nurturing and supportive as mothers.
- Common signs of acute distress include: crying, protest, clinging, difficulty settling, and being hard to console.
- Common signs of prolonged distress include: lethargy, sleep/feeding disruption, blunted interest in the environment.

Risk factors to keep in mind:

- Infants and toddlers who, by temperament, react strongly to any change will have more problems with separations and other disruptions of divorce.
- The effects of divorce on infants are indirect and will likely augment other more general risk factors such as prematurity and developmental delay.
- A caregiver suffering depression or emotional unavailability during this crucial early phase of life can lead to later psychological problems in the child.
- The lack of siblings increases the risk that the child will become the focus of the parents' conflicts.
- Poor parental communication can lead to misinterpretation of normal ups and downs as being due to the other parent.

Protective factors include infants who have a calm temperament and seem to adjust naturally without showing signs of wide variability in adjustment. Certainly, the presence of siblings is often missed in terms of its supportive function even with babies. Older siblings can have a calming, ameliorative effect even when transitional adjustment stresses are higher.

Supportive caregivers besides parents, including nannies, grandparents, and daycare providers, among others, can make a big difference in terms of baby care and help absorb any transitional flux created by marital break-ups. What matters most, it appears, is that the parents can cooperate rather than compete for the same space with the child. In this regard, they need to use a reliable means to share information about their young child. In infancy, this will include feedback about feeding, sleeping, and other physiological parameters. If communication is accepted as the priority (*vs.* struggle and competition), then the child will be much better protected.

There are often special considerations that need to be considered before an appropriate care arrangement can be implemented. Breastfeeding, for example, is a complicating factor although not insurmountable in the right context. Breast pumping, freezing and storing breast milk can prepare the way for the father to care for the baby.

I have seen numerous situations in which there was no actual viable relationship between the parties existing prior to the birth of a baby. This is particularly difficult because neither party has any real sense or trust of the other nor have they had the chance to develop a relationship capable of supporting the infant's care. In one such situation, the birth of the baby coincided with almost instant legal pressure to take the baby for an extended outing from the hospital. The mother perceived the father as a threat and she effectively shut him out. His legal protests were mainly sporadic and ineffective. The child grew up without knowing that this man who occasionally appeared was her father.

First time parents who lack knowledge of baby care also create special circumstances that need to be considered. Looking after an infant takes knowledge and skill. Hence, some experience helps and builds confidence.

Finally, problems such as post-partum depression or medical illness in the primary parent could also present special circumstances that would shape what is asked of the other parent.

As mentioned above, marital separations and infancy mesh awkwardly simply because of the youth of the child. The confluence of developmental considerations, father's rights, legal, and gender politics make determination of custody/access in this situation very difficult.

Let's take an example to illustrate the problem. In this case, we have a baby born to a couple whose union did not survive the first year of marriage. Nevertheless, based more on hope than track record, they did marry shortly before becoming pregnant.

Janice, an accountant, took parental leave while Albert, self-employed, did the same. Post-leave, his schedule remained flexible while her work facilitated part-time hours. In this regard, they were both much more available to provide care than most couples.

Albert demanded equal time with their infant child. This severely stressed Janice who asked for a graduated schedule that allowed for equal time at a later stage of development. Although the baby appeared to cope with the two rotating caregivers, the same cannot be said for Janice who suffered enormously. The court ordered interim shared access on the grounds that both parents were willing and able to provide care.

Whether this was the correct approach or not is open to debate. My own concern is that there was no sensitivity to the fact that not all infants would have coped so well. A more insecure infant with less stable attachments or a different temperament could have found this too unsettling and the result could have been damaging. Moreover, there is always the concern that a child faced with excessive disruption would experience repeated loss more than stability.

When it comes to infants in the first two years of life, these issues need to be addressed in a cautious manner with particular attention to the child's habitual functioning, temperament, and needs. There is no case for deciding access on the basis of adult rights or some overriding principle of parental equality.

It takes many years to grow a person, which is something often missed by disputing parents seemingly in a hurry to assume their rightful place in their child's life. Separating couples with infants need to act prudently together with the understanding that they will optimize care in their young child's best interests and that this will evolve. As such, there is no problem with broad sharing of care even for infants but only with a child who can handle this regimen and thrive. Otherwise, having at least one secure and steady attachment figure would work best until stable functioning of the child is achieved.

Overnight care—babies and young children

As overnight care with respect to babies and young children is a controversial issue, further discussion seems warranted. The main reason for controversy appears to be that overnight care, especially during infancy, tests the limits of the shared parenting model now favored by social and behavioral science as well as some legislatures.

When policy is guiding planning, space has to be left for appreciating the diversity of individual and family differences. These are factors that cannot be legislated or generalized and underscore the need for a sensitive and flexible approach to managing the care of babies and very young children in the separated situation.[6]

In constructing parenting plans for children, especially in the first two years of life, the initial objective must be to protect the safety of the child. This includes providing opportunity for parental comfort as well as maintaining stress levels as low as possible. Safety, in this respect, includes physical, psychological, and environmental factors. For instance, it is no use dwelling on the benefits of a particular parent child relationship if that parent lacks the knowledge, skills or appropriate environment in which to place a baby for the overnight period.

Assuming that this baseline criterion is met, however, the next planning step would be to ensure that any access arrangement supports the development of secure attachments to both parents. This should include opportunities for each parent to provide direct care, which involves playing, feeding, soothing, and supporting as well as exploring the outside world.

There is often insufficient attention paid to the transitioning from one parent's care to the other. Young children need ample reassurance and time to settle as they navigate between households. They are particularly sensitive to the relational climate between the parents and will learn to dread transitions if hostility and tension is high. In this case, regression will be observed—crying, clinging, temper tantrums, refusing to let go, and other such manifestations. If very young, they will not be able to verbalize what they feel but this does not mean that they lack an experience of the transition.

The key to ensuring successful care and interchange is when both parents are able to coordinate efforts at a pace truly compatible with their child's needs and adjustment capabilities. Parents who are more attuned to their presumed rights than to the child's needs tend to confuse their interests with those of the child. In my experience, parental teamwork is essential at this stage of development when the child is so dependent and reliant on the basic framework of care.

A lack of concordance between the parents and their caretaking will upload stress to the child. In this state of misalliance, the parents will not be able to guarantee the essential safety, calmness, and reassurance, which is the first step in caring for young children post-separation. They might argue about whether the child is stressed and, if so, who or what is responsible. Such parents tend to underestimate the real impact of not working in concert and doing their best to harmonize care.

It is also important when caring for young children in the separated context to understand parenting at its most pragmatic and systemic level. Hence, the time traveling between households matters, as do other practical considerations such as the availability of the parent and availability of other family and non-family caretaking resources. As a general principle, the goal should be to maximize the amount of time that the child spends with each parent or, if required, other family members or trusted caretakers. Parents should work together to build a sense of teamwork when it comes to child rearing.

It is important to keep in mind that children differ in their attachment styles and rapport. Some will do well with either parent and simply need one or the other available to feel secure, comforted, and connected. Others might require the primacy of one caretaker over the other for a period of time in order to ensure that at least one attachment relationship is securely established. This could lead to delay in fully integrating the other parent into the care system but the child's nature should take precedence over any value ascribed to parental rights or ambitions.

It has been my observation that high conflict couples with young children are often not able to provide a secure enough container to settle their child. Of course, this leads to heightened conflict itself, which only worsens the vicious circle that quickly evolves. The risk is that the child will be unable to form a secure attachment to either parent and this would certainly have long-term consequences. Further, professional support is often beneficial when there is a history of psychopathology, substance abuse, and violence between the parents or in the case of deeply troubled relationships where rapport is absent or minimal.

In respect to overnights, it is important to recognize that the separated or divorced situation creates added emotional hurdles for young children. Having the comfort and security to drift off to sleep requires a degree of contentment that occurs when a child feels safe, protected, and confident. Not all babies or little children can master this step right away although almost all will in due course.

It is not a reflection on the parent or the child if there is a delay in reaching this developmental capability. Not all children go to sleep easily even in the intact family situation. Development is rarely smooth and continuous. When we ask a child to master this hurdle in two homes with two parents who potentially have different styles, we can appreciate the complexity. Hence, planning for overnights needs to keep this general developmental appreciation in mind so that it does not become a contentious issue. There should be no inherent contradiction between optimizing parental relationships and providing a care regimen for young children at a pace and rhythm that meets their developmental needs.

Toddlerhood

The emphatic "no" of the two to three-year-old announces the emergence of self and the beginnings of autonomy. This needs to evolve within a safe bonded relationship. The child becomes more aware of absence and loss. The parent strikes a balance between allowing exploration and autonomy while remaining present and attentive. The stability of primary attachment(s) remains crucial. The child is developing a sense of self and an ability to interact with others. This is the phase of toilet training in which the child assumes control of important bodily functions. This maturing physiological control supports self-development. An awareness of gender differences and beginnings of genital curiosity arise during this period.

Principles and observations to help construct an appropriate care arrangement include:

- Separation anxiety can still be expected as self and emotional maturation lead to feelings of aloneness and loss although by age three this factor should greatly lessen.
- Leaving one residence and going to the other can be stressful, as it is associated with loss. The toddler is reluctant to leave where they are and resists change.
- Attachment (bonding) is not restricted to one parent only but needs to be secure with at least one caregiving adult.
- Mood states of clinging with regressive behavior alternating with states of independence and assertion can be expected.
- Signs of aggression including kicking, biting, and temper reactions are common and not necessarily a symptom of divorce.
- Overnights with the non-residential parent in children under three have been found to strengthen the involvement of that parent in the future.
- Overnights for infants and toddlers merit caution and needs careful consideration of factors including breastfeeding, the

child's capacity to handle separations and the other parent's aptitude and comfort with young children.

- Toddlers can usually handle one or two consecutive overnights away from a primary caretaker if they are with another established attachment figure.
- More than two consecutive overnights from the residential or primary parent are generally not indicated. This would cause too much disruption and create stressful re-entry problems.
- Three to four days without seeing the other parent could lead to distress in the toddler and preschool child.
- Visits need not be long but they need to be regular.
- The capacity of the non-residential parent to provide nurturing and competent care is an essential consideration.
- Presence of multiple attachment figures does not diminish the importance of the primary caregiver(s).
- Having a single home or anchor in terms of stability is only one factor. Other factors include a stable parental presence, good quality parenting with consistency of mood and technique, regular meal and sleep schedules and a warm, accepting parental attitude.
- Common signs of distress include: temper, severe obstinacy, clinging, extreme tantrum, self-injury, fecal smearing, regression in toilet training, urination in peculiar places, hurting pets, destructive behavior, and lethargy.

Some risk factors that come to mind include:

- A propensity to regression in the child and lack of stability in maintaining mood and behavior.
- Protests around exchanges or transitions, which are then misinterpreted as a reaction to the quality of the parent–child relationship and become a source of parental conflict.
- Presence of any evidence of abuse or neglect.
- Social, emotional, and economic factors that impact negatively on the capacity of the parent to provide a supportive childrearing environment.
- A lone caretaker that lacks social and/or family supports, especially if that caretaker has emotional and adjustment problems such as being regularly irritable, stressed, impatient, and reactive.

- Parents who are verbally hostile with each other in the child's presence and who chronically poison the inter-parental climate.
- Socially anxious children who might need more regular contact with a primary caregiver without this being seen as reflecting poorly on the other parent.

Reliable frequent contact with both parents is certainly a protective factor in divorce involving children in the tender years, including toddlers. As care is physically demanding at this stage, the participation of two parents can take the load off the shoulders of any one caretaker. Certainly, professional daycare facilities are also part of the support system in many instances allowing both parents to enter the workforce.

The younger the child, the more imperative the need for accurate and conflict free real time communication between the parents. Having this capability for sharing information and observations is a major step forward for a separated couple with a child of toddler age. This leads the way towards cooperative parenting and decision-making throughout the age span.

When parents have similar styles, values, and emphases, there is a uniformity of approach that aids development. In particular, the capacity to provide warm, steady, and secure parenting is likely a protective factor in divorce as compared either to overly rigid and strict parenting, or its converse, indulgent and/or erratic parenting. Part of the issue concerns the parenting style itself but another part relates to significant discrepancies in approach between the homes. Hence, for example, a strict and somewhat rigid parent in one home and an indulgent, laissez-faire parent in the other would be hard for any young child to integrate.

Certainly, the capacity to maintain a consistent routine is associated with fewer social problems. This does not imply that exceptions cannot be made but it does indicate that routine is an important factor in healthy development for young children. Routine provides a constant that is reassuring particularly when the toddler is confronted with flux from divorce as well as the rapid pace of early development.

Finally, there is a body of child research that focuses on "resiliency" as an independent protective factor. Some children are simply born resilient and this natural resilience is associated with low anxiety and strong coping skills. Although it is certainly possible to foster resilience to stress and conflict by enhancing coping and relationship skills, individual differences matter. Parents who have resilient children who appear to handle life adversity should not view this as license to take their children's coping for granted. Children who are more reactive and easily rattled or overwhelmed need help to develop appropriate coping skills and, hence, develop greater resiliency. This preventative work can pay dividends in handling future stresses.

Regarding other considerations, some toddlers are still breastfed at decreasing frequency although in a divorce situation, this can be seen as a ploy to limit access to the other parent.

A more mobile child capable of ambulation also creates increasing safety concerns. This can become an issue when parents are unable to properly supervise or otherwise maintain an appropriate environment for a young child. Sometimes this can be aggravated by emotional or personality problems in the adults. When one parent mistrusts or fears that the other cannot maintain a proper frame for safety, this can add greatly to divorce tensions. Having a proper car seat and following precise instructions goes a long way to assuaging anxieties in skittish parents worried about their child's safety when not under the primary parent's direct control.

I am a proponent of parenting classes that are available in most communities. These are especially useful in the early years and can offer essential knowledge and techniques to assist adults in becoming responsible and responsive parents. Parent resource centers and family service centers routinely offer such courses. There are even online resources although the in-person experience additionally allows for sharing with other parents in a similar situation.

Preschool

The three-year-old child is old enough to attend "preschool" and has formally moved beyond infancy. There are occasional regressive moments in preschoolers especially when coping resources are strained but on the whole, preschool to first grade children are busy developing skills and competences. Play is initially more parallel than interactive but this quickly matures into the first steps of peer relations. Imaginative play and self-development evolves within the context of a secure family. Needs for emotional and psychological support from parental figures and teachers are high, as identity formation and the capacity for initiative take hold. Gender differences are often apparent in play although with wide individual variation. Relations with each parent evolve while the child becomes more aware of separate parental relationships. In a divorce situation, children become increasingly sensitive and reactive to tensions and outbreaks of hostility or stress.

Some signposts to be considered when developing a parenting plan for children of this age range include:

- Quality of parent–child relationships is key to child development: warm and firm leads to better adjustment than overly strict, indulgent, or detached approaches.
- Some disruptions are inevitable in any post-separation care arrangement. These are not necessarily harmful to the development of the child.
- A non-residential or secondary parent's involvement, even when pre-separation participation is low, is associated with positive child adjustment.
- Common signs of distress include: emotional upset, problems separating, nightmares, aggression towards peers, school refusal, resistance to sleeping alone, non-compliance, and lack of fantasy play.

Risk factors that need to be considered include:

- Inter-parental conflict especially when the atmosphere is chronically hostile. It is an urgent priority to address when entrenched.
- Chronic exposure to parental hostility is related to childhood behavior problems and poor psychological wellbeing that can be enduring at all age levels.
- Separated parents who allow outbreaks of fighting and conflict in front of their child often leading to increased

fearfulness during the day and at bedtime, worries about loss of a parent, yearning for the absent parent or increased aggression directed at the parent providing care.

- Parents who enlist their children to provide comfort and nurturing in what becomes a role reversal.
- Preschoolers in particular will become attached to other caring adults such as a new partner. If these relationships end, they can react to the loss of the new partner.
- Parents who impose step-parents on children still adjusting to divorce rather than letting them adjust more slowly.

One protective factor in particular should be mentioned, which concerns the parent's capacity to support the child's relationship with the other parent. This often manifests through an ease of contact between the households, allowing for quick check-ins in a conflict-free and respectful atmosphere. This is very helpful, comforting, and protective of children's wellbeing.

Among special considerations, we should not forget the higher frequency of multiple births today due to advances in reproductive technologies, fertility treatments and the fact that age is associated with increased occurrence of multiple births. Besides the much added workload in multiple births, twins and triplets are not necessarily first children, which creates risks of parenting disruption for young singletons in particular.

Health concerns such as asthma, allergy, and gastrointestinal vulnerability, including reflux, often add to the complexity of parenting post-separation. Medication management and keeping track of symptoms requires a higher level of communication and coordination. Not all divorced couples can readily meet this standard and this can have negative consequences for offspring. There is no guarantee either that the parents will agree on the threshold for what constitutes a symptom change. Hence, one parent might be ready to take the child to the doctor or emergency department far more quickly than will another. This can lead to heightened conflict and accusations of negligence.

Divorced parents that are physicians or other health professionals are often accused of under reacting to health concerns in their own children. In other words, this can be a complex area that takes special consideration and planning. Separated and divorced health professionals should always scrupulously follow professional guidelines regarding treating family members.

My suggestion is that parents articulate as concretely and clearly as possible a way of reporting symptoms or health status so that they can at least use a common language or framework.

Further, in our pluralistic world, it is more common for people of different faiths or different degrees of observance of the same faith to get together and have children. When these relationships end, the implications of these differences become more apparent and potentially significant. Will the child attend Sunday school every second Sunday post-separation, for example, or will the less religious parent continue to honor the commitment even on their weekend? A woman who converted to Islam and agreed to raise the child in that faith could have second thoughts when she personally discards the religion after the union ends. Or consider a Protestant father who wants to take the child to his church while the Catholic mother wants the child raised and confirmed in the Catholic tradition.

Finally, we could mention the problem of shift work and its impact on parental availability and scheduling post-separation. Of course, this has repercussions at all stages although it is particularly challenging in the case of young children. Airline pilots and flight attendants, nurses and other health care workers, police and fire fighters, among other occupations, often live their lives on a shifting work schedule. Trying to harmonize these demands with a parenting schedule can be challenging. It takes flexibility and a willingness to make adjustments to make it work.

Nevertheless, in the context of poor or damaged rapport between the ex-spouses, it can be a source of ongoing stress. This is particularly apparent when the parent subject to shift work is insensitive to the demands and disruptions this places on the other parent and automatically expects every accommodation no matter how last minute. Tact, respect, and patience are the hallmark of the good divorce. Stressed parents invariably means stressed children, an obvious connection that can however be missed.

School-aged

Childhood from seven to eleven years is marked by an emerging independence and focus on peers, tasks, extracurricular activities, and skill development. The child has a stable sense of identity separate from parental figures. They have greater ability to cope with their own emotional life and to develop themselves as learners and social beings. They increasingly become a part of their neighborhood and school. Mid-childhood is marked by a rapid growth in coping skills and socialization, which is often accelerated through the wide availability of social media. Talent and skill development becomes apparent and accomplishments can be substantial.

Some considerations and observations to help guide developing a suitable care arrangement for this age range include:

- Create a neutral space between the parents allowing the children to go back and forth freely.
- Convey a positive image of the other parent. Leave room for the child to have a relationship with the other parent.
- Focus on the child and contribute to the child's life rather than fixating on personal rights or entitlement.
- Pay attention to the child's history of attachments and peer relations, anxiety control as well as adjustment to other settings such as school and extracurricular milieus.
- Note that the absence of specific risk factors in the parent(s) such as personality disorder, mental illness, substance abuse, and family violence will contribute to good adjustment.
- Create fair and balanced parenting plans so children will not be drawn into their parents' conflict especially in the older segment of this age range.
- Note that common signs of distress include: prolonged emotional upset, conduct problems at school and/or home, nightmares, sleep problems, loss of appetite or emotional eating, digestion difficulties and stomach aches, night time enuresis (bedwetting), constipation, nervous symptoms

such as tics, coughs, aggression towards self or others, excessive fear of making mistakes or being "bad", stealing, excessive masturbation often at inappropriate times and places.

Be aware of the following risk factors:

- Stress or psychological duress is often channeled through one child in particular and not shared equally among siblings.
- Children are most likely to feel guilt or responsibility for the break-up or responsible for the parents' welfare.
- Loyalty conflicts may be present.
- Continuing parental anger is associated with strain in children who become co-opted as advocates and caregivers.
- Exposure to family violence pre-separation leads to negative effects on children's development.
- Risks are greatly increased when violence occurs within a pattern of abusive domination or when parents have no means other than violence to settle disputes.
- Spousal abuse post-separation is associated with increased negative consequences.
- Prolonged high conflict that pervades a family environment post-separation is also a demonstrated risk to child development.
- School stress related to learning disabilities or social maladjustment can put extra strain on child and parental communication.
- Parental disagreement about choice of school program can create instability for the child.

Among protective factors, successful academic adjustment is often an asset for a child even when the home environment is turbulent and stressful. School can be a reprieve from family tensions and a positive milieu representing emotional control, neutrality, and peace.

Moreover, children definitely gain self-esteem from extracurricular activities such as sports, dance, and music. Not only do these contribute to life enhancing skill development but they also allow for engagement with trusted adults other than the parents and provide another positive and supportive environment. Extracurricular activities also facilitate children's friendships and a sense of belonging to community, which is another important aspect of identity.

Special considerations are hard to anticipate in advance. Certainly, children with behavioral and learning difficulties present a special challenge in divorce. For instance, even a mildly autistic child would need particular attention to their adjustment and a slower cadence to implementing changes. Differences in routine are relatively easy for most children to handle but an autistic child could have real problems as a result even in the best of circumstances. In my experience, mild autism is often associated with acute sensitivity to inter-parental tension and conflict. These children simply cannot handle it and an adverse emotional climate in the home will result in behavioral regression and disorganization.

Learning disabilities are common enough to be a frequent consideration in divorce. Thankfully, psychologists have made great strides in identifying these problems and specially trained educators have developed effective strategies to help the learning disabled child. In terms of divorce, however, the challenge is to provide continuity of support, appropriate vigilance over school matters and follow through between the households. Sometimes an external tutor who works with the child in both homes is an apt solution but this is not always affordable. It could take a greater degree of cooperative parenting and oversight to ensure that divorce does not add to the risk factors faced by a child with learning disabilities.

Pre-adolescence

Pre-teens from eleven to thirteen years are a more culturally defined group in recent years. Wide exposure to social media and opportunities for broad life experience lead to greater sophistication and at times precocious development. Certainly, the peer group becomes increasingly important and there is a shift away from the family as the central focus of life. The family, however, remains the anchor. These pre-teen children often have a healthy and at times inflated sense of their capacity to make their own choices. On the other hand, they can be responsible for their chosen activities and schoolwork.

Puberty with or without burgeoning sexual interest often arises during this period. It follows that this is an age of expanding self-consciousness, which can also be associated with increased body image sensitivity. Children reach puberty at different times, girls usually preceding boys but with wide individual variability overall. This adds to the social and psychological complexity of this age with children at different points in development interacting daily. Complementing these changes, children's cognitive development allows for more abstract thinking and more sophisticated intellectual processes.

The onset of puberty is associated with increasing demands for independence and input on decisions. Parents must be attuned to their children, able to maintain a structure without becoming overly rigid or misinterpreting autonomous strivings as necessarily rebellious. It can be a time of flux for some children but certainly not all.

Some principles and observations to help guide establishing appropriate care arrangements in this age group include:

- Pre-teens can appreciate complex life situations and often demonstrate poise and sensitivity in the face of regressed and struggling parents. This is in contrast to younger children who are more likely to be bewildered and disorganized by parental turbulence.
- Anger may hide deeper sadness and distress. Older children can articulate their anger.
- Identity is still defined by the family so that children of this age experience their world as shaken when parents break up.
- Headaches, stomach aches, and other psychosomatic symptoms are common at this age as a reaction to divorce.
- They can become valuable allies of one parent against the other if exposed to distorting influences that embroil them in the controversy. Alignment with one parent against the other is a type of maladjustment in most cases unless the children are exposed to actual violence.

- Common signs of distress include: push for premature autonomy, behavior problems, power struggles, excessive concern/worry for parents' wellbeing, clinging, insecurity, fearfulness, precocious sexuality, smoking, drug and alcohol use, harm to self or others, food or eating preoccupations.

Some risk factors that can complicate a child's adjustment include:

- Weak, conflictive or shaky relationships with one or both parents prior to the separation.
- A history of intense conflict with a sibling.
- Vindictive adults who seek alliance with a child for manipulative and strategic reasons.
- Pre-existing weaknesses such as academic or social difficulties, which are worsened by divorce strains.
- Parenting that is overly rigid, increasing conflict with pre-teens.
- Parents attempting to curry favor by offering excessive freedoms or socially desirable material items.
- Early unsupervised access to social networking that can put the child at risk for precocious sexuality, peer harassment, or acting out.

In terms of protective factors, strong parent–child relationships in which the child can express their real feelings are essential. Communication between parent and child is an essential tool to aid adjustment during this complex phase of development. It helps, therefore, when parents demonstrate respect for each other's roles and relationships with the children despite divorce.

Because separation and divorce can be stressful on families, peer support through friendships, school, and extracurricular activities assumes particular importance. Children with strong peer relations have a natural buffer to help absorb the shock of divorce and any ongoing strains that occur as a result. The peer group will help emotionally contain children whose parents have separated. They might not say a lot to each other but the knowledge that one is not alone in this predicament can be a great comfort.

Finally, parents who stay on the same page and offer independence to their child in manageable doses help protect their child's development. Supervision and structure are still very important but are not to be confused with hovering and control, or the opposite, total freedom without the accompanying maturity to handle it.

Adolescence

Teens from fourteen to eighteen years are the group most obviously affected by divorce. It can be interpreted as a major intrusion into what is already a complicated and full-time developmental endeavor. They need support and understanding as much as it should be them and not their parents claiming center stage at this time of life.

The peer group is firmly established as an extremely important reference group. Sexual interest heightens and romantic relationships evolve. Cognitive potential develops further to include greater capacity for abstract thinking. By the end of this period, adolescents develop a relatively stable self-identity with some degree of physical and emotional independence from parents. The capacity to work and to love takes a major step forward. There is certainly a continuing need for parents to provide structure and offer guidance and support. Adolescents are coping with rapid changes in the complexity of their lives and they welcome parental support as long as they do not see this support as controlling or infantilizing.

Some observations and principles about adolescents to help guide parenting at this stage include:

- They are the most likely age group to judge parents and become polarized in dispute.
- They can assume the role of caretaker for younger children and parents.
- Resentment can arise particularly when the teenager views the parent as usurping their right to be the center of concern or preoccupation.
- Loyalty conflicts are also common.
- Access cannot be imposed unilaterally and often requires the adolescent's consent and cooperation.

- Some adolescents will show remarkable initial maturity while others will become aloof and withdrawn even if they were not so before the break-up. This does not always improve with time.
- Adolescents often cope best when the separation seems warranted or justifiable in their eyes particularly if the post-separation emotional climate is improved.
- Disillusionment in terms of the dependability of adult relationships can affect teens and have emotional consequences.
- Common signs of distress include: acting out, addiction, running away, truancy, refusal of contact with a parent, anxiety and/or depression.

In this regard specific risk factors to keep in mind include:

- Acting out as a real possibility and a common sign of maladjustment to the divorce.
- Separation leading to depression, withdrawal or anger and disdain for the parents due to disillusionment.
- Slow and difficult adjustment especially in the first year if the break-up is sudden and not comprehensible to the teenager.
- Parental violence as the teen can become involved.
- Feelings of rupture and loss for a long period afterwards particularly in close-knit families with a strong family feeling pre-separation.
- Preoccupied or dysfunctional parents, which may lead to adolescents falling through the cracks.
- Long-term role reversal can lead to emotional burden and fear when the teen feels protective of parents and willing to give advice.

Parents with teenage children that are separating are naturally interested in any protective factors that could mitigate the sizable downside risk facing this age group. For one, continuity of parenting is essential. The parents need to be able to establish and maintain firm and consistent limits. An adolescent who feels that the parents are so caught up with each other and their drama that they virtually abandon their parental role could easily react adversely. It is natural for some temporary lapses in coverage during the acute phase of the break-up but the extent to which the parents can maintain the frame the better it is for teens.

Second, parents need to preserve a clear divide between their own relationship and those with the children. There has to be a mutual agreement that neither parent will appeal for sympathy or allegiance from their children or involve them in the separation. Children who perceive this boundary take obvious comfort.

As a corollary, break-ups that are scripted as moral narratives in which one party is the abuser and the other is the victim limit the capacity of children to stay out of the fray. Of course, there are situations that legitimately could be framed as unfair treatment and even abuse. Hence, I am not speaking of how one adult might feel towards the other from whom they are separating. Mainly, it concerns parents who use this model of victimization as their standard template to claim the "good" and attribute "evil" to the other. Adolescents can be influenced if they feel that they have to serve as one parent's champion.

In terms of protective factors, however, parents who are able to establish a firm barrier or boundary between the marital union and their children are protecting their offspring. Here is an example.

Jerome and Danielle had a turbulent relationship with three children, all teenagers at the time, before degenerating into a high conflict divorce. The father rebounded and quickly regained equilibrium while the mother was obviously deeply disturbed by the divorce. She felt severely abused emotionally and believed that she had suffered psychologically as a result of the bad treatment. The oldest child, a daughter, continued to see her dad but eventually ended visits when she complained about her father's critical attitude. A second daughter went to live with her dad only after declaring that in her mother's house there was no space to love both parents. She felt harangued simply for wanting to see her dad. The youngest child, a son, turned on his dad soon after the marriage ended, and, although he continued to see his dad infrequently, also identified totally with the mother and felt equivalently abused by the dad.

The example illustrates the fusion and confusion that arises when internal family boundaries break down. In this case, there was no insulation between the parents' divorce and the children's lives. Two children were effectively lost to the parent perceived by the mother as an abuser and the sole source of her mental injury. It was a family that fragmented rather than held together as if the schism affecting the parents came to include the children as well.

Parents who can continue in their parenting roles while separating are in a much better position to meet the psychological needs of the children following divorce. It can be difficult to predict how teenagers will respond but parents who remain available and attuned continue to support the family framework that in the end makes all the difference.

One factor that can certainly impact on teens is the financial limitations and pressures that often occur as a result of parental divorce. This might entail moving to a smaller home, having a smaller bedroom or having to adjust to less disposable income in one or both homes. For some teens, this is a small issue and not a major problem while others take it personally and feel let down. From the child's perspective, the parents could appear to place their own needs selfishly ahead of their offspring. Of course, child–parent and adult relations are different dimensions of family life but some children are bewildered and angered by their parents' actions.

Intolerance of the separation is most common when the teenager cannot accept the parents' rationale for ending the union. This can be especially challenging when there has not been open discord or a long period of obvious marital struggle. In the case where struggle and relationship failure have been obvious, adolescents are capable of acceptance and even relief despite any deeper longings for parental love and unity.

As much as remarriage and blended families are increasingly common, this can present special considerations. There is a major difference between children of divorce who have had several years to get used to parental break-up and those who are thrust precipitously into a merger with a step-parent and his or her children. Needless to say, such a venture takes tact and talent from the parents to read the teenager's signals to facilitate some form of integration. There are few challenges in divorce as complicated and difficult as blending two families into one.

Another special challenge that would also count as a protective factor is the parents' capacity and willingness to work with a teenager's wishes and preferences in helping craft a post-separation parenting arrangement. Parents who can manage this process well will find their children grateful for the opportunity to have input. Teenagers in particular need to feel heard by their parents and they carefully gauge whether they are being treated respectfully as autonomous young people who have a right to their own views and needs. Adolescence is a swing-stage between an anticipated adulthood with its many demands and entitlements and childhood dependency with its anchor in the family and its protective layering of parental reliance. Attuned parents are able to appeal to both constituencies in the same teen: address the adult they want to be and the child they very recently were.

A further special consideration arises when divorce leads to change of neighborhoods and sometimes even communities. Again, this cuts across what an adolescent most needs, which is environmental stability in order to deepen social bonds and adjust to life and scholastic demands. Of course, a child with social difficulties might welcome a change in schools or neighborhood but, for the most part, this would likely not be perceived as an opportune development. Adolescence is a full-time job and teens usually prefer their home life to be the constant in the midst of developmental flux. This does not mean that change is impossible and sometimes there is simply no choice. Every situation is different as is every child. The goal is to have support from both parents who demonstrate understanding and a willingness to accommodate, support, and remain sensitive to the impact the situation has on the teen. This is far different from the parent who takes the position that bad stuff happens in life and it is solely the child's role to accept and accommodate.

Conclusion

"The best interests of a child" principle guides the family law process that determines the best plan and schedule to care for children after their parents separate or divorce. Determining "best interests", however, can be a difficult process that is anything but straightforward. Although the principle is clear, the application can be complex and controversial. There are numerous dimensions to be considered including who will make key decisions and how differences or conflicts will be resolved.

Under usual circumstances, the parenting schedule should reflect the needs of a child to have a relationship with both parents within the framework of child development and any specific circumstances or risk factors that need to be taken into account. Developing a parenting plan then should have less to do with parental rights than parental obligations to provide psychosocially for their children over and above their own comfort or interests.

Presumption of joint legal custody has been enshrined in divorce legislation in some jurisdictions and this is impacting generally on care arrangements post-divorce. It is intended to overcome maternal supremacy as an underlying cultural and legal preference. In principle, there is merit to the position that both parents should participate equally in raising children. It works well for the broad majority of divorced couples that should choose this model anyway. It does little, however, to solve the problem of dealing with those conflictive and complex family scenarios that frequently find their way to the courts.

Nonetheless, it is a useful proposition that all post-separation care arrangements should be optimized to suit the children of the union. Nevertheless, the analysis should begin with a clear and honest appreciation of the risks that the children face and not the rights of their parents. Risk analysis would need to take into account intrinsic factors such as age, temperament, and relationship to siblings. It should also include developmental jeopardies that the child might face anyway such as learning disability, hyperactivity, and susceptibility to anxiety, social problems, and medical issues. Then there are risks that arise from the way the parents deal with each other and the extent to which they can successfully accommodate, respect, and cooperate together.

In the ethical divorce, there is an appreciation for risk rather than a focus on entitlement. The children are seen as independent of the parental relationship and their needs can be addressed on their own terms. In contrast, however, the problematic separation or divorce often features little differentiation made between the child's best interests and what the parent might want. The complication then deepens when family law and the parent both make presumptions that might not apply to the situation in question. In this regard, the risk in the family law system is that the child's needs disappear behind the parent's who serves as apparent spokesperson for the child. Judges, lawyers and mental health professionals, however, are aware of this possibility and will often take steps to ensure that the child's voice is heard.

The presumption of joint custody and shared parenting can serve as a corrective for parents who keep a tight hold on their children and make it very difficult for them to go back and forth in optimal frequency. Risk analysis is especially tricky when it is the parents' own behavior that is the source of the gravest risks.

What is most positive is when parents come together post-separation to work out a flexible and sensitive parenting plan that respects their limitations and strengths, their children's realities and contextual factors such as finances, lifestyle, and work demands. It is a "child first" perspective that is enormously comforting for children who sense that their parents are still responsibly in charge.

CHAPTER SIX

Divorce, parenting, and families

Families contain, hold, organize and identify us within a specific social context. In this regard, they are more than just an amalgam of related or linked people of different generations. Although the current model of family is apparently a relatively recent phenomenon in social history, there is enormous importance given to it in society. Family has become our shared cultural antidote to loneliness and isolation. Although modern pluralism has expanded the notion of family, it has also solidified this concept as central to human togetherness and the main focus of our celebrations. Whatever the religion or tradition, the notion of family will be found at the crux.

With divorce and remarriage, an increasingly common phenomenon, new pairings of adults create opportunities for novel family groupings. This can be as simple as a new partner joining an existing parent with one or more children or as complex as two multi-children units merging due to a new partnership. It takes sensitivity to boundaries, existing loyalties, communication, and interpersonal relations to make a success of such a venture. When blended configurations work, it can be a terrific addition to family life. They are a huge challenge, however, and often take patience and special skill.

Although I tend to see the more troubled situations in my practice, my impression is that there is often an expectation that the new blending be accorded immediate validity not only in the eyes of the child or children but also in the eyes of the former spouse. The implicit notion is that the new family has completely replaced the old configuration, which is supposedly relegated to history. It is inevitable then that conflict erupts mainly because the original family cannot be renounced without weakening the cornerstone of a child's identity. One telltale sign, for example, is when a divorced and re-partnered parent insists that the child spend half of Mother's or Father's Day with the respective step-parent. Another indication is when the parent who has re-partnered closes off entirely and refuses to deal with the other parent.

Part of the ethics of re-partnering is to continue to acknowledge the original family identity that remains operative. There is still a mother, father, and child who together form a unit even when the parents have separated and re-partnered. When the parent forecloses on the original family grouping and demands that only the new blended family has any validity, the children will be inevitably torn. Loyalty conflicts are not simply restricted to parents but can extend to deeply held loyalties to the original family with all its hopes and dreams. Children will hold onto a scene, real or fantasized, containing the parents' love for each other and the child. If one or the other parent denies this in their actions and attitudes then the child might react adversely. Refusal to visit might be labeled parental alienation but could actually stem from the child's deep anxiety about being with a parent who needs to renounce the other parent and everything seemingly to do with that person and their history together.

As an example, eleven-year-old Steven was telling both his separated parents that he wanted to spend less time with his dad and the dad's new partner. This sharply escalated the conflict between the parents mainly because the father blamed the mother for their son's attitude. His contempt for Steven's mother was palpable. His new partner appeared to mirror this negative attitude towards the ex-wife. The man could not forgive his wife for an affair she had or communicate with her other than through lawyers. Steven indicated that he was not allowed to call his mother while with his father and that if he raised his mother's name there was a deep chill that he found disturbing and at times frightening. He indicated that he would prefer not to go at all but would accept a reduced schedule.

In major part, what happens in such situations depends on parental motivation and specifically on the capacity to mourn, which is central to resolution. In the best of situations, the new couple gives their children and ex-partners a chance to adjust. Children actually have no say in the matter and are together as a sole consequence of their parent's choice. In other words, whether the children embrace the other adult as a step-parent will depend on numerous factors. It takes tact, sensitivity, and diplomacy to make a success of this blending process. The final result is not guaranteed especially with older children and teens.

Steven had little emotional connection to his father's new partner. She had no seeming ambition to be a step-parent. My understanding was that Steven's father had been devastated and injured by his wife's actions and handled it by a form of emotional amputation that severed her completely from his life and from his discourse. Unfortunately, Steven was a continuing reminder and underscored that he could not kill his ex-wife off in his mind and life without threatening the wellbeing of their son.

My approach was to encourage the husband to deal with his ex-wife in joint sessions where he could work through his feelings and find some capacity to acknowledge her. He was also able to link this reaction to his own childhood experiences of unexpected loss due to the death of a parent when he was a young teen. The couple sessions helped lance a boil and it freed up some potential in the inter-parental space for Steven to go back and forth more freely.

In some instances, blended families can be very complex amalgamations that have their own social organisation and dynamics. They are very much a project.

Jack and Amy grew up in a blended family. They were preschoolers when their mother left their father. Their mother was living independently for several years when she met and then cohabited with a recently separated man with two children. It was a blended family of four children. All four, however, saw their other parent half time. Weekly rotations were not always synchronized so that for stretches there was a minimum of overlap. Moreover, Amy and Jack went to one public school while the other children attended a different school. Nevertheless, it could be harmonious and stimulating when they were together for occasions.

Their father divorced and remarried several times before Jack and Amy were grown. Hence, they had a stable stepfather in their mother's partner and unstable stepmothers in the women their father married. Ultimate allegiances though were really with the parents.

The boys had a challenging relationship with their stepfather and no lasting closeness with either stepmother. Step-sibling relationships were not particularly enduring although their mother formed an especially close bond with a stepdaughter. Amy's rapport with her father was rocky in later years while Jack got along well with his dad. According to Amy her father expected a lot from her and suffered from disappointment in her choices.

The children's mother communicated as much as necessary with her ex-husband. The stepfather had a conflictive relationship with his ex-wife that was aggravated by litigation and there was no real capacity for communication. Moreover, the stepfather's ex-wife blamed Amy and Jack's mother for interfering in her marriage and effectively stealing her husband.

The mother and stepfather in this case had very different styles of parenting. The stepdad had little sensitivity and could be heavy handed or dismissive with Amy and Jack. Jack in particular resented his stepdad and made no secret of his authoritarianism. Amy got along for the sake of getting along and not provoking unnecessary disturbance that would only make it more difficult for their mother. In turn, their mother tried hard to create an overall family identity that bridged differences. The blending, however, was far from ideal although everyone managed.

Successful blended families fare best when they have the support of the ex-spouses on both sides. When this doesn't occur, fragmenting influences will thwart the degree of cohesion needed to forge a new family reality. Hence, James and Jonathan went their own way in life although sharing time and space with three others who also found little to preserve over the long term.

Of course, this is but one example. Even in biologically related families, siblings might not get along or parents might not relate harmoniously with one child as compared to another. Blended families represent amalgams forged by re-partnering of two adults. One or both will have pre-existing children and they might have children together as well. They could be a gay or lesbian couple, officially married or simply cohabiting. The children can be genetically related to one of the parents or adopted. In other words, blended families are unique social structures that serve the collective purpose that all families serve. In today's shifting world of divorce and remarriage, the stepfamily circumstance is an important area of study. In theory, the blended family can make good sense while in practice it takes tact, delicacy, communication, great conflict management skills, respect for boundaries, and an abiding affection for all.

Of the sixty million American pre-teen children, one-half are currently living with a natural parent and that parent's current partner. The 1990 US census estimated that by the year 2000 there would be more blended or stepfamilies than original families. Approximately thirty percent of children in total are living within a stepfamily environment. As mothers are still more likely to be custodians, the majority of these blended families involve a stepfather.[1]

Indeed, Americans marry, divorce, and cohabit more than any other Western society.[2] Hence, the stepfamily in its various configurations is a reality in the life of many people. The Pew Research Center reported in 2011 that forty-two percent of American adults have some type of step relationship either as a step-parent themselves or as a stepchild.[3]

Statistics Canada reports that married couples and children remain the dominant form of the family, accounting for sixty-seven percent of families in the 2011 census. Nevertheless, the trend is downward with increasing common law couple families, lone parent families, same sex couple families and blended (step) families. Indeed, 12.6 percent of all families counted in Canada in 2011 were stepfamilies either where the children were the biological or adopted offspring of one partner (simple stepfamily) or where the children derived from previous relationships of both partners (complex stepfamily). In Canada, 5.3 percent of blended or stepfamilies were of the complex type.[4]

Even without adding the new layer of the blended family, the divorce situation alters basic family relationships. This is especially true when one parent becomes "non-residential" but it even applies, as in the case of Amy and Jack, when the parents share the care. It is a huge adjustment for many parents not to see their children daily. If the children are young, this can be wrenching and destabilizing for the adult, not to mention the children. The accessing parent who sees the child regularly, according to a schedule, must adapt to a different rhythm and different relationship dynamics. How does one speak about raising a child that is not seen daily? When parents and children live full-time under the same roof the core relationship can be more or less taken for granted. This is not the case when contact is interspersed with absence. The parent must devote considerable time and energy to sustaining an affectionate tie and keeping up with the child's current life and involvements.

As a baseline, however, the story about parents and children after divorce begins with how they manage during the period in which the union is failing. Although there is usually much attention given to the effect of divorce on children, many parents are able to maintain healthy and responsive attachments to their children even during rough times when there is outright conflict between the spouses. Moreover, some parents become very close to their children during break-ups with the child–parent relationship serving as a buffer against the turmoil of loss, instability, and rejection.

Lisa's marriage to Tim was successful on the surface. The couple had two children, a boy and girl, and both parents had excellent jobs. Nevertheless, an undercurrent of discontent pulled at Lisa. An old boyfriend lurked in the background and an affair with him sealed her intention to leave. This man shared Lisa's cultural heritage and would probably have been the choice of her parents. She had no overt complaints about Tim but bemoaned the lack of passion. When the affair was discovered, the marriage ended as Lisa proved unwilling to cut her ties with the other man.

Tim reeled in the aftermath of the failed union. He had no preparation for what was occurring. Lisa alternated between remorse and defensiveness. She forced Tim to accept one day less than her in the care schedule but they agreed to joint legal custody.

Tim's bond with his children strengthened enormously as he found the wherewithal with psychotherapy to accept the outcome and acknowledge a world that might not always be loyal. His reliance on his children was obvious but did not amount to overtly leaning on them. In other words, although the children appreciated their vital importance to their dad, they felt validated and loved rather than burdened. It was, thus, a deep bond more than a deep dependency. In this regard, eventually Tim successfully remarried although not with the naïve trust that characterized the innocence of his first union.

Nonetheless, failing unions can certainly impact on quality of parenting although not necessarily affecting both parents equally. Much can depend on the pre-divorce parent–child relationship as well as priorities post-break-up. In the above example, Lisa's romantic rapture displaced attention from her children's need for reassurance. Her daughter, in particular, experienced her mother's absence deeply, which damaged her trust in her mother. The son weathered the storm more easily in that his same-sex parent represented stability and continuity. The daughter found it harder. Although it could be too reductionist to attribute a one-to-one causality between the mother's perceived abandonment and the daughter's struggles, the rupture with her mother altered the girl's certainty and control over her environment.

Sometimes the shifts are more subtle but nonetheless perceived. Even transitory depression, impatience, emotional instability or distractibility can lead to an experience of parental unavailability. Children can usually ride out these periods unscathed when the psychological base is otherwise firm. Older children can be amazingly supportive and generous. Yet, this breach in the protective link with needed parents can be experienced traumatically with psychological consequences such as increased insecurity as well as anxiety and depressive states.

The most troubling issue and the hardest to shake for children is open and hostile fighting between parents. This violence will not necessarily extend to the children but even witnessing it can be deeply disturbing and frightening. Sometimes, though, the parents can be very harsh with each other but still kind and supportive to their offspring. This does not cancel out the impact on the child but it can mitigate some of the potential damage. Violence post-separation is particularly dangerous and always very disturbing and damaging to children. Where children are targets of aggression, the effects are multiplied and always traumatic.

Often the most fragile period is when the parents have effectively separated but not concluded a Parenting Agreement to permit physical separation without prejudicing the legal case of the relocating parent. Hence, they continue to live under the same roof. Usually the relationship is at its lowest ebb and the parties are depleted, angry, threatened, and fed up by this point. It is a potentially volatile mix of helplessness and vulnerability. They are essentially trapped in the same space. They usually attempt to create rules to divide the space but it is an imperfect solution. Even in unions without any history of violence, the potential exists and emotions can spill over and become physical leading to rapid escalation of the conflict. The best approach is to conclude an interim arrangement that allows the parties to physically separate.

Parental relationships

To fully grasp the complexities of family configurations post-divorce, it is important to understand parental relationships themselves. In the gender politics of divorce, there is too little appreciation for human development and too much emphasis on competitive jousting. This becomes particularly conspicuous when babies and young children are involved.

It is a very different mindset between parents who negotiate roles within a partnership and parents vying for the same space and role. The former is a formula for complementarity while the latter is a formula for struggle and impasse. Divorce does not negate the need for complementarity of roles although in the push and pull of divorce negotiations divorce will often trump development. For example, the mother of a twenty-month-old will likely feel completely unready to send a child off to the other parent for half the time. Everything in her will rebel at the thought simply because of the nature of attachment during such tender years. The separated father (or non-birth mother in a same-sex situation) will often view this resistance as a bid for control through achieving initial advantage, setting a precedent that is then hard to reverse.

There is no easy way to address this issue other than by first separating the two narratives: divorce and development. Of course as children grow and reach middle childhood, parents are more interchangeable. Gender role and identification are still important factors contributing to development but raising children is less shaped by gender role. In this regard, it matters that humans come into this world after being incubated within the mother's body. Biology is destiny at least in respect to origins.

As I have emphasized previously, however, this certainly does not lessen the importance of fathers (or the parent in the role of "second other"). Children without fathers in their lives suffer and have a harder time finding themselves in the world. Nevertheless, when we are speaking of infancy this is not the issue.

Mothers and fathers enter the parenting world through different portals. This creates differences that should balance each other and not clash. Of course, it does not take maternity to change a diaper any more than it takes paternity to earn a pay check. So I am not speaking about culturally assigned roles but to the core identity of motherhood and fatherhood and how this serves the development of children.

Motherhood and fatherhood—core identity

Motherhood begins at the frontier between the physical and psychological. Maternity situates the baby in closest relation to her and gives her the difficult project of bringing a newborn into babyhood and beyond. Maternity is more than a body doing its thing. It is a psychological shift that defines motherhood itself. This core identification extends to those children designated as children whether they are biological, adopted, fostered or any other relation.

From the child's perspective, there is never anyone else who can compete with the mother's unforgettable place in our psyche. Separation from her and the mourning this entails is essential to psychic development but it should come slowly and in micro-doses. Although motherhood has traditionally been associated with ideals of responsiveness, empathy, and relatedness, so called idealized feminine attributes, this might imply wrongly that men cannot embody these traits. There is very little if any difference on the nurturing capacity scale between the sexes.

Caution is required though not to idealize maternity in a way that fails to take proper account of individual variation. Indeed, there are women who do not make the psychological transition to motherhood as much as there are men who withdraw completely when children arrive and who remain absent. One person's greatest moment of rapture is another's existential crisis. Indeed, there are women (and men) who experience considerable psychological distress when they become parents and this might have nothing to do with hormonal side effects of the birth process. Yet there is value still in trying to isolate distinctive features as long as it is also clear that these are descriptive and not intended as an ideal template against which women or men should measure themselves.

Apart from this caveat, my impression is that there is something fundamental to the maternal, which is quite separate from the care they provide. When women, social scientists, politicians or the courts equate the maternal with care, there is an understandable backlash from women who feel stereotyped and pigeonholed and from men who feel disenfranchised on hollow grounds. In other words, men perceive an idealization of the maternal that sets it apart from fatherhood and creates a significant bias in the courts. The idea then is to speak about maternal and paternal at the level of essence rather than in terms of caretaking.

When we speak of the primal relationship between mother and child, we need to start before birth. The pregnant woman must give herself over to the life of the baby. As a woman, she will never be the same. Her body is marked by pregnancy and her primal responsibility to this infant stems from this primal relation and continues after birth. The maternal, therefore, is created when the mother gives herself over to sustain the baby's being either before or after birth. Whatever caretaking the mother provides renders her a parent in the general sense whereas this primal contract sealed and delivered with her own body makes her a mother.

In the case of adoption or surrogate birth, the psychological process of "giving oneself over" is the same although identification replaces pregnancy. It still remains a fundamental maternal act. Little girls in the four to five-year-old range become aware of an internal bodily space capable of growing life. This miracle of femininity shapes the female psyche and whether she actually grows the baby inside her body or adopts, the same process of exchange occurs.

In the same vein, it is important to distinguish the essence of paternity by separating it from the role the father plays or the caretaking he provides. Fatherhood is based on a very special relation between father and child that lends full support and imagines a future for that child. Paternity is thus transformative for the man.

Of course, mothers and fathers both sustain a baby's life and both imagine a future. It is not a question of exclusivity but of essence. In terms of fatherhood, we can see this occurring in many ways. When the father intercedes between mother and baby and promotes psychological separation, he is directing the child outward towards autonomy and future. There is much research demonstrating that father absence in divorce is linked to low self-esteem and depression in children. Apart from the magnification of loss in this instance, fathers foster exteriority and pave the way for the child to join the world. It will not be long before neuroscientists map the brain consequences of this role.

I would note that paternity does not actually depend on the body and therefore the "paternal" is not necessarily restricted to men. It is a way of relating to the child that begins with vital support and protection of the mother, allowing her to give all to the baby's needs. Paternity, therefore, also defines a protective presence and way of relating that helps the child be in the world.

Maternal and paternal thus represent a special relation that leads down different channels of development. Maternal preoccupation with the infant recognizes the primary immaturity of the baby and charts the process of becoming a subject. Of course, the mother shares the baby with her partner but remains for a period in the bubble of maternity, which gives the baby the means to emerge as a healthy infant and toddler.

Paternal presence protects the mother whose preoccupation with her baby is initially all encompassing. If she relates through the viewpoint of interiority, the father represents the external world, the world beyond mother. He watches over mother and infant both as a sentry and guardian of the baby's future. The baby senses him from the beginning as a special other-than-mother but initially the infant's exploration is focused on the mother's body. Later, however, exploration moves into the environment and the father promotes the forward process. Of course, both parents provide care and both are likely to work outside the home while raising their child.

This conceptualization of maternal and paternal independent of care helps with visualizing the optimal care system in divorce. It has implications for how parenting should be constructed particularly in the case of infants and preschool children.

The essential step forward in development is when the child achieves "object constancy". It is attained gradually over the first two years of life although more fundamentally during the first year. Object constancy refers to the child's capacity to maintain an internal image of the parent in the parent's absence. If separation stresses are too frequent, too long or too disruptive, emotional harm can result, impacting adversely on acquiring object constancy. The harm would result from perceived losses that would exceed the child's capacity to tolerate.

There has to be at least one stable anchoring presence but more than one works well. In other words, there is no absolute requirement that a stable mental representation be established solely with the mother. On the other hand, where the mother is available, it should begin with her. The problem arises when divorce demands lead to very young children being passed back and forth without any stable presence. The issues are complex and it is best to err on the side of caution rather than expose babies and young children to severe separation stresses before object constancy is well ingrained.

Both professionals, Anna married Richard mainly on the strength of a dream that they would be a happy couple embracing a child. They had little history and no formal union when Anna became pregnant with their daughter Gloria. In an act of good faith, they merged their lives and prepared to welcome their baby. Shortly after, however, the relationship floundered and, by the time Anna delivered, the union was essentially over. They managed to stay together until Gloria was one and then separated. Richard seized the legal initiative and demanded joint custody and shared time. He articulated in court papers his desire to care for Gloria at least half time.

At court, Anna argued that Gloria needed a measured and appropriately paced separation from her. She acknowledged the joint custody but felt that sharing the care at this stage was potentially harmful to their child. Richard convinced the judge that he was a modern father and did not want to wait his turn in any respects. The judge agreed with his petition and ordered a schedule where Gloria was changing caregivers frequently.

Anna was devastated. Everything in her experienced the event as a rupture and ripping away of her child. She became depressed, angry with the family law system and deeply threatened by Richard who claimed victory on the legal front.

Emotionally, the impact on Anna was significant. To what extent this also impacted on Gloria will only become clearer in the future. From Gloria's standpoint, she was saddled with having to make ongoing adjustments outside of any control, as she was tossed like a football between her parents.

What can we say about this situation? In my view, the judge took a significant risk without any evidence that the child would handle this arrangement. He made his decision on the basis of parental rights, not a nuanced, careful, developmental perspective that would have included Richard from the outset while giving Anna and Gloria a chance to find their mutual footing and establish necessary equilibrium and harmony. At least one psychological attachment needs to be steadfast in the sense that it is continuous presence that in the beginning is not marked by strain or rupture.

What often works best in the case of babies and very young children is a stepwise model that introduces overnights as soon as possible but mainly keeps absences and separations short and manageable. Gradually between birth and three years of age, the psychological subject emerges and basic internalizations (object constancy) allow for much greater leeway in divorce provisions. Building towards a shared two-parent system should be gradual with development trumping divorce in the earliest phase. It takes many years to grow a child and it is best to ensure a solid foundation with at least one parent before insisting on equal everything.

How this translates into actual parenting agreements depends on individual factors and the expectations of the two separated parents. The arrangement needs to be constructed from the child's perspective and not the parents. Even though in principle the best interests of the child govern decision-making, the adults and their legal adviser have louder voices than children. It is not always evident that the child's needs are being considered particularly because separating parents can find it exceedingly difficult to distinguish their interests from those of their children.

Hence, a father will demand shared parenting of a six-month old because he has parental leave as a work benefit and the breastfeeding mother can readily pump breast milk. A mother of a two and a half year old will insist that even one overnight would be far too much because the child has never been away from her before. The parents, of course, claim to represent the child's interests but are basing their views on over or underestimations: the father greatly underestimates the benefit of a foundational, stable and anchoring relation to the mother as bedrock while the mother greatly overestimates the child's need for an exclusive bond with her at the expense of the father.

Increasingly the issue of whether motherhood is divisible has been coming to the fore in divorce struggles involving two female parents wherein one is the biological mother. The non-birth parent might insist that gender alone qualifies her to be a co-mother on entirely equal footing with the birth mother. If we revert to the core understanding of maternity, however, motherhood is very much tied to the body leading to a primal relation between mother and child. This usually occurs in utero although not always. Optimally, the mother gives herself to that baby's survival. Hence, maternity is a transformation of womanhood and should not be reduced to gender alone. In this increasingly frequent scenario, the other woman can certainly function equally as a parent but there is only one mother. This other woman, however, is well positioned to provide the "paternal" function, which is a special relation in itself. Of course, roles are not mutually exclusive and both parents provide nurturing. Moreover, this has no bearing on what name the child would use to differentiate the two parents.

Yet, we cannot avoid the complexity of the situation if we also acknowledge that women are very capable of a psychic incubation in the absence of actual pregnancy. Hence, why wouldn't the non-pregnant partner achieve the same maternal end point in her identification with the child? Perhaps she would or at least would assume this position but from the child's perspective the need is for two parents rather than two women competing for the same maternal space. In the instance where two women adopt a child, distinctions could be negligible from the child's viewpoint although much would depend on the parents' personalities, capacity for nurturing and natural attunement.

If we switch examples to consider two men in a gay union who adopt a child and separate, then the care would be apportioned although not along maternal lines. An observer might predict that one of the couple is more "maternal" but this would underestimate how nurturing, supportive and caring men can be with babies and young children. In the same way, the confidence a mother shows in her child can contribute greatly to the child's confidence in dealing with the world. Roles are not exclusive. Consequently, motherhood and fatherhood are not categories defined by function but are based on a foundational way of relating with deep psychological roots.

In terms of male same-sex couples, the issue of whether paternity is divisible is unlikely to arise mainly because identification, the core of fatherhood, has no gender base. In other words, two men could co-father without one having to claim the inside track of primal parent.

From this perspective, paternity has least to do with the genetic contribution needed to achieve pregnancy. It evolves post-birth although some men might indicate that they felt strong paternal stirrings even during the latter phase of their partner's pregnancy. It is identification with that child and that child's future that shapes and motivates paternal relationships.

I recall treating a man who felt barred or excluded from the register of men. His disenfranchisement was so great that his only outlet was to hire young male escorts to describe their sexual exploits with women. We understood this symptom as a way of putting his ear to a railway track to hear the train coming. Although direct heterosexuality eluded him, he found a resolution by becoming a devoted father figure to a niece and nephew, a boy and girl, whose parents had died in a car accident. Paternity opened a door for him and he fully supported the children through their schooling, and eventually into married life. It was a solution based on paternity not sexuality in the narrower sense of the word.

In today's way of thinking, all sorts of absolutes are questioned and there is a rejection of categories or distinctions. Hence, the modern father is no longer simply the provider and the modern mother has a career and work aspirations beyond her children and mate. Raising children is a joint project of parents and children without needing to resort to authoritarian values and forms of child rearing. In many ways, these changes have made a positive difference for children and families if only because they encourage participation and promote equality. The risk, however, is that the complementarity of roles is eliminated because important guideposts are viewed as prejudicial or old fashioned.

I am certainly not suggesting that society return to a pre-feminist era of father-knows-best or to maternal supremacy in all matters related to children. Women and men are working out the best ways to combine forces to solve today's challenges. I strongly suspect, however, that women are still more comfortable with childcare and do more of it than men overall. Moreover, in the United States and Canada, women head eighty percent of single parent families, which creates a special risk for boys if there is no father involved. Fatherlessness remains a serious issue with major implications for children and families.

On the other hand, when separated fathers are involved, they are understandably often not willing to play a secondary role in which their relationships with their children are artificially squeezed into narrow visitation regimens. These trends contribute to a complex albeit necessary dialogue between the genders to sort out how to protect children's interests when the parents separate or divorce.

The divorced family, especially when there is remarriage and blending, can actually assist children in adjusting to a pluralistic world. It greatly expands the notion of family and suggests that a collective of people can come together in a meaningful way and make a life together. This includes the prior children from both parents along with any additional children from the new union itself. This expansion of the concept of family to encompass different groupings apart from the basic heterosexual nuclear family is well suited to divorce and re-partnering with children. It has helped to legitimize blended families and provides support for new family constellations.

On the other hand, it can be difficult to maintain the structure of parenting across households. The inclination is to strengthen bonds within each household rather than working on the coordination between households. There is a need to work with the other parent and not simply rely on children to bridge solitudes. When there is support from the former partners, however, the new constellation is further validated, which is usually important for children.

Indifference to the other household or simmering hostility and mistrust put pressure on children and psychologically intensify the divide between the homes. Sparks fly between the parents in this cauldron but also impact on the quality of step-parent relationships. Fractures and estrangements can easily occur, which can then lead to more blame and division. It is a vicious circle that usually does not end well.

Fundamentally, if we conceptualize the model as one "meta-family" with two sites then we can better appreciate that they need to have some sense of belonging to a single-family system. The parents do not have to live in each other's pockets or portray an illusion of unity but they do have to respect the overall system and retain a functional connection that spurs cooperation and communication across as well as within each unit.

It becomes clear, therefore, that the work of divorce is not restricted to adjustments only at the time of break-up. The challenges might change but there is always a challenge. Professionals in the area of divorce and custody often observe active resistance to any contact or communication with the other family unit when both parents have re-partnered. This forces the children to live in a split and discontinuous world without any real peace.

Here is a typical example.

Arnold and Marilyn had two teenage children, a girl and boy. It was a sudden and acrimonious break-up when Arnold started an extramarital relationship. Subsequently, Arnold married the woman with whom he had the affair and they had a daughter together. Marilyn also successfully remarried a man with prior children who were older. Problems arose when the older teenage daughter was hospitalized for a depressive disorder. She said that she felt unwelcome in her father's home and passed over. She did not want to stay at her father's any more. The parents had no communication during this period apart from official counseling sessions at the hospital. The son continued to see both parents although he refused to abide by a schedule and took personal control of where he stayed.

What was apparent was that the initial split and break-up between the parents had resulted in a gulf that was never bridged. There was absolutely no contact or communication between the ex-spouses. Emotions remained raw and unprocessed. Behind the deep chill was lingering fury related to separation trauma that had never healed. Whatever we could surmise about the children's issues, the model of two parallel units without any space for détente and dialogue created an unworkable system that was bound to come off the rails. It was unworkable precisely because it eliminated a key connection to make containment possible. They had no means to join forces and help their daughter work through feelings of paternal rejection. The dad was in over his head in dealing with these emotional issues and mainly defended himself against his daughter's grievances, which did not help the situation. The mother was interested in communication but joined her daughter in blaming her ex-husband for his "habit" of rejecting women close to him. Meanwhile, the son took charge of the schedule and spent much less time with his dad than previously.

The operative word is "containment". This refers to the capacity of the parents to respond as a parenting team to their children's needs and issues independent of where the children are residing. Containment is thus a capacity that only evolves when there is recognition of an overarching family system. In order for this to happen, the former partners have to progress from being disappointed, hurt and often angry ex-spouses to co-parents who empathize with each other and acknowledge connection. There is no way possible for any form of co-parenting to occur unless there is an empathic reconnection on the level of belonging to an overall family system.

In the example above, the couple would not be able to deal with the major problems facing their children and the broken family system unless they could find this thread of connection through a process of self examination and reflection. If their relationship was frozen in time at the very moment of rupture and betrayal, then how could they possibly tackle issues facing them currently? Sometimes you have to pare back to find a point in time of working together to raise the children. If the parties can make contact with this bedrock then they might use this as a bridge to overcome the hurdle of hurt and rupture. Where there was never a period of harmony then professional assistance is usually required to construct this capacity anew through mutual awareness of the interests of the child or children that join them.

Co-parenting cannot exist without this empathic identification between former partners or, as I have described previously, there has to be a remainder, surviving unscathed, that reflects this co-parenting feature. Without it, there can be no co-parental capacity. If present, however, co-parenting remains in reach.

Stepchild, step-parent and stepfamily

Thirteen-year old David was small physically but he had an easy-going affability and resilient personality with a keen sense of humor and a personal flexibility that served him well. He shared the household with his sister Linda, three years his senior. Linda was less outgoing than David but an excellent, focused student and violinist. David preferred sports but had always been a great reader. He had little interest in the self-centered video games that were so popular among many of his classmates.

From David's point of view, there was no real hint of problems or unhappiness in his parents' marriage so it was a huge shock to him when they revealed that they had been negotiating a break-up for some time. To their credit, the parents called a family meeting and told both children together. Nonetheless, it was a shock to have them announce that it was a done deal with a short timeline before the family broke up.

David learned that his mother would be leaving and that the family home could be sold in the future. For now, however, his dad would stay with them and mom was prepared to settle in a two-bedroom apartment with bunk beds. Within a month of his mother leaving, however, David learned from his sister that their mother had a serious boyfriend.

The news was hugely discomfiting to David. For one, he was deeply embarrassed that his mom, seemingly the guarantor of family stability, was behaving in this apparently errant way. He also felt angry with his father for failing to make his mom happy and angry with his mother for "ruining the family". David was troubled by intrusive thoughts and felt quite anxious and overwhelmed. In contrast, his sister Linda seemed to go on with her life and appeared less bothered. She spent increasing time with her friends and David felt her absence as well. It was as if all the certainties and anchors he had always known had evaporated.

Over the next year and a half, the family re-established some form of equilibrium and, superficially at least, David also found his footing. His mother had been living with her new partner for six months and David had a ten-year-old step-brother whom he liked. David spent alternating weeks with each parent but identified his father's house as home. His dad arranged to keep the matrimonial home by buying out his ex-wife's share. Although his mother spoke of the children having two homes, David resisted what he felt to be his mother's propaganda.

The parents must have felt that the worst had passed and that they could breathe again. The business dealings winding up the union were handled relatively easily. His mother embraced her new "family" configuration while his father appeared to accept that this is what his ex-wife wanted. David was less accepting, however, as he could not understand why his mother would discard what she had and why his father did not fight harder to keep the marriage together. From David's perspective, there was plainly no need to replace anything and he harbored resentment against his mother for her alleged "selfishness".

David's mother encouraged him to explore a relationship with her new partner and referred to this man as his step-father. David, now fourteen, bristled when she used the term.

He treated the man cordially but emotionally kept his distance. His mother sensed her son's aloofness and found it disconcerting and perhaps a little rude. She finally confronted David and told him "to get with the program." This confrontation, however, pushed David too far. He exploded with anger and his resentment poured out at his mother who was shocked and taken by surprise. David was sent for psychological treatment and this is where I became involved.

David made it clear that he saw no need for psychotherapy. I thought it best not to challenge him but suggested that we still use the opportunity to review what had happened and see what this meant to him. We "contracted" to meet three times and then see where we stood. This gave David control while giving me a chance to secure his cooperation in the short term.

David was surprised that he was still emotional when he described the family meeting at which the divorce was announced. He related that events occurred rapidly after Linda and he were told, as his parents had already formulated their plans. He recalled a dream in which he was standing on a hill that instantly turned into a diabolical mudslide. He knew it was just wet slippery mud but it felt "all evil" and threatening. David understood that he felt out of control at the time.

David's current feelings, though, seemed to focus on his mother's choices and attitude towards him and his sister. He felt that she had simply replaced his dad with a new man and expected the children to go along without question. He felt betrayed by his mother. It bothered David that, from his perspective, his mother wanted him to forget about the family he once had and embrace this new reality. David wanted none of it. He especially objected to her elevating her "boyfriend" to the position of stepfather. David insisted that he was not interested and resented the imposition.

As we explored his feelings, it was evident that David was not necessarily experiencing a loyalty conflict. Indeed, the divorce had not drawn him closer to his father but neither was he looking for any supplemental dad either. He did not actually dislike his mother's partner but he was definitely put off by his mother's insistence that a new and valid family unit had been formed.

David confessed that before sleep he would often search for happy memories of the family together before his parents' divorce. These memories would soothe him and allow sleep to take hold. He felt that he had lost his actual family and that his mother had casually put an "X" through the very entity that had defined him. He was very annoyed that his father did not fight harder.

It was clear that David's mom had a new paradigm in mind. She envisioned a new family emerging from the ashes of her divorce from David's father. She had exercised the option open to adults who feel unfulfilled or unhappy in their unions. In this regard, she expected her children to go along with this decision. At the same time, she did not stand in the way of David or Linda's relationship with their father. She was content to share the care and control of the children despite the fate of the marriage.

With three sessions under his belt, David decided to stop meeting. He found it helpful that I had given him the control he needed over the "contract" particularly in light of how powerless he had felt regarding his parents' divorce. It was not the last time I saw David, however, as he came infrequently but regularly over the next six years until he left to attend university in another city.

As a nineteen-year-old, David was more philosophic regarding the situation but he never came fully to embrace his mother's partner as a stepfather. On the other hand, he could also appreciate that this man had been helpful when asked and was overall a benign and supportive figure. In other words, David's construction of family remained loyal to the original family unit and did not shift on an emotional level.

David retained the impression that something was lost in his life as a result of the divorce that was not replaceable. I would summarize this essentially as a trusting innocence and belief in the immutability of relationships. Nevertheless, David valued the solid friendships made during his high school years and he was in a relationship with a young woman who would be attending university near to where he would be going.

He was aware that trust remained an issue but he found it helpful to discuss these feelings with his girlfriend and relate them to his personal experience. He looked forward to his future.

Parental desire and expectation

There is no sidestepping the fact that parental desire and expectation is imposed on children at many levels of experience. It is parents who name their children, often with someone revered in mind or as a way of situating them within the continuum of the generations. Thus, even the child's name can carry important messages about what parents want or expect. It is the same parents who impart a wealth of other influences from unconsciously mediated needs to openly expressed demands and expectations.

When parents divorce and re-partner, expectations on children are bound to follow. At minimum, they want their child to adjust readily to this change and make room for the new partner and new family configuration. Young children often have less difficulty complying and adapting than older children and teens. The younger child looks to parents to define the framework of their lives and they will generally adjust without much upheaval. The older child, however, can be a different story.

In the case of David, for example, we can easily identify his mother's expectation that he would adjust to the new reality and readily include a stepfather and stepbrother in his life. David's resistance, however, proved to be formidable. Moreover, despite the power of adult expectation and privilege, stepfamilies must fundamentally be created in the child's mind. It is the child who ultimately determines if the new partner is or is not a step-parent. Indeed, if parental desire or demand supplants the child's right and need to "choose" on her or his own terms, loyalty conflicts and outright refusal become much more likely.

David's mother did not appreciate that the perceived dismantling of the original family unit would have major implications for her son. In this regard, she did not expressly negate the family identity that included her ex-husband and children but neither did she refer to it or give it credence. She was much more interested in forging a new family entity with its own validity and continuity.

This clashed head on with David's need and orientation. Instinctively, David pushed back not because he was opposed to the new partner or his son but because it usurped his need to ground himself and his development in the family that brought him into the world and raised him. He was insulted and threatened by his mother's seeming inclination to overthrow what had been his family for something entirely new. Of course, this new reality was a fait accompli by virtue of his mother's choices. Nevertheless, It was never something that could be psychologically foisted on David. He had to come to it of his own accord.

Identity formation

What was at stake for David or other children faced with this challenge? There are a number of factors to consider. In particular, I would focus on the issue of identity, which links to the fundamental importance of origins.

Identity formation is an evolving process that begins with the baby's initial self-recognition reflected in the gaze of the loving parents. As such, the baby is not only welcomed into the world but also welcomed into the family. Identity is the cohesive sense of sameness about the self that arises through the course of life. In the layering of identity occurring throughout development, family is elemental. Thus, it should come as no surprise that children beyond the pliable early years might not be so prepared to embrace a change simply because it reflects parental desire and is imposed unilaterally on them.

Of course, children love their parents and will make an effort to comply as long as there is a basic respect for timing and process. There is no doubt, in this regard, that adapting to the stepfamily reality can be difficult. Children often long for their parents to reconcile even when there is no chance of it occurring. They long for reunification not because they would want their parents to return to a deeply unhappy union but because this is the fundamental unit that defines them. They want them to reconcile for the children's sake. Parents enter marital relationships voluntarily while children make no such choice. There is a permanence regarding family that is not negotiable even under the onslaught of divorce.

It matters little or not at all whether origins are biological, adoptive, gay or lesbian. There is still a creative coming together of the parents that produces a child. It is a primal scene that is important because it is installed at the base of identity. We are first and foremost the children of those who conceived us in desire. Even before they conceived us, they conceived of us. We were an idea born of parental union. This original reality has staying power and does not mesh well with later parental revisionism.

In other words, when parents separate and re-partner, children can feel stressed when the parent appears to ask the child to shift their entire frame of reference from the original family constellation to the new one. The demand stems from the parent's desire to "move on" and to validate the new family situation. It might not be intended as a negation of the past family entity but it can feel like that to the child. Adults who were unhappily married, especially those who experienced emotional and especially physical abuse, will have little desire to continue to validate these origins. They will be on a different page from their children who could have a very different experience and mindset.

"You are not my mother/father" is the rallying cry of those children of divorce struggling with the step-parent situation. It can occur when the new partner tries to discipline, set any rule or even advise in a parental fashion. "But I am not trying to be your mother/father", is the usual retort. Sadly, it rarely soothes. The child is often sore that the parents took this drastic step and put them in this complex situation in the first place.

So much shifts when non-related adults and children endeavor to form a family. Rules and traditions change as well as the rhythm of the family. For instance, I recall a woman relating that following the break-up of her marriage, she developed a casual, rather laissez-faire way of living with her school aged son and daughter. When she remarried, her husband's very structured and organized approach to living represented an initial shock to her and the children. He made a list of groceries to buy based on a prepared weekly menu. Chores were assigned and life became more ordered and predictable. This worked out in her case but the woman was clear that the children expressed reservations and to some extent felt usurped by what they experienced as a new regime. She had a hard time describing exactly what kind of relationship her children shared with her husband although she described it as positive.

Loss and uncertainty

Whereas adults grieve following failed unions, especially when not the initiator, the fact that children might need to mourn is often not taken into account. Sadness is the telltale emotion that describes most children after their parents separate. They feel the loss as well as the uncertainty. Of course, they still have two parents and life goes on but something is lost, namely the united family they have only known. Divorce creates disruption for children and they frequently feel adrift. The introduction of a new partner, especially when the timeline between the end of the marriage and re-partnering is short, would almost certainly complicate the grieving process.

Further, how the new partner comes into the parent's life can also matter. When this new partner is associated with the break-up of the former union, such as a prior extramarital relationship, loyalty pressures on the child can be increased. On the other hand, when there is a reasonable gap between the end of the marriage and the gradual, measured intensification of a new relationship, the psychological climate could well be very different.

If identity can be represented as a self-portrait then the family would be the picture frame. Indeed, the photo has no ability to be self-standing without the frame. It gives the photo definition and emphasis, and outlines the contours that separate photo from surround. This helps visualize how family serves as an anchor, a source of stability, continuity and sameness against the backdrop of rapid change that characterizes development.

The vital need for the sameness of family that cradles the psyche is disrupted by the divorce and then step-parent encounter. Shifts are major and minor, anxieties new and old, relationships change and are tested. David's relationship with his father, for example, was measured differently in the light of living alternate weeks with another man who was father to his own son. He wanted more from his father and felt disappointed that his father seemed passive and unmoved by the presence of this other man in David's life. Further, David found the spark and newfound joy of his mother disconcerting. He was glad that she was happier but reacted anxiously to his mother's overt affection for her partner. It felt weird from his perspective.

In respect to the stepfamily, thus, the child alone must come to value it and make it real. This is more a process of inclusion than one of radical redefinition. In this regard, the child needs to accommodate and validate the new partner in a way that feels meaningful and natural. Hence, becoming a step-parent is always in the control of the child and represents a process not an anointing by adults. Stated otherwise, before there is a step-parent, there must be a stepchild. It is the child who must appoint the new partner and conceive of them as a step-parent. Parents who attempt to impose this on children will often meet stiff resistance. Further, this could well add to family instability and emotional problems that might be blamed on the divorce.

Part of the problem in discussing stepfamily situations is the variability and timing in how they arise which makes generalizing difficult. Each situation is different. Nevertheless, it is clear that society has witnessed a burgeoning of stepfamilies. When these are stable and longstanding, families have the opportunity to adjust. For some children, however, there can be repeated separations and re-partnering, which almost certainly adds to family instability and impacts on wellbeing.

Remarriage is not a one-time event with a brief adjustment period. It occurs as a process that can take several years, particularly with older children, before equilibrium is established.[5] Younger children accommodate more quickly while complex stepfamily scenarios take longer. It helps considerably if there are family and community supports in place and if the ex-partner supports the new arrangement or at least is not hostile to it.

Denise met and married Richard after a brief failed union with Paul with whom she had a son. It was not long before she was pregnant again and gave birth to another child. This time it was a daughter.

Denise felt very happy with Richard and was glad to relegate Paul to the dimly recalled past. Nevertheless, the son provided an ongoing link that made forgetting impossible as Paul was clearly treated as persona non grata. Denise made no secret that she preferred Richard in every way as a role model for her six-year-old son and viewed Richard as the legitimate male parent. Understandably, this upset Paul very much and the conflict between the parties ramped up dramatically.

Matters reached an impasse when Denise requested that her son spend half of Father's Day with Richard given the paternal importance his stepfather was playing. As a young and malleable child, the boy was open to relationships with both men. He would have naturally accepted a stepfather as well as a father in his life but his mother's radical position created an internal conflict.

Paul's reaction to the situation did not help matters for the boy. Paul refused to refer to Richard in his son's presence and demanded that Richard never be involved in any transition. He pressured the child's school not to allow Richard to attend parent-teacher meetings and transitions became particularly tense until Denise decided that she would wait until Paul pulled up in his car and then retreat into the house leaving the son alone as his father approached.

The boy became increasingly more stressed, as he felt caught in a situation he could not understand. He began to confabulate stories that placed Richard in a bad light. For instance, he told his father that Richard had thrown him down some stairs and blamed him harshly and wrongly. Richard would also strike him for no apparent reason. These events supposedly occurred when Richard was left with the children and Denise went out.

Paul wrote accusatory emails to Denise and the situation deteriorated further. Lawyers were engaged, the local child protection agency contacted, and eventually the entire family was referred for psychological therapy.

Here we can appreciate that Denise's wish to leave her marriage to Paul behind went well beyond the usual dimensions of simply leaving. Indeed, she wanted to radically expunge Paul from her memory as if this union was a mistake that never happened. Of course, the son was living proof of the contrary. It was an existential fact that could not be denied. Notwithstanding, Denise's profound negation and attempt to replace Paul as the father of record simply placed the boy in an emotionally untenable position.

Paradoxically, there could be no easy acceptance of a stepfather precisely because of Denise's attempt to foreclose on Paul. The boy's story telling was an attempt to appease his father and to reassure his dad that there was no positive man in his mother's home whom he could also love and emulate. Of course, this was untrue. Richard and the son generally did well together, which added to the complexity.

Yet, the situation was headed for disaster and the risk was that the boy would have no man that he could love and admire unequivocally. If he loved Richard as a stepfather, he would be betraying his actual dad and if he loved Paul he would be defying his mother's wishes and acknowledging the importance of a man she was working to totally forget.

In remedying the situation, roles, boundaries, and relationships had to be clarified within an ethical framework. Denise needed to accept that Paul was the legitimate father and that her feelings about this relationship could not be confused with the son's need of the father he had. Richard had to step outside of the role Denise had prescribed for him and accept that he could meaningfully serve as a supportive adult without having to compete with Paul for ascendancy in the child's life. It would be the child who would decide on Richard's role and designation in his life, as he evolved. In turn, Paul had to appreciate that he was trapping his son in the middle and pressuring him to become an informant in order to relieve his father of any idea that he liked Richard or appreciated the relationship.

We can understand from the example that parenting can suffer in the period after a remarriage. Of course, this is not inevitable but in Denise's case, her capacity to distinguish her son's needs from her own diminished once she was married to a man she could defend as a proper husband. If the situation were allowed to fester, the child would have had enormous difficulty as he developed finding a secure place between his father and stepfather. Nevertheless, when the problem was addressed, there was no doubt that Denise felt very confident in her union with Richard and she could only imagine how miserable and potentially poorer a parent she would have been if she had stayed in the marriage with Paul.

The step-parent role is not an easy one and it lacks clear definition or description. As I have indicated, it is really a construction of the child and should not be imposed or preconstructed by adults. Legally it can also be ambiguous depending on the jurisdiction. Mainly, when remarriages end, the best interests of the child prevail and if this includes maintaining a relationship with a step-parent, the courts could well order it. On the other hand, there is no automatic right and when second unions fail, which is not uncommon, the step-parent might well be lost to that child.

Step-parents also differ in their degree of engagement, aptitude, and interest. They could be experienced parents in their own right or completely inexperienced. If we define a step-parent as a person married or cohabiting with a legal parent, whether natural or adoptive, the term has to be understood with some elasticity. In this regard, some new partners are involved only peripherally with the existing children while others become fully implicated even with their own parents serving as step-grandparents. Thus, there are many permutations and each stepfamily has to be understood in its own context.

Blended families

Although the term "blending" implies merger or fusion of separate elements into one, the word also suggests a hint of deception. In other words, the blend of one with the other gives the illusion of unity that when tested over time does not hold. Thus, when we mix oil and water, we have a transitory mixing that will soon separate into strata—to each its own. Of course, ideally the fusion of substances is more stable and the mixture achieves a novel and lasting balance. Mixing salt and water is a good example. They seem made for each other and the result is a transformation.

Likewise, the blending of families is a complex and at times uncertain business. It takes considerable work and patience to achieve a good result. Even then it is not always possible and the constituents have a way of separating into strata—to each its own. In some cases, however, something very positive, nourishing, and healthy emerges that enhances life for all family members.

The relevant issue appears to be one of identifying best practices rather than trying to isolate each and every issue, as if these would have their own discrete solutions. In this regard, there can be many problems that arise in blending. The stage is set for conflicts of values, cultures, religion or religious observance, favoritism, jealousy, envy or competitiveness, among other possible challenges. Many issues could arise in regular families but there is no doubt that blending heightens risks and raises the level of difficulty.

In the blended family, there is a demand on the participants, adults and children alike, to behave as a cohesive family without a clear rulebook or set of traditions designed to govern what occurs. Moreover, in the case where two previously divorced adults, each with offspring, get together, schedules might differ dramatically adding logistical complexities to how holidays and regular care are handled.

Susan's mother was widowed at a young age when her husband died of brain cancer at thirty-two years of age. At the time, her mother had one child, a son. Her mother's second husband, Susan's father, was divorced with three sons when the two got together and had Susan followed by her brother Sam. The blend created a new family unit of six children and two parents. Susan was the only girl and the apple of her father's eye. Nevertheless, he worked long hours in several jobs to support his large family and was often not home. When he was home, he had favorites, which, surprisingly, not only included Susan but his one stepson.

Susan's mother was determined not to let her daughter's special status go to her head. She was especially severe with Susan as if to compensate for her preferred status with her dad. From Susan's perspective, her mother was deeply jealous, which impacted on their relationship and undermined Susan's confidence and sense of security.

Susan was left unprotected and one of her father's sons, sixteen at the time, molested her on several occasions when left to babysit. She kept this dark secret to herself for many years until marital issues as an adult brought her into psychotherapy. Susan's adult life had begun early when she became pregnant as an eighteen-year-old and was essentially evicted from her childhood home. Susan's adjustment had been rocky in her twenties but gradually good choices replaced poor ones and her life improved.

There are many books written that prescribe how best to handle the blended situation. In my experience, the key to successful blending presents a seeming paradox: blending is mainly about respecting boundaries and understanding the limits of relationships. In this regard, blending is never about dispensing with differences and limits but of accepting them as a key part of the new family order. In terms of the necessary toolbox, there is only one tool that is indispensable for family blending, which is communication.

Second, the blended family can never be fully separated from other family units to which the children belong. In this regard, it is important to situate the child in the full context of their lives and not act as if all that matters is the new family unit created by re-partnering or remarriage. When the child's full existential reality is denied or only paid lip service, the child inevitably suffers. Thus, the meaningful family unit for any child of divorce includes all home environments in which they regularly participate. Although parents naturally expect autonomy and privacy within their respective lived environment, they do need to appreciate that the children are also part of another entity that defines and sustains them.

Of course, Susan's experience of sexual abuse underscores the complex and occasionally dark forces that can erupt in any family situation but are far more likely to plague step or blended families than families headed by both natural parents. The 2010 Fourth National Incidence Study of Abuse and Neglect published in the United States found that children living in a stepfamily with a married biological and non-related parent were eight to nine times more likely to be sexually abused. A child living with a single parent with a partner was twenty times more likely to be abused.[6] The essential message from such alarming statistics is that blended families must be constructed carefully with clear communication between the adults and children, respect and appreciation for the need of boundaries and awareness that it takes much real experience together within a process measured over time to construct a functioning stepfamily or blended unit. There is no shortcut or instant version and the adults must enter such a process with their eyes open to the complexity of the task and with a mature appreciation of what is involved. We should also keep in mind that although reporting relative risk helps to see the significance of the problem, it does not provide any information about actual numbers.

Diana's first marriage ended in divorce after a brief union. The couple had one baby daughter when the relationship fell apart. Diana's husband stayed in the city where they had moved for his job but Diana returned to her hometown. One year later, Diana was grateful to meet Harvey, a fun loving and robust man with a big heart. He found it very easy to embrace Diana and her daughter. In time, Diana and Harvey had another daughter as well. Diana was clearly an attuned and devoted parent who enjoyed an excellent rapport with the girls. She loved and respected Harvey and gave him huge credit for his contribution to their cohesive family life.

It was difficult to discern any difference between Harvey's treatments of the two girls. He respected the relationship his stepchild had with her birth father while she obviously adored and felt very safe and loved by Harvey. The stepdaughter visited her father regularly in the city where he continued to live. The two girls proved to be excellent students and Harvey made sure that both had fully paid university educations, which he was the mainstay in providing. Nevertheless, Harvey would be the first to acknowledge that his stepdaughter had her own dad and that his role was defined or crafted on different terms.

The difference between the two examples is striking. In Diana and Harvey's case, respect for boundaries and differences do not preclude a lasting closeness and affection for all family members. Harvey did not replace his stepdaughter's father but simply made his own contribution on independent terms. The children could share a father in their primary home even while the differences in origins were openly acknowledged. Harvey allowed his stepdaughter to shape the relationship with him on her terms while he provided the level of care and support that expressed his values and understanding of his role.

In the case of Susan, however, we can perceive the opposite circumstance. In this instance, boundaries dissolved while jealousies and destructive currents erupted. There was an absence of respect both between and within the generations. Children were left unprotected and subsequently preyed upon. Communication was stunted and dark secrets prevailed. The adults had preferred children and treated others either harshly or with indifference.

Clearly, an assembly of adults and children does not necessarily constitute a family. Families emerge from a set of values that put the best interests of children first while promoting respect, structure, communication, and affection. Children feel held by these values and learn to express themselves with confidence within it. Although love serves as the bedrock of parental acceptance, step-parents and stepchildren do not need to match the natural parents. Of course, affection, communication, respect, and tolerance are essential but these relationships must be constructed on their own terms. Whatever solidity and permanence evolves stems from the adult and child building a real bond rather than responding to some imposed expectation or label. Step-parents, who do the work with stepchildren in careful, measured ways guided by the child, have a good chance of experiencing good results.

The parent/step-parent relationship

Remarriage where one or both new partners have children from a pre-existing union creates the double challenge of forging a strong union and, simultaneously, a viable family unit.

Although optimally, these two tasks occur concurrently and smoothly, these can also be perceived as opposing priorities. In this regard, the need for a strong intimacy could feel quite urgent considering the previous marital failure. The partners might have endured sexually and emotionally depriving relationships with ex-spouses and now feel a deep hunger for love-making and mutuality that could at least temporarily put their children second on the list. This can add to the dislocating impact of remarriage on children whose normal anchors are broken.

Further, there is no guarantee that the natural parent will remain as focused on the children as was the case previously. Indeed, parenting can suffer after remarriage due to distraction, preoccupation with the new partner and the presence of stepchildren. Financial strains could be greater and the remarriage of one ex-spouse might lead to fears of being displaced or supplanted as a parent in the eyes of the other. This can add to inter-parental tensions in some situations or lead the other parent to withdraw.

I can recall numerous children of divorce over the years relating that they were used to having an open door to their parents' bedroom but now had to contend with a locked door or a keep out sign. If the old conflictive or empty marriage allowed the children to feel first, the new regime feels quite different. From the adult's side, a new partner who is a non-parent might view the children of the first marriage as rivals for the spouse's attention and have little patience for their demands or intrusion. Yet, if this same couple has a child of their own, the former non-parent could well undergo a complete turnaround to the dismay, envy, and distress of the non-related children. There is no pre-existing template for how to organize and run a stepfamily and certainly none for how to feel, relate to others or coalesce. The ground rules must be established for each situation based on the many factors that come into play.

One can appreciate how complicated the stepfamily can be for children and adults. For instance, the legacy of the failed marriage can be borne by a child of divorce who is alternating between the parents' homes. In other words, the child can symbolize the ex-spouse to the remarried parent in a way that shapes parental feelings and how the child is treated. Here is one example that comes to mind.

Morris's parents had lived for twenty years in virtual silence and emptiness before the union sputtered to its demise. His father's quiet non-participation contrasted with his mother's more passionate investment in his life and activities. Nevertheless, when his father remarried he responded to his new wife's support and became more engaged. Morris had no experience with this type of involved father and mainly stuck to his mother as his anchor and life source. His father became furious and accused Morris of treating him with the insulting indifference of his mother. It was as if Morris became the symbol of the father's grievance against his ex-wife. He found it hard to be civil with Morris and this ironically sparked conflict with his new wife who found her husband harsh and unfair to his son.

When I saw the couple, the father's raw pain was palpable. It was clear that he had suffered in his first marriage albeit in silence, and could barely tolerate seeing his ex-wife during transitions. He understood that his longstanding withdrawal played a significant role in why Morris was seemingly so aligned with his mother. He was able to associate to his own family of origin and the void that characterized his own childhood. He had learned as a teenager that his mother had engaged in a multiyear affair during his childhood, which explained why she was never home, while his father seemed oblivious. Hence, Morris became a lightening rod for what this man had endured in his childhood and his marriage. It was essential that he free Morris from the projections that belonged elsewhere.

Adding to the mix is, of course, the ex-partner who often remains a vocal force in the new family's life. In this regard, stepfamilies are never fully independent from the primary family units that preceded them. The ex-partner can have a major impact on what happens in the new family home. This is especially evident when there is continuing post-divorce conflict or endless negotiations that sap energy and make decision-making perilous. Depending on personalities and circumstances, the ex-spouses might get involved in struggles over support payment, discipline, homework, extracurricular activities or whatever issue divides them. Intensified conflict between the parents, with the step-parent(s) involved and joining the fray, is never good for children and undermines security and stability.

Competitiveness is especially problematic and seems to be a major source of discord that affects new family configurations. It tends to occur in individuals who fear losing and who perceive their children and stepchildren's fidelity as winnable in the divorce/remarriage context. Competitiveness can focus on who has more money, a bigger house, more pets, more electronics or a more exciting lifestyle especially with respect to vacations. It tends to morph into power struggles and feeds on underlying hostility and preoccupation with loss. The lingering effects of divorce, including sensitivity to failure and loss, can fuel competitiveness between ex-partners.

As seems evident in many of these divorce scenarios, how the parent proceeds to re-establish their life and integrate new partners with existing children can have a major bearing on outcome. Sarah's concerns centered on her ex-husband's lingering bitterness over the break-up and his brainwashing of the children. Her twelve-year-old son, Raymond, would tell her daily that he wanted to be with his dad. The ten-year-old daughter, Dorothy, was more compliant but Sarah felt it would be only a matter of time before she joined her older brother in demanding to live full-time with his dad.

Unlike Sarah who had in her words "moved on", her ex-husband seemed content to make the children the focus of his life. Sarah was sure that he was inducing the children to ally with him and filling their heads with ideas.

When I spoke with the children, however, the picture changed from what Sarah was presenting. Raymond explained that his mother had initiated numerous conversations in which she would sketch out a supposedly hypothetical situation in which their father or mother had a new partner. She apparently related that this person would become a step-parent and the family would be assembled anew.

Dorothy and Raymond had been raised to expect the full attention of their parents. The marital rupture was extremely threatening from their perspective and disrupted all the anchors that they had previously known. They had not witnessed serious fighting or discord and did not really see this coming. Moreover, their mother seemed entirely different. It felt like she had replaced them with the man she would meet in her future. They had no wish to follow their mother down a path that they felt was unjustified. In contrast, life with their dad had continued much as it did before.

When Sarah did attempt finally to introduce a man into her children's life, making good on her promise, Raymond, in particular, resisted and became very hostile. He demanded to stay with his dad more and refused to cooperate with his mother's plans. It was unclear what role the children's father was actually playing but, in truth, he did not have to do much if he actually wanted to scuttle this new liaison. Sarah demonstrated precisely how not to succeed. First, she did not allow her children to grieve and gradually come to accept the fate of their parents' marriage. Her focus was already on replacing their father in her life. Second, she underestimated their needs for security and continuity in the immediate post-separation period. Third, her own emotional needs took command of her judgment, which led to preoccupation with replacing her partner that broke the trust and goodwill of her children.

Succeeding as a step-parent

From the parent and step-parent's perspective, having the right attitude and understanding goes a long way towards improving the odds of success. In this regard, we can highlight the following guidelines:

- Keep expectations modest
- Keep in mind that stepfamilies evolve over a long period of time
- Take your cue from the child and accept that the stepfamily must first evolve in the child's mind
- Be sensitive to special occasions like Father's Day or Mother's Day although accept graciously if a child presents the step-parent with a token of their affection and esteem
- Allow boundaries to exist between step-parents and non-related children and view these as natural and healthy

- Begin with "friendship" as a benign, supportive, caring adult figure with no emotional demand placed on the child
- Expect older children and young adolescents to have the most difficulty due to loyalty conflicts and identity issues
- Expect younger children to accommodate more easily as well as older adolescents who are often less defined by family or as intensely invested
- When children are older, facilitate communication about roles, duties, expectations, and ways to resolve conflict
- Establish some link with the other natural parent based on the children's welfare and demonstrate a willingness to be respectful and helpful.

Many children these days are being raised in new family constellations that fit the broad definition of stepfamily. It is certainly a difficult area to research primarily because there are so many variables and permutations possible, all falling under the same general category. Families are complex relational structures and step-parent/stepchildren relationships definitely add to this complexity.

Nevertheless, a positive step-parent in a child's life can do an amazing amount of good. Generally, this is a benign individual who is sensitive and perceptive to a child's needs. This positive step-parent waits to be asked and sees no need to impose or assume an importance in the child's life. Perhaps because of this sensitive and empathic caution, the child feels safe to approach, to love and to cherish this relationship as a meaningful and fulfilling part of his or her life. Moreover, the natural parent feels hugely supported by the step-parent who never tries to take the place of either legal parent. The child embraces the relationship, first as a friendship based on respect and helpfulness. This gradually evolves into a meaningful, valid parent–child interaction that is not perceived as threatening to the non-resident parent.

Perhaps the reason why it is not threatening to the non-resident parent is that it has no purpose outside of the relationship itself. In other words, this step-relationship is not involved in the divorce or any competition for the child's affections. It resembles the child's relationship to other beloved adults such as some teachers, grandparents, and other relatives in their life. Children respond very positively when they feel respected and accepted. The good step-parent does not choose one child over another and knows precisely when to stay back and let the parents come to the fore.

Conclusion

Parent–child relations are altered by marriage break up. It is very different, for example, to be a woman in a partnership with another adult caring for a child than a single parent having to provide the mainstay of care while working at the same time. It is a quite different matter to be a father in daily contact with a child *vs.* seeing the child only in prearranged windows of access. Special attention needs to be paid to how divorce rearranges these core relationships between parents and children and how this could affect parent–child relations and general outcome.

Sometimes it is not the actual amount of time difference in the care schedule that is so crucial but simply that one parent has more time with the child than the other. Freud referred to this as "the narcissism of small differences".[7] In other words, the parents' pride and personal value is focused on the disparity rather than on whether each has a reasonable block of time in which to enjoy a full relationship with their child. The politics of divorce are powerful and overcome any rational analysis of what might be best for a particular child at a certain age or stage of development.

Part of the challenge facing Family Law is that although it is structured around the doctrine of the best interests of the child, having the child's needs and priorities clearly recognized and differentiated from the parents is another matter. Each parent has to be able to recognize and accept the child's need for the other parent even if this means accepting personally less time and less exclusive duties. Of course, shared care, fifty-fifty, could be seen as the one answer that avoids such determinations but there is no panacea in divorce and not all situations fit with this ideal.

What then is the desired outcome as children, parents, and families re-group post-union? It is hardly different from the intact family situation. The only real distinction is the further goal of avoiding negative repercussions directly attributable to divorce. As I have said previously, divorce itself might not be as calamitous an event as how it occurs and how it is handled. Outcome is likely to be affected when parental rights and entitlements or residual relationship trauma blind parents to children's needs. Sadly, this happens frequently enough although it is usually greatest in the minority of high conflict and disputed cases that preoccupy the courts and mental health professionals.

Of course, many of the examples I report focus on this more extreme population. This approach could be seen as a limitation although I hope that it also helps document the pitfalls in order to expose and examine underlying issues and themes more clearly.

Gender, parenting roles, and custody have become hot button issues as feminism gave rise to its counterpart, paternal rights. Care is not gendered and can be satisfactorily provided by men or women within same-sex or heterosexual unions. So from this perspective, there should be no question regarding primary parent, primary residence or whether mothers or fathers have an inherent edge on the other. So why is there still an issue within society and the courts?

Certainly, how women and men come to parenting is different. For women it begins with the body and the inherent capacity to grow a baby inside them and give birth to new life whether this is actualized or not. Men come to parenting through their deep identification with their child. Allotting any preference to gender differences in parenting, however, might miss how much there is in common. It is the grey area in between mothering and fathering on which much of the controversy turns.

In terms of origins, it is clear that children need both mothering and fathering in the layered approach that would optimally occur in the intact family. Mothering and fathering comprise one system and not two parallel tracks with built-in redundancy. On the other hand, even this statement becomes controversial in the hard-knuckle legal and societal struggle where men experience extreme negative bias based on maternal supremacy. Breastfeeding aside, say father advocates, fathers and mothers are interchangeable in any context. They both provide equivalent care. The fear is that any concession to difference will serve as the slippery slope back to maternal dominance.

Psychoanalytic research certainly allows for differences between the sexes and between mothering and fathering although not at the expense of a more general theory of parenting. In this regard, infants and babies require a layering of care in order to establish basic harmony, attachment, and equilibrium with caregivers. Layering of care sustains mother and baby in the first months and evolves in graduated steps from the mother to the father or second parent in evolving steps towards the wider external world. Layering is protective and complementary. It is absolute at the beginning and relative as the child grows.

Starting with mother as first or primal other, even though the father is certainly also present from the beginning, could be cultural and not hardwired at all. Maybe this is so but it is hard to separate out the various strands. Certainly, support for this position of some difference is not political; it is relational. Babies appear to internalize and differentiate between caregivers. The mother's breasts and skin provide a unique perspective for the infant giving nutrition a distinctive human face.

Marital breakdown encompassing infants and very young children creates a distinct situation and accommodation is required. Nevertheless, care systems post-separation should not disregard development in favor of parental rights although such arrangements should take advantage of the resiliency and flexibility possible when babyhood is behind and childhood beckons. In other words, even if we agree that mothers and fathers have somewhat different roles at the outset of life, this should never be interpreted as giving cause for either gender to possess the children or undermine potential contribution of the other parent.

Finally, modern life with its ease and acceptance of divorce has given rise to many forms of family re-arrangement following divorce. The stepfamily has emerged as a major social unit although one that defies simple generalizations. These new family configurations bear risks for sure although they can succeed when the parents are able to build and sustain positive, affectionate relationships with their children and stepchildren. The larger the unit of course, the more of a challenge this becomes.

The realities do not always fit the ideal and the outcomes can be painful for some children and adults. Sometimes parents will treat their own children better than the stepchildren. It might even be the reverse. Moreover, not all step-parents will feel a moral obligation to treat all the children alike. They can pick and choose favorites. Step-siblings might have problems getting along and this could create tensions between the step and natural parent. In other words, the challenges are daunting.

Further, there are no clear social norms or guidelines for how blended families should function or behave. Hence, there are few challenges in life that can match the blended family situation.

On the other hand, the presence of a step-parent can also contribute extra resources to a family situation. Social, economic, and emotional support can be strengthened. The mature, ethical step-parent approaches the challenge with tact, respect for boundaries, realistic expectations, and a place for a child to mourn, protest, debate or withdraw as needed in the accommodation phase. Kindness, affection, and tolerance can go a long way to smoothing the way.

The ethical step-parent supports their new partner with the children and does not create conflicts forcing the partner to choose him or her over the children. It is my impression that stepfamilies succeed to the degree that they can transpose to the new configuration values of fairness and equity that are the accepted framework or expectation for families in general.

Yet, step-parents and stepchildren meet as strangers. These are relationships that must be built on their own terms. Moreover, re-partnering can also alter parent–child relationships. The children's natural parent might not have happy memories of the union that created the child. It is a lot to consider as anyone who has gone through the experience can attest. The divorce and remarriage process is a long one indeed for both children and adults.

In approaching the step-parent role, we must acknowledge that there is no particular social tradition that defines it. Nonetheless, when the child is allowed to shape the relationship and the non-related adult is committed to fairness, affection, and openness, the situation is surmountable and the outcome can be positive. Much as a special teacher during childhood can have a lasting impact, so a step-parent can be remembered in the same way. It is often an important role even if it is so hard to define, characterize or explain.

CHAPTER SEVEN

High conflict and the pathologies of divorce

Failure of divorce

Ideally, the termination of troubled unions would create the conditions for stabilization and a return to life harmony. No matter how difficult the break-up or unfulfilling the union, going separate ways should address the crisis and permit healing to occur. Children have no say in these matters and are required to adjust to the consequence of decisions made by one or both parents. Generally, they manage this task although some children have more difficulty than others. In a minority of cases, however, divorce turns out to be one juncture in a saga that won't end.

If divorce is the remedy for a failed marriage, then high conflict and the pathologies of divorce represent the failure of divorce to solve the inherent problem. When ex-couples realize that break-up is insufficient to heal what ails them, there is often panic and rage. Torrents of blame spill out and more drastic solutions emerge. So-called "parental alienation" is one such possible outcome and it should be understood in this context. Chronic power struggles, paranoia, and misuse of police and social service agencies are other forms of outcome.

There is widespread agreement among researchers that children's adjustment to divorce is largely determined by their parents' ability to safeguard them from parental conflict. In most circumstances, the capacity of each parent to foster a loving relationship between the child and the ex-spouse or partner helps the child to adapt and get on with developing.

In high conflict families, however, this capacity to safeguard children defies containment and is missing or grossly inadequate. The parties lack the skills either to disengage or to transcend the dynamic that locks them into chronic blame. The marital and post-marital relationship assumes the status of an intractable symptom and there is too little capacity to protect children from its impact.

Of course, some conflict is part of most marriages and certainly exists in marriages that end. It is not inevitable, however, and the rule of thumb is that the separation will mirror the union: quiet, calm or empty marriages result in quiet, empty divorces whereas stormy, conflictive marriages end in kind. The timbre of the break-up is always a reflection of what was evident during the union.

When we speak of "low" or "high" conflict, however, we are not simply referring to the amplitude or noise factor. It is the immersion in conflict that defines high conflict. It simply never ends and one cannot usually trace where it began either. It is conflict that exists on its own terms, which saturates everything the former couple tries to do together. There is no interaction that is not bathed in duress.

In a general sense, some degree of divorce conflict is actually productive. It can foster distance and protect from over-internalizing the inevitable guilt and shame of marital failure. Despair, despondency, and a sense of inner catastrophe are a much greater menace to mental health than is conflict. As such, a little conflict can go a long way to help separate self from other. Normally, it dissipates in intensity as the parties settle their differences. Conflict is sobering and can facilitate accepting what has occurred and getting on with life. In turn, this helps the offspring adjust.

Conflict tends to peak at the point of rupture of the union when there is a realization that the relationship is over. It is inevitably traumatic to divorce; we never part easily from what we love or even once loved. This point of rupture may or may not coincide with the physical or legal separation. If there is no clear rupture, then the couple was either never really emotionally married or they will get back together. Sometimes, though, the deep emotional rupture occurs belatedly when, for example, one party starts a new relationship. It can be hard to predict what will actually represent the point of rupture but it often does not coincide with the physical break-up.

We should always keep in mind that as much as high conflict is negative for children's outcome in divorce, it is not the only important variable. Empathic parent–child relations are protective even in the face of parental psychopathology and conflict.[1] Nevertheless, high conflict is a major risk factor for sure in the wellbeing of children and families.

Perhaps it would help to say something briefly about conflict in general. Conflict enters human social development during the toddler stage. It serves the purpose of self-differentiation, me *vs*. not me, as a means to consolidate a sense of self. There is no "conflict" per se as long as there is no self to defend. The more "self" there is to defend, the greater the likelihood of conflict particularly when there is a perception of threat to the continuity and/or integrity of self-experience. Later, conflicts arise over higher order themes and values held to be dear to the self and its goals and ideals. Whenever the other is perceived as responding in a way that does not mirror the elemental emotional needs of the self, there is a risk of conflict.

Whatever the precise formula to foster a healthy union, having a good marriage is very positive for most people. We are better people because of our spouse or partner and for this we are grateful and loving. When the hurts, disillusionments, and disappointments predominate, however, exit from the union is more likely. In a healthy although disillusioned couple, divorce provides the remedy that marriage failed to provide. Most often, conflict fades with time, as there is no longer an expectation being dashed painfully against the rocks of empty hope.

In some cases, though, separation and divorce fail to provide the solution. The couple discovers that the sole social remedy open to them, divorce, is not enough to stem the tide of hurts and wounds. Indeed, what they need most, which is to separate emotionally, eludes them. Couples in this situation are notoriously unable to differentiate their children's needs from their own mire. They require help to disengage, to stop projecting and counter-projecting blame, or at least to allow the intervention of a third, which is usually a therapist, mediator, parent coordinator or judge. We are now in the range of high conflict whereby the conflict seems to be fed by deeper personality pools.

In all divorce involving children, however, identity is very much linked to the parenting arrangement of custody and access. In this regard, divorcing couples can clash over these matters precisely because role and identity are intertwined. In high conflict, these clashes are more extreme because the threat to identity is so huge. Divorced couples in general might speak about being forever linked through their children but high conflict ex-couples perceive themselves as chained together in a perpetual nightmare. Indeed, although the chains are not visible to the observer, they cannot psychologically separate and exit the nightmare. Indeed, they are chained by their insistence that only the other can make it better.

For instance, one couple had adopted after going through the rigorous steps of qualifying and locating a child. Nevertheless, now bitterly separated and contesting custody, the wife described an abusive ex-husband who had repeatedly diminished her while he emphasized how fault finding, blaming, and controlling his ex-wife could be. If she felt discarded as a wife by him, he felt rejected as a worthy parent. Trust was non-existent between them and each feared the worst about the other. They were locked in a mutual nightmare while they tried to remain calm and peaceful in the life of their child. It was a tightrope that was increasingly failing. In spite of their best efforts, each was desperately hurt and enraged by the other's inability to provide the love and containment that their fragile personalities required. They were not sick people but their destructive interaction was eroding the neutral ground required to raise a child. What seemed especially tragic was how much they needed each other's love and support.

In this type of high conflict, the consequences are significant. The parties cannot separate from the very struggle in which they are drowning and pulling down their children with them. Here we find represented the classic themes of divorce conflict, now taken to a very high degree and enacted repeatedly. These include:

- Fears of merger ("I can never get away from this person, as we are forever conjoined by our children")
- Domination/subjugation (I am overpowered and controlled and have lost all freedom to determine my life)
- Rejection (I feel unloved, humiliated, deeply betrayed, and unlovable)
- Competitiveness (only I can offer authentic love and serve as the anchor and mainstay for the children).

High conflict arises when there is inadequate means to establish healthy boundaries. Such boundaries are essential to forming healthy attachments. As I have indicated, the couple cannot actually separate even if they are causing pain and distress to each other. Merger fears concern the issue of identity or loss of individual destiny. In this regard, any perceived "loss" of the child of the union carries the deep fear of loss of identity. Hence, the threat level is enormous.

Fears of domination or subjugation are at the core of paranoid fantasies. The individual feels attacked and is sure that the ex-partner is out to destroy them. This is associated with powerlessness and helplessness for which the only recourse is to attack.

Rejection goes very deep in high conflict cases. Divorce is naturally associated with rejection. It is unavoidable and goes with the territory. On the other hand, in these cases of high conflict, the rejection is so profound that the person feels all value has been stripped. Humiliation runs deep and there is a feeling of self-endangerment.

The main challenges for anyone trying to help such high conflict ex-couples is not to overestimate their capacity to manage post-divorce or underestimate the challenges to resolving their high conflict enmeshment. Most often there is huge resistance to making things better despite the obvious advantages. The sharp conflicts that arise do not reside in issues as much as they reside in the interaction of the two people. The problem is that they still need each other or fear they do. Consequently, the only way to actually extinguish the conflict is to change the interaction. At the same time, it is important to find the thread to disentangle them from each other. The question is how to do that.

If I can generalize for a moment, I would note that most of these cases feature a high degree of vulnerability in both parties. They are constantly disappointed and have trouble understanding their ex-partner's or their partner's sensitivities and needs. They are prone to emotional injury and are not easily open to self-examination. In this regard, they fail to appreciate the situation beyond their own needs and perspective and yet they feel oppressed and held captive by the demands of the other. If only the ex-partner would take responsibility for what they are doing to them and the children, the reasoning goes, all would be okay. There is often a deep longing for some reparation that is rarely acknowledged. A history of traumatic disillusionment in childhood repeated and compounded in the union itself is common in my experience.

The ruptured relationship comes to resemble a toxic abscess while fear, loathing, and longing make it impossible for the couple to mourn. One cannot mourn someone who is both needed and reviled.

Here is an example that helps put these issues in more concrete form.

Samuel and Maya met in the shadow of a loss in which Samuel's older parents had both died within a year of each other. His adjustment had been shaky beforehand, however, although he described himself as an entrepreneurial dreamer with a lively temperament. Maya's parents had a volatile and conflict-ridden relationship that marked her childhood and teenage years.

Both were energetic and gregarious although emotionally brittle and reactive. Neither had the means to contain or settle the other and the relationship never achieved a working harmony despite the birth of two children. They would have wanted more but the relationship floundered as both sought comfort in extramarital affairs.

When the marriage finally burst, it was mayhem. Scenes erupted in the unlikeliest of places such as the local grocery store parking lot. The children's school, child protection authority, and the police became involved. The parents fought a shrill, self-defeating legal battle that quickly exhausted their financial means. The children were bright, effervescent, and creative like their parents but badly needed structure and stability as much as their parents did. The children did benefit from counseling with a social worker that provided essential continuity and consistency. Maya and Samuel also understood the need for routine and to the extent that they were capable provided this for the children.

Conflicts in this case were turbocharged with drama and there was no effective barrier between children and adults. They were each involved in a flurry of communications that expanded beyond the family circle. There was no actual rule of law within the family or at least ground rules on which everyone could count. Hence, if a scheduling issue arose concerning how a child might get to a certain event, this would become an opportunity for chaotic negotiations based on brinkmanship and accusation.

The guiding principle in helping such high conflict cases is to specify the care schedule in such detail that there is no room for interpretation (and therefore discord). Naturally, this can help but conflict will still likely target the inevitable grey zone. Maya and Samuel were failing at divorce as much as they had failed at marriage. They could not live apart and could not live together.

Yet, underneath all the noise, they were thrilled with their children and occasionally openly celebrated the union that created each child. Hence, they loved each other in a deadly sort of way.

Often the best one can do in such a situation is to provide the children and parents with as much support and decision-making assistance as possible at least to where the children can be successfully launched. High conflict families deplete money and legal resources at an alarming rate and they often end up self-represented in the courts.

High conflict is a closed system that feeds on itself; it has no built in end game or purpose. These couples do not hold onto the marriage; they hold onto the divorce or at least can't let go. I do not see them as unable to give up their illusions and dreams regarding the marriage. Rather, I see high conflict as a failure of divorce, amounting to the disturbing realisation that divorce is no more possible for them than was marriage.

This is why any intervention, therapeutic, mediational or judicial must be aimed at promoting divorce. The incapacity to divorce leads to the scene of two boxers pummeling each other while holding on and blaming the other. It is the sadomasochistic position of divorce trauma: a union in which pain has replaced any vestige of love or companionship and becomes the medium of exchange.

What are the cardinal signs that a divorce process has finally occurred?

- Blame is no longer the sole subject of the ex-couple's discourse
- Calmness in the presence of the other
- Emotional control, appreciation for boundaries, without the need to vent to third parties
- Factual, reality-based communication and an actual capacity to make decisions
- Capacity to support the other parent in the children's eyes and when required in daily life
- Ability to put children's wellbeing ahead of the pleasure of recrimination.

In dealing with high conflict cases, finding the thread to pull is not an exact science. In most cases, however, the parties need to be encouraged to account for their own behavior and not to justify how they behave based on the alleged abuses and misdeeds of the other. They should be urged to speak about themselves and not about the other. If it takes "two to tango", the high conflict participants insist that they are an exception and, even if they can see their part to some extent, they will still feel at the mercy of the other. Blame feeds denial of responsibility and lack of insight. Such individuals use the other to handle what cannot be tolerated in the self. It is not so much about blame as avoidance of self-responsibility.

Personality disorders involving acting out of divorce tensions are an especially difficult form of high conflict that can get out of control. The goal, in these extreme cases, should be to use sole custody and very tight and detailed access regimens as a tool to foster separateness and limit interaction. These have a habit of not getting better over time. The risk or history of violence is another important limiting variable. It is from this group that violence can be a more systemic problem and therefore much more dangerous over time.

Jo and Paul's marriage was short lived. There were twin seven-year-old girls at the time of the break-up. Jo was coping poorly and needed psychotherapeutic help. She was the primary parent and Paul harangued her incessantly in court for interfering in the relationship between him and their daughters.

Adding to the mix of problems were Jo's longstanding self-esteem issues, and poor judgment in personal relationships with men. Paul proved to be a deeply antagonistic character who regularly exacerbated conflict. The court finally fixed access at less than what Paul was requesting. It was unclear, however, what would be the long-term outcome as this sustained high conflict struggle was fuelled by two vulnerable personalities.

These severe cases of high conflict are the most problematic for mental health professionals and the courts to handle. The following complicating factors come to mind:

- Psychopathology can be underestimated, which can worsen the situation considerably. Community mental health professionals might not be trained to identify accurately what amounts to the conditions for poor prognosis.
- Appeasement or accommodation of inappropriate behavior could be perceived as a worthwhile strategy out of fear of provoking a worsening conflict. This almost always backfires.

- Litigiousness can be very high in this group and they are prone to complain and abuse the mechanisms available to them to settle their problems. This includes complaints made to regulatory bodies about mental health professionals. Afraid of repercussions, the practitioner might understate the pathology out of need for self-protection, which inevitably leads to worsening of the family conflict.
- Working with these very high conflict families exposes the professional to a ghoulish inverted world where adults make hate, not love and where children are being buffeted by uncontained forces instead of being held within secure, safe bonds.

We should be clear when we speak of "high conflict" that we are not referring to acute conflicts that focus on a particular issue at the time of divorce. Such conflictive states may be very intense and loud but they do not fit the definition of high conflict.

What characterizes high conflict is that it saturates all aspects of a separated couple's dealings with each other. They fight about everything and no detail is too small to ignore. There might be particular areas where conflict peaks but in all such cases conflict permeates the entire spectrum of interactions. Where there might be some live and let live and identification with the ex-spouse as a co-parent, there is only mistrust and hateful fury.

Brian lived through his son's superlative tennis career; the narcissistic investment was extraordinary and all encompassing from summer tennis camp to tournaments to special master classes. As he noted about his son and tennis, "unless I give him every opportunity to excel, I may regret it." His son might not have felt the same about the sport but this was immaterial. The dad was fully invested in this son.

Ex-wife Marion fought against Brian's over identification. In her late forties, the constant wrangling depleted her and created a state of desperation. Agitated, furious, and drained, she could still never let go. It seemed that the struggle was interminable. The parents fought about everything and when not quarrelling, they fought with their parent coordinator.

Here we can see the telltale signs of high conflict: sustained battle where fighting itself is the primary mode of relating despite the hemorrhage. Divorce is not a remedy in these cases but a battleground. As much as they rail about emotional costs and the failures of the system, the other is viewed as totally responsible for the mess. The struggle has no end and no beginning even when an observer can identify specific issues.

Neither party, in this case, could disengage not because anything was getting solved but because neither had any real emotional autonomy on which to leverage a divorce. Indeed, their failure in marriage paled against the failure to divorce. The tennis star son became a shared symbol of what they could not relinquish. In the curious logic of high conflict divorce, perpetual struggle was the preferable outcome to the experience of loss. In this respect, intense and prolonged fury and angst masked an unacknowledged inability to mourn what was perceived as essential to the self. Thus, Marion harbored powerful fantasies of reunion with Brian while his over-identification with their son led to many excesses and much extra conflict.

Clearly, as we can see, not everyone has the personal wherewithal to divorce. In other words, it takes certain requisite skills of which three come to mind:

- Capacity to imagine oneself autonomously
- Capacity for self-responsibility, which means tolerating the weight of guilt and shame arising in divorce without falling into the black hole of blame
- Capacity to tolerate mental conflict and, thus, to assume responsibility for what has happened and for charting a course for the future.

Clara and Ronald married solely because Clara became pregnant after a few years of on and off dating. The relationship soon crumbled in a hailstorm of accusations and acting out. Ronald was obsessed with his ex-wife's alleged impropriety. He judged her completely unworthy, while she wielded a skillful political instinct that tied him up in knots legally. His inability to reflect on himself coupled with a deep intolerance of guilt helped fuel a morality play that took on absurd proportions. In Ronald's eyes, he was close to heaven while his ex-wife inhabited hell. If the wife needed to be right, then he needed to be righteous. Conflict was not a symptom of unresolved issues but a symptom of the enmeshment itself. This is the defining characteristic of the "high conflict" couple.

High conflict is not the same as sharp or focused conflicts. These can be very intense divorce related conflicts, as usually one party is demanding what the other is resisting. They are usually perceived as crucial by both parents. High conflict, however, is global, saturates the field and involves minutiae. It is the medium of discourse and spins on its own momentum. As there is no capacity for disengagement, there can be no negotiation, communication or conflict resolution.

It is a shock as the couple falls into a maelstrom of repetitive turbulence. The one social remedy open, divorce, proves useless to stem the tide of hurt and rage. This is the realm of high conflict. As much as these cases represent a small minority, they occupy a majority of family court time and often require judicial case management and professional intervention.

In high conflict, there is no sense of cooperative engagement and affiliation. In the worst cases, it can feel like a fight to the death where only one parent can survive and claim the children's love and loyalty. In this mindset, the other parent is devalued sometimes to the point that the assumption is that the parent can be excluded without any loss to the children's welfare. Cases of "parental alienation" are based on this distortion.

High conflict functions as a closed system. It is fed by deeper personality pools and creates its own dynamic and energy. The high conflict exists in anticipation of the issue and not because of it. In other words, it is not the issue that leads to conflict. High conflict expects and feeds on failure. Thus, the goal is to open the system because it dissipates with success. The mental health professional or coordinator has to promote successful divorce no matter how vehemently the ex-couple opposes it.

Some say that disengagement is the first order of business and I agree with that. Working on firm boundaries, clear procedures, and lack of ambiguity in separation agreements is an important task. High conflict seeks out ambiguity and makes any loophole the cause célèbre. Hence, to the extent possible, this has to be removed. High conflict couples should be encouraged to tailor their separation agreements over time to remove as much grey area as feasible.

High conflict also exists in the realm of the negative. It reflects perpetual unraveling leading to a widening scope of damage. In this regard, I view it as the major pathology of divorce. How does one know when this label applies? Common indications for high conflict include:

- Lack of self-responsibility for any part of the problem
- Issues migrate from one concern to another without any specific focus
- Inability to let any matter go; nothing is too small to ignore
- High jacking of communication tools such as email so that these serve the conflict
- Inability to solve disagreements, which inevitably fester and fuel conflict
- Need to involve third parties in the conflict including school officials, friends, health professionals, and relatives
- Erosion of neutral ground in which the children are likely to become drawn into the conflict
- Interaction that is fearful, enraged, and embroiled without any empathy for the former partner or awareness of consequences.

Helping high conflict families is always a labor intensive process that takes patience and focus. Nevertheless, they can be assisted over time particularly after a basic post-union parenting plan is in place and there is less likelihood of court involvement.

As much as I would label high conflict as a pathological state of divorce, this is not the same as saying that each member of the couple suffers from emotional pathology. Sometimes it is the case but this is not inevitable. Rather, the high conflict is stirred from the nature of the union that subsequently infects the disunion. In particular, high conflict couples cannot separate because they have no psychological basis on which to anchor their autonomy post-relationship. This might arise for a host of reasons. For instance, there could be a history of childhood trauma, problems coping with adult demands such as work, issues with self-esteem and mood stabilization, addictions, unresolved dependency needs, and many other individual factors that undermine psychological autonomy. In other words, there is an emotional vulnerability that arises in the union and increases dramatically during the break-up.

Transitional object

The pediatrician and psychoanalyst, Donald Winnicott, described the infant's need to use a soft toy or blanket to tolerate painful feelings of loss or separation that occur in the mother's absence.[2] He called this a "transitional object". The transitional object is the first "not-me" possession that the fragile child can hold onto that provides some comfort to counter feelings of isolation or loss, longings for affection, and deep need for mutual recognition that arise in the experience of absence.

We can use this concept to understand how couples need to have some later day transitional object to buffer the trauma of loss and separation. In healthy cases, the children provide such a comfort or buffer against feelings of fragmentation and catastrophe. To be sure, all individuals need some creative outlet to allay feelings of loss and to leverage a separation. In high conflict, however, there seems to be no substitute for each other, which is the dilemma they face. True paranoia is when a person senses that the very person they most need is the one they can least trust. It is a formula for perpetual endangerment and helplessness.

Apart from the children, separating adults usually take with them favorite pieces of furniture, paintings, photos, memorabilia from happy times or from childhood. These becomes sources of comfort and help weather the storm of rupture that arises in divorce. Some parents fear the emptiness when the children transition to the other parent. In this way, there are moments of loss and emptiness that need to be handled through transitional phenomena much as Winnicott described. Indeed, this is true throughout the life span.

The worst scenario for high conflict couples is to be left alone without any means to manage their situation with each other. They need the intervention of a third, usually a mediator or family therapist, to serve as transitional object. Mediation implies conflict resolution of an issue but, in the case of high conflict, resolution must be systemic. There is no substitute for working to deconstruct the situation with the couple over time. Of course, there are techniques and strategies, some of which I have noted but basically the mental health professional must create conditions where autonomy can take hold.

Serving as the transitional object means that the couple gradually learns to make use of the therapist to allay problems. This capacity to "use" the therapist is not available initially but gradually evolves. The therapeutic space serves as an important buffer and attenuates fears that inevitably fuel conflict.

Marla and Morley presented as an anxious, threatened parenting couple with a two-year-old son. They were enraged with each other, threatened and fighting endlessly through lawyers. Marla had always depended on her parents who were devoted to her and this now extended to their grandson. Morley had a strong relationship with his own parents though they seemed to have no means of resolving differences or conflicts however small. From their description, the union hadn't quite survived the wedding planning.

One can perceive that Morley and Marla have no basis for togetherness or separation. Neither has any comfort or fall-back position on which to build a solid foundation. Everything feels up for grabs and nothing can be assumed in terms of graciousness from the other. There is only one possibility, which is for them to engage in a process that gradually includes a capacity to use a therapist as a source of rational guidance in order to be able to co-parent their child and co-exist with each other. As such, the therapist serves as a transitional object reinforcing the accountability and emotional autonomy of each parent in a context where neither has the psychological means to acquire autonomy on their own or to imagine the other and their child in the same way. In such a case, the child has no independent standing between the parents either, and is treated as an extension of one or the other in the push and pull of high conflict.

Parental alienation

Alienation of affection describes parents who go out of their way to denigrate the other parent's value in the child's life. Not all alienation of affection, however, will lead to a radical breach in a parent–child relationship to which the term "parental alienation" refers. In order for alienation of affection to translate into parental alienation or estrangement, the child must somehow collude and play her or his part. A more descriptive term and perhaps one less value laden is "refusal to visit".

One exception occurs when the alienating parent is psychotic and the children are young and become swept up in the parental delusion. In this case, the child protection authorities usually become involved as initially the allegations against the other parent are often accepted as valid. Only with time does the underlying delusional disorder become clear and appropriate action can be taken.

For example, I became involved with a family where the wife accused the husband of sexually abusing the children. He had to accept supervised access but she kept insisting that even under professionally supervised conditions, he could sexually violate the children faster than the eye could see. She had also been observed by neighbors hammering boards over the children's bedroom windows to prevent him from entering at night, which she had reported to the police. She was sure, however, that he could evade any defense that she could muster.

In most instances of parental alienation, the child is older or a teen and together with the primary parent, usually but not always the mother, completely blames and devalues the other parent as worthless, harmful, and failed. The child's point of view is offered without any hesitation or nuance. There is no lingering affection for the spurned parent who is deemed to have absolutely nothing of value to contribute. Any loss of relationship is perceived as meaningless to the child's welfare and the eradication of that parent is complete. Indeed, continuing to see the parent would constitute suffering and harm, according to the child, who might threaten severe action, including self-harm, if they were coerced into seeing the rejected parent. The alienating parent either actively backs up the child's conclusions or passively concludes that the rejected parent has solely earned this fate.

Although there could be cases where the rejected parent is totally innocent of contributing to the problem, most have some basis but rarely enough to justify forfeiting a parent. Moreover, there can be too much emphasis placed on the alienating parent and not enough on the motivation of children either to come to the aid of a vulnerable parent or serve as shock troops in the favored parent's divorce.

As an example, consider a family where there are two children and the parents' marriage ends in a flurry of accusation and recrimination after eighteen years. Police, child and family services, and the courts try to bring some sense of closure and structure but soon after the break-up, the eldest child, a son, stops seeing his dad. One year later, the other son ends his visits although the reasons are vague. The two sons, both of high school age, convey the usual pattern of seeing no value in continuing a relationship with such an unworthy father. The mother distances herself completely from her ex-partner. She refers to him by the title "mister" and never questions the judgment of her sons.

Each situation is complex and needs professional help to unravel and repair. Alienated children are deeply resistant and hold onto their negative views with the tenacity of a delusion. In the above example, the father's family of origin was replete with examples of uncontrolled jealousy and conflicts. He had poor relationships with his own siblings and tended to withdraw in the face of conflict. The mother denied a traumatic history but considered that she suffered irreparable harm as a result of her supposedly abusive marriage. It was difficult to discern the kernels of truth in each narrative and differentiate these from the hyperbole of high conflict. Meanwhile, the two boys were scathing in their contempt for their father although they did not go as far as some who change their surnames to eradicate lineage to the spurned parent.

What struck me about the boys was that they were actually well adjusted in terms of their own lives. They were polite, respectful, and productive students preparing for their future as adults. In contrast, when it came to their father, the boys insisted that he was only abusive, selfish, insensitive, and even cruel. Their mother insisted on respect for others despite treating the targeted parent as a special case that required extraordinary measures including total banishment. This is the core then of what is pathological: a fixation on the "badness" of the rejected parent as a repository for everything failed and broken.

The children's rhetoric in these cases usually lacks any doubt or evidence of mixed feelings. The protected "good" parent is idealized and there is usually a powerful alliance with that parent that shores up the parent's identity. The targeted parent has no recourse and no defense. The protected parent is given every benefit of the doubt and the children are likely to see that parent as having been victimized by the rejected parent.

Even in cases where progress is made, the floodgates rarely open completely unless there has been an opportunity to successfully treat the preferred parent. The alienated child might begin to visit the other parent but restrictions and limitations often remain in place. It can be a struggle and very difficult for the spurned parent who is often placed on probation for perceived sins. When these children become adults and free of parental influence, they start to understand the destructiveness of what happened to them. They are usually scarred by the experience.

Although researchers have described the different ways that alienating parents manage to turn the tide against the rejected parent, my sense is that it is not simply behaviors that are involved. There is an underlying personality factor that makes the child's loyalty and exclusive affection essential. Often the preferred parent has an underlying emotional vulnerability and the child willingly serves as the transitional object on which that parent can solely rely. Sharing the child's affections with the other parent would be experienced as too dangerous although this is never acknowledged. The psychological vulnerability, if recognized, is interpreted as a consequence of bad treatment at the hands of the ex-partner. Of course, the child knows none of this although the role of protector is deeply empowering and fulfilling. The alienated child turns on the spurned parent with a fervor that is at least a match and often exceeds the vitriol of the "good" or chosen parent towards the ex-partner.

Rejected parents respond in various ways. Some are quite passive while others resist legally and go to great lengths to see their children. Assessors often leave it to the children and rejected parent to sort out but this rarely works because it ignores the fundamental role that the preferred parent plays. It is wrong headed in my view to single out the rejected parent for the job of finding a solution. The rejecting child will resent the imposition and it often sets up the spurned parent to fail and still be blamed.

At the same time, it is important for the rejected parent to receive help and guidance. Often this parent had no idea during the union how to cope with their partner's vulnerabilities or needs. There could be problems with insight, capacity for reflection, and sensitivity to the consequence of their behavior on others. In this regard, estrangement is not necessarily about right or wrong. Moreover, some cases of estrangement are entirely realistic and based on real issues such as family violence, incest or other serious, and often criminal actions. Naturally, it is essential to sort out first whether the estrangement is realistic and, if not, what is the dynamic fueling the fire.

Although "reunification therapy" appears to be the most common recommendation or approach favored by mental health practitioners and the courts, I have not found it a useful strategy. Mainly, children feel coerced, resist, and resent the intrusion. Further, they frequently blame the rejected parent for forcing their will on the child. Moreover, leaving the preferred parent on the sidelines reinforces the view that the rejected parent is solely responsible and accountable. Of course, there could be mental health professionals who have found a better way to achieve unification results but it remains that these cases are often extremely recalcitrant to change.

Although reunification has many problems and seems ill suited as a remedy, there is certainly an indication for individual therapy for the child if only because these children bear an emotional load from the unrecognized psychological needs of the chosen parent. In cases where the good parent has been highly manipulative and even sociopathic in pursuing an alienating agenda, the child will obviously benefit from having one therapist to see over the longer term. This would help bolster individual thinking and autonomy. It can also provide a neutral adult who can focus on the child and not the parents. This can aid in developing a capacity for reflective thinking, which is essential for mental health and resiliency. Working with teenagers from such troubled and polarizing families can serve their long-term benefit but it takes time.

Whenever there is a rejected parent who is scorned and discarded by a child or children for unspecified reasons that do not amount to realistic cause, the focus in terms of understanding should be the family. This does not mean that the whole family should or would agree to be in treatment. The rejected parent, however, should have as much information and feedback as possible about the child to keep abreast of the child's life progress. Moreover, the preferred parent should be helped at least to see the folly and destructiveness of a child severing contact with a parent.

Offering psychotherapy to alienating parents whose children are refusing to visit can also help turn the tide for the children. It can depressurize the family environment and lead to different messages and cues. Improvement tends to happen on its own, which is the optimal outcome in many cases. It often occurs out of the limelight and apart from professional intervention.

As I have indicated, the only poor plan in my experience is to saddle the discarded parent with the responsibility of making it better. This puts parent and child, who are already in one emotional cauldron, squarely in another.

Conclusion

Divorce is many sided. It is concurrently a state of mind, a legal status, and a process of disengagement. Why divorces fail or succeed may not have much to do with why the marriage itself failed. On the other hand, divorces fail when the former partner cannot be given up, not necessarily because of desire but because the loss of self or identity would be too great to bear. To repair the situation, scattered elements of self must be returned to their rightful owner. Identities must be reinforced and boundaries strengthened. Each must learn to speak from the position of his or her own self. It is the art of disentangling two people who cannot on their own part ways.

Parental alienation is a further variation on the same theme. The preferred parent will say that they have nothing in common with the discarded parent but nothing could be further from the truth. Indeed, they identify too much. The preferred parent fears being bereft and alone, void of identity and parental role. Hence, they possess their children and suffocate the space for the other parent to be loved. In the paranoid encounter of high conflict in all its forms, one loses and the other wins. The alienating parent is well aware of these forces and decides well in advance that the abandoned parent will never be him or her.

So we come full circle back to the first fear in life, separation anxiety, the fear of being alone or abandoned in a state of helpless need. Marriage offers the promise of permanent fellowship, a companion and stopgap against the existential dread of aloneness. Nevertheless, this stopgap remains precarious and requires strengthening even in psychologically healthy individuals. Divorce removes this assurance. Within the high conflict population, survival fears and threat are higher than normal with the entire onus or blame placed on the former partner.

Children can help mitigate the unbearable state of aloneness but then one has to share the child with the other parent. Moreover, children grow up and leave. In other words, having children is not a perfect solution to address this existential threat. Pathologies of divorce defend against such dangers to identity and existence either by clinging to the ex-spouse through interminable conflict or clinging to children to the point that there is no space for other loves.

There is no sure fire way to avoid high conflict. Divorcing couples destined for this road readily find it. Solutions must be personal and not interpersonal. Each participant must be prepared to reflect inwards, finding a place for thinking about the self and not the other. This takes huge effort especially with individuals who feel completely innocent and bullied. The desire to focus on the faults and crimes of the former partner exerts a fundamental pull that rivals an addiction. Yet, when the individual can be freed from this one-track focus and turn thinking inward, the possibilities for change multiply.

The best divorces are healed by creative efforts to learn from experience and chart a new course. High conflict is contrary. It traps the person in the old relationship and works against separation. There is no exit even from the union itself. In such a scenario, despite the apparent narrative repeated endlessly by the participants, the only hope is that the other will change. Such is the irony of high conflict that it places hope in the very person that failed to be a lasting partner in the first place. In this respect, high conflict joins those conditions of self-defeat that litter the field of human behavior.

CHAPTER EIGHT

Space for discovery

It is not unusual to treat people a number of years post separation who are still experiencing considerable psychological distress: depression, anger, and feelings of vulnerability, low self-esteem, and preoccupation with loss, loneliness, and aging. Of course, there must be individuals not seen in the clinic who proceed happily into the future without looking back following marriage break-up. On the other hand, this conclusion might be overly optimistic. The truth lies somewhere in the middle. Despite the plethora of self-help books, there has been no major breakthrough on how to make divorce less difficult and taxing.

Many find it very tough to part ways. They engage in highly ambivalent forms of involvement with ex-partners regardless of how they might feel about the divorce decision. These relationships can be extremely hard to mourn. The more significant the emotional investment in the love relationship, the more difficult it is to leave it behind.

Despite this sobering perspective, divorce can also open up real opportunities for deeper emotional change. Achieving this potential requires the courage to keep a space unfilled. Spaces for discovery are necessary. Questions and not answers should prevail. Internet dating and meet-up sites invite and build on the illusion that gaps can be filled with a click and a few promising emails. Getting answers without having to reflect on difficult questions is alluring but profoundly unrealistic.

Mary asked for help after her eight-year marriage ended with Raoul. They had a six-year-old daughter. According to Mary, Raoul's turn to Christian fundamentalism coincided with an insistence on patrimony. He was the "head" of the family and determined what choices they would make. He rationalizsed that this was the "Christian" way and represented conservative and time-honored family values that she was expected to obey without fail or question. Indeed, in his court demand for custody after their relationship imploded, he cited her "disobedience" as a major reason why he should assume care and control of their boy. Mary felt forced to find refuge in a women's shelter in order to finally get away.

Mary faced many questions about her self, as she had to wonder why she had so willingly surrendered to such an extent. It had been a major overestimation of her capacity to change Raoul, to soften his domineering character and to modulate his profound sense of entitlement.

But Mary could not stop there in her self-analysis. The wish to change Raoul had deep roots for Mary who was a middle child and only daughter. Her parents were salt-of-the-earth people who were devoted to their children. As devoted and affirming as the parents were with their offspring, however, they were fragile, apologetic, overly wary of offending, and both insecure.

Mary's natural warmth and gentle spirit made her the "love child" of the family. She had a way with her father and mother. Indeed, Mary silently stood guard for most of her childhood, lest her parents have difficulty coping with life or each other. Mary developed a potent capacity to charm, appease, comfort, and mollify in the name of family peace, love, and goodness.

It was precisely this powerful tool that Mary brought to her marriage to Raoul. As she had been a significant resource to her vulnerable parents, she reckoned that she could bring the same potent medicine to her relationship with Raoul. She would attempt to soothe and pacify him. She failed miserably in this task, which was perhaps something to be thankful for in the end. Mary was unaware of how much she lent to the service of the other, how sacrificial her unconsciously motivated mission was and how unfair it was to her welfare overall.

Divorce opened a space for self-discovery. It was up to Mary to find the truth about her self and not focus solely on the failings and excesses of Raoul. She needed to foreclose on the possibility of immediate answers. Of course, she could easily have a found a new partner but she would have been doomed to repeat the only dynamic she had ever known, which had led her to accept the imbalanced, tyrannical, and emotionally depriving relationship with Raoul in the first place.

Gradually, Mary came to appreciate that her warmth and tenderness were an authentic part of her and did not preclude her receiving love and tenderness in return. Moreover, Mary was able to understand more deeply how she allowed others to set the terms of engagement and viewed her function as one of accommodation rather than self-expression and self-affirmation.

When Mary eventually did meet a man she liked very much through a mutual friend, she described him in glowing terms. I told Mary that she casts her spell on those on whom she is most reliant; a seeming idealization that is hard to resist. Such psychodynamics ran deep in her case and simply exposing her logic in one context did not necessarily slay the dragon overall. It had to be rooted out in every corner where it resided.

Mary's idealization was her way of ensuring or at least trying to ensure that her needs would be met. In historical terms, she had to reinforce and elevate her parents so that they would be the parents she needed. The "wonderfulness" of the other was a necessity of her psyche. She was not prepared to live without this illusion, which defied extended or distorted reality. Mary had to keep a space for discovery and this included allowing significant others to succeed or fail on their own terms. She had to accept that this was not something she could or should control. I stressed to Mary that we only know others through our experiences with them. This takes time and cannot be short-circuited.

Mary is not dissimilar to many. Marriages collapse but the real issues are found in the unseen layers of the personality. Liberation from a bad marriage does not in itself translate into the kind of freedom that allows for discovery. To Mary's credit, she took the opportunity to better understand her self and what was motivating her. She came to appreciate that she rarely felt relaxed and suffered from low-level anxiety due to constant vigilance. The gains in her case were manifold.

In a romantic union, the space for discovery is a dividend of the healthy relationship. Each subject brings a unique history, perspective, and ideas, needs, and emotions to the encounter. If there is positive synergy, something creative occurs, which is attributable neither to one or the other. The space for discovery amounts to a shared space for creative play. This can also be described as a "baby".

Indeed, there must be a "baby" in order for the relationship to flourish. This symbolic baby cannot be reduced to one or the other but is a creation of the couple. They might identify it as their "relationship" and treat it as something precious to be nurtured, nourished, and cared for. It has a unique status in their lives.

If there is no "baby" in this figurative sense or if the baby withers from anemic input and expires, the relationship will fail. Couples that get together and, in short order, bear a real child without the relational baby in place are invariably in trouble and likely to disappoint each other. Let's take a typical example that I have observed on many occasions.

Jim and Laura worked in the same office building although for different companies. They would meet occasionally in the coffee shop or elevator. Laura had recently exited a long-term relationship that fell short of union. She did not feel in a good space when she began dating Jim but thought it might boost her self-esteem and confidence.

Effervescent and outgoing, thirty-four-year-old Laura tended to be noticed. In contrast to Laura, Jim had never actually been in a long-term relationship although he had considerable experience dating. Fastidious to the point of being set in his ways, women lost patience despite his nice appearance and successful career.

Part of Laura's concern was that the optimal window of opportunity to have a child was fading. Jim was not completely negative about the idea although he had no exposure and no real appreciation of childcare. Whether it was by miscommunication, design or mishap is unclear but unprotected sex led to pregnancy and a daughter was born.

Without a stable relationship on which to build a life, however, problems between Laura and Jim occurred almost immediately. They joined households just in time for Laura to give birth. Following the birth, Laura felt completely unsupported by Jim. His life seemed to continue as before: sports on the weekends and at least one workweek night out with the boys.

After much cajoling, though, Jim did try harder and there was some initial success as the child neared her first birthday. It warmed Laura's heart when Jim would play with their child and took her to the park. Nevertheless, Jim protected his former lifestyle as much as he could and he was reluctant to pay for baby supplies, toys, and general infrastructure needs. Laura was put off by his cheapness. He counted every expense and demanded parity even though she was on reduced income from parental leave benefits.

Moreover, Jim complained that Laura was often short-tempered and not the fun woman that attracted him in the first place. In turn, she felt lonely and isolated. From Laura's perspective, it was as if she had two children at different stages of development. In turn, Jim felt constantly chastised.

When Laura returned to work, family demands increased once again and Jim balked at the workload. Deeply frustrated and feeling overwhelmed, Laura lost her temper repeatedly. Seeing the writing on the wall and unsure what to do, Laura consulted a family law lawyer. She had not made up her mind to do anything but she was preparing for the worst.

When she finally told him of her doubts and that she had sought advice, he blew up. Laura tried to explain why she was unhappy, unsettled, and insecure in the relationship. Jim felt betrayed and blamed for her constant negativity and intolerance. He insisted that Laura was never happy with anything he did and that he felt doomed to displease her. He was sure that she had used him to have a baby and was now plotting to discard him apart from the child support payments he would have to make. Caught in an angry maelstrom, the relationship imploded. Jim demanded shared legal and physical custody, which Laura found preposterous considering his track record. It took two years finally to sort out.

Clearly, relationships must bear fruit before they bear babies. It is the synergy of the two participants—the creative chemistry of two subjectivities—that creates a third entity depicted as the "relationship." If there is no synergy, no meeting of minds and desires, then there will be no fruit or symbolic baby.

Laura and Jim stumbled into their encounter, which never really achieved the status of a dynamic relationship. Neither could take comfort nor be confident that they felt enhanced in the other's company or that together they created something beyond themselves. Jim's lack luster relationship history suggested deeper personality issues while Laura had yet to sort out what she really wanted. Neither had taken steps to open a space for discovery to deepen self-knowledge and enhance personal insight.

Looking more deeply into the respective history of each, Laura suffered episodic stress and stomach reactions while Jim's early parental attachments had been affected by a stormy divorce. While Laura's reactivity fed her anxiety and high reactivity to feeling unsupported, Jim was too wary to trust and in many ways preferred antagonism to any underlying sense of weakness. He kept his distance and placed heavy emphasis on financial security and self-control.

In contrast, healthy relationships evolve in the potential space for discovery co-created by the couple. Much like two children in a sandbox intermingling imaginations, the area of creativity lies outside each subject although still being a construction of mind. This is what British psychoanalyst Donald Winnicott meant when he described "potential space" as an intermediate area situated between reality and fantasy.[1] It is where play occurs as well as intimate relationships, including therapeutic ones. Fantasy enriches reality rather than being opposed to it. Thus, each couple must share a dream that is mutually constructed from the amalgam of their desires.

Returning to our example, the problem was not so much that Jim and Laura had a baby as much as that they failed to have a mutual dream about their relationship. Of course, they would have dated, talked, and become intimate physically but nothing evolved to launch them into the shared space for discovery where relationships must bloom. They had too much reality and too little fantasy, too little play and too little opportunity to build something together that would have supported the heavy load of a new child.

Perhaps popular literature makes too much of finding the "right" person as if the answer to our lives somehow lies principally with the choice of other. Of course, the choice of mate is not irrelevant even if it isn't sufficient to ensure success. What matters is that the interaction of the partners has the potential to create from the outset. Something new is added that is enriching to both. It is the mutually enriching creative process that comprises the "something more" that underwrites successful relationships.

Self-discovery

At the individual level, the "something more" is found in the zone of being where we are most likely to achieve insight through personal self-discovery. Whether in communication with another or in some self-directed process such as journaling or any form of self-directed communication, there is a need to move towards some new understanding.

The popularity of journaling, in this regard, is understandable for its potential to create "spaces for discovery". Simply recording one's thoughts and feelings is an invitation to think about what we have written. What is mandatory is the external relation that pulls us away from the here-and-now of behavior to the realm of reflected experience. This is a fundamental condition for new learning.

Using this example of journaling, we can identify three points of perspective in what can be visualized as a triangle. First, there is the subject who is experiencing life in a more or less spontaneous and unexamined way. Second, there is the text on which expressed thoughts are put to page or tablet. Third, there is the opportunity for thinking about what was written, which comprises the real work of mental processing.

We often don't know precisely what we are thinking or feeling until we speak our thoughts to someone or put pen to paper and ponder what was said. Thinking elaborates and expands on thoughts. In order to be useful, thoughts require a thinker, which requires a mind capable of mindfulness as well as the willingness to contemplate. By adding the third dimension of reflection, a space for discovery arises. In other words, it is the process of thinking about our thinking that opens the window to what we might learn.

The "thinking about" then creates a new dimension independent of the original speaker and the text. This opens the potential of something beyond. As much as this form of reflection is very helpful at any point in life, my premise is that it is critical to recovery after long-term unions and marriages end.

It is surely no accident that much of great poetry has been inspired by lost love. Human motivation requires us to go beyond mere expression to evoke images that bring us closer to what we might learn about ourselves. Hence, everyone at times needs to become a poet. But what differentiates poetry from banal narrative? Poetry is its own discourse. It is more than the sum of its words. The poet paints with words, metaphors, and analogies instead of brushes. In this way, it has the potential for discovery of something beyond, which is as yet unknown. Even though we might never reach some ultimate truth, we are uplifted and gain personal power and scope through deeper self-knowledge. This is the spirit of all self-discovery including the best use of creative journaling, which focuses on experience and not events. As such, effective journaling is closer to poetry than prose.

Pamela ended a five-year relationship with Henry, the father of her daughter. She was forlorn, harbored unrealistic wishes for reconciliation, and her family physician wanted her to take antidepressants. Pamela, however, thought that she needed to understand herself better before she did anything else in her life. She began to journal. Her initial entries were more journalist than personal diarist but she gradually stopped editing as she wrote and allowed herself to compose and then perceive her own experience.

"It all began", wrote Pamela one day expecting to link with her experience of supportive parents who raised her. Yet, she ended the sentence with "bed-wetting". She was shocked, as she really had not expected this association. Pamela had been a bed-wetter as a child. She had to acknowledge to herself that she had never shared this part of her life with her ex-partner. Pamela heaved with emotion. It touched a deep well of shame and mortification that prompted her to seek psychotherapy.

Pamela related that Henry had often complained about her lack of spontaneity during lovemaking. Pamela's counter argument was that she could not trust him. Henry was a spendthrift and unreliable. There were too many unwelcome surprises. However, this gnawed at her for there was some connection with her unconscious shame.

Of course, the trust factor was also important but Pamela's attention did not remain focused on Henry's failings. Rather, she associated with the flaws and imperfections of her own body. These shortcomings assumed huge importance in her psyche. She admitted to covering up, hiding, and fearing exposure of what tormented her about her body's failings.

Pamela noted that she had also been briefly bulimic during early adolescence although not a committed one. What should have been a celebration of womanhood had been suppressed by fears of a body out-of-control that cannot be trusted or loved. It had been a struggle in her relationship to Henry to handle these feelings. Henry's problems with money and reliability were a preferable focus to her own struggles with an imperfect body that she viewed shamefully.

When Pamela began to address these body issues, she was able to begin thinking about it. Previously, stark negative body images existed outside of thinking. These negative body images were saturated with mortification and had never seen light of day. They were more like frozen slides than thoughts. Hence, new insights and perspectives followed from bringing these troubling "truths" into the open. This included awareness that perhaps Henry's overspending and unreliability had something to do with his own reaction to Pamela's deep physical inhibitions and the part this played in the couple interaction.

Pamela and I constructed a language together to fully describe her inner world. In other words, although originating in Pamela's experience, we were able to construct shared images that were neither Pamela's nor mine alone. Nevertheless, they were powerful symbols that Pamela identified with the severe conflicts that had troubled her since childhood.

Pamela met the test of the newly separated person who found a way to expand her consciousness and open her mind to new meanings. She had begun with Henry but ended with Pamela. Making a space for discovery offered a sizeable dividend that changed how she saw her self and added clarity and scope to her relationships with others.

Search for new meaning

There are times in life that call out for the search for new meaning as a way of fostering emotional and even spiritual growth. Divorce appears to be one such situation. Perhaps it is because there are few life experiences that are more potentially rupturing or life bending. Divorce does not necessarily teach anything. Indeed, there is a huge difference between being rocked by experience and learning from it. Learning increases our sense of agency or freedom. Helps us not to feel controlled or coerced by external or internal forces.

A space for discovery is needed if lessons are to be learned. This takes an open exploratory process with no set or pre-determined conclusion. It follows that anything that limits or shuts down this process of new learning will work against best interests. For example, pervasive blaming severely narrows the field of discovery and basically eliminates the capacity to think about the self other than in victim terms. The sole conclusion possible in the blame mindset is of being wronged, betrayed or otherwise affected by forces beyond the self's control. It might feel better short-term but creates sizeable long-term risks.

Moreover, blame reduces the sense of will, self-direction and self-observation. In contrast to blame, finding new meaning in an event, especially one as difficult and precarious as divorce is self-enhancing. It augments the sense of will and ownership of our actions, which is crucial to new learning.

In his existential treatise on meaning, Victor Frankl observed, "When we are no longer able to change a situation ... we are challenged to change ourselves" (Frankl, 1984, p. 51).[2] This is precisely what I mean by finding new meaning. Divorce requires us to change ourselves not simply as a matter of turning a page but of retelling the story through the lens of greater self-knowledge. The change in question is not biographic but, rather, existential. It is related to understanding ourselves better.

Life is a narrative that merges past and present while in the process modifying both. In the example of Pamela noted above, the past helped her understand the circumstances of her relationship with Henry while the present revealed and helped modify the past. Her early traumatically inflected feelings about her body impacted on her capacity to be authentically open and present in her union. By being able to reinterpret her past, she was able to change the present and give new meaning to her life.

Perhaps the biggest threat of divorce would be that it would have no personal significance or meaning. For instance, the individual would conclude that the break-up had nothing to do with them. They might say that they never really knew their partner or that the person changed dramatically and this was beyond their control. This need to disassociate self-responsibility, as if to eliminate any contribution to what transpired, also removes any chance for new learning. Denial in this case is so great that it creates a void where new meaning might otherwise develop. The individual is left at the mercy of the other mainly because the self is excluded from the event.

This dynamic of extreme self-evasion is certainly evident in high conflict divorce. We might surmise that most divorce pathologies represent a gross enactment of the need to avoid any personal significance or acknowledge any contribution. For instance, it very much describes what is seen in so-called parental alienation. The alienator is fundamentally alienated from their core self. There is no search for personal meaning while inner life is excluded from discourse or reflection. Denied an inner world where individual security could be established, the alienator is pulled to the outside world and, thus, appropriates the children as an exclusive source of comfort and meaning. The children are possessed more than loved. There is no room for rivals to that love and no capacity to share the children's love with the other parent. In this respect, the children take the place of the inner self from which the alienator is estranged. The alienating parent cannot afford any separateness from the children without feeling hopelessly alone.

As we develop understanding and glean personal significance and value from even something as difficult as divorce, we can come to own the event. It is no longer something that simply beset us but, rather, is an experience which informs the self. The past becomes clearer and, as a result, so does the present.

It can be hard sometimes to locate the self or find the inner solitude to sense our own individuality. There can be too much noise and pressure generated by others particularly at a time when a life partner likely rocked our world. Of course, we are forever tied to otherness. We are born into a world of others that welcomes us, names us and is responsible for our survival. Adult love partnerships cement the importance of otherness in nourishing and sustaining personal identity. Nevertheless, as much as marital rupture seems so traumatically focused on the other, the real challenge is to find a means to put this aside in order to ponder and re-find the self.

An essential "selfness" is crucial to the human enterprise and this selfness is associated with achieving a capacity for aloneness that supports emotional autonomy. This autonomy is most readily experienced at moments where we have found solitude and the capacity to be alone. In this state of equilibrium, there is no desperate attempt to pursue the other or find a replacement as quickly as possible.

This capacity to be alone is so fundamental to psychological adjustment over all that it can be seen as a key developmental and emotional acquisition. Indeed, there are two fundamental tenets of relationships that could be explained in this context:

- No union is possible without the capacity to be alone
- No healthy divorce can ensue without establishing the capacity to be alone.

Psychoanalyst Donald Winnicott wrote an evocative article in the 1950s entitled, "The capacity to be alone".[3] He was interested in the basic situation in which this capability evolves. Winnicott noted that the capacity comes about paradoxically through the experience of having someone reliably present during early childhood. The child sitting on the floor can focus on their toys and, when he or she looks up, they see the parent. Gradually, the child internalizes parental presence and this internalization creates the capacity to be alone. It is at the core of self-soothing and permits separation from the other.

Hence, "I am alone" is a developmental achievement and not something to be taken lightly or for granted. Not everybody can be alone without becoming too lonely, panicky or threatened. Loneliness, which is a part of everyone's experience, can become extreme if the person has no sense of a center or internal presence of a soothing other. Solitude is too threatening. We can consider, as an example, the recently separated woman or man who is desperate to replace what was lost, as if only the physical presence of the other will plug the hole and relieve a dire loneliness.

In an unhealthy context, "I am alone" can also mean to be undefended and at the mercy of a hostile world. This should be distinguished, however, from the capacity to be alone, which is the essential ingredient of emotional autonomy and allows for healthy alliances with others. Without this capacity, relationships are either very insecure and dependent or very frightening.

Following any traumatic life experience, divorce very much included, there is a need to establish or re-establish healthy internal solitude, which is a dividend of the capacity to be alone. This is essential in order to experience life in a direct and meaningful way. It takes the desperateness out of the situation and allows the self to serve as its own anchor.

I am reminded of the 2000 Tom Hanks film *Cast Away*. The volleyball, "Wilson", floats to shore in a FedEx package. Hank's character, Chuck Noland, paints the face with his own blood when he injures his hand trying to make fire. Wilson sustains Noland not by simulating companionship like an imaginary friend but by serving as an external point of reference in which Noland can experience and reflect on his own thoughts. Wilson is reminiscent of the parent whose presence is reassuring and permits the child to learn to tolerate aloneness. It is a togetherness that supports solitude.

Thankfully, there is no need to follow Tom Hanks' character to a deserted island to discover merit in solitude as a means of consolidating the self as the first order of business following separation. Moreover, I am certainly not equating aloneness or solitude with social isolation. The issue is not one of social withdrawal but of emotional consolidation through reinforcing the capacity to be alone.

Perhaps the biggest error made following divorce is to perceive the problem as one of otherness whereas it is really the problem of the self. There can be no end to the repercussions of divorce without establishing a healthy solitude. Blame is the major remedy preferred by those who are certain the problem concerns the other. Divorce can also be negated through rapid re-partnering but it will never be resolved. The self will remain vulnerable to repetition with the separation trauma just beneath the surface. This can easily feed into subsequent relationships, serving as a destabilizing and undermining force.

In terms of what specific path to follow to establish this healthy solitude and find personal meaning in the experience, this is really a matter of personal choice. Some people seek programs that promote mindfulness, meditation, and focused self-reflection. Others see counselors or undertake psychotherapy based on need and extent of suffering while some rely on self-generated approaches such as journaling or structured workbook approaches available in the self-help section of bookstores. All these approaches recognize that the self needs its just due after committed relationships or marriages end, not at the expense of others but in order to participate in a fuller or more confident way in the future.

The notion of "space" in space for discovery is another vantage point to understand this process of adjustment more fully. We tend to stress the issue of space in human discourse. The expression, "I need my space", or "give me space" are well-honed metaphors that link the self and body to its immediate surroundings. Space for discovery suggests a different kind of space—mental in form—as if we can be crowded mentally as well as physically to the point that we are pushed completely out of our own internal life space. There is recognition thus that self-discovery depends on having a solitary space in which creative and meaningful thinking can occur. This is a space that we must value and protect rather than forfeit even for the chance of quickly being with another.

Seemingly paradoxically, we are no less lonely with someone with whom we do not share emotionally than when actually alone. In other words, those who make every effort to quickly fill a hole in their social life, as if this is the immediate remedy, are at risk of interminable loneliness. In contrast, relationships that begin when we are grounded, secure in the merit of self-connection are much more likely to succeed. Not only are we in a better position to make good choices but, as well, there is better reason to trust these choices. This has ethical implications as we are in the strongest position to honor the person we choose and simultaneously to represent our best interests.

How individuals can accomplish this vital task is an important issue. Friends or family who can provide a watchful but non-intrusive presence or influence can be very helpful in this regard. The concept of "holding" is relevant. Holding provides attentive, empathic contact but does not impinge or coerce the individual to do this or that. The notion of easily dispensed "advice" such as, "get back into circulation", or whatever, is basically unhelpful. Each person faced with severe disruption must find his or her own way back. Primarily, they have to connect with themselves before they attempt to re-engage with the world. This self-connection then is what secures a foothold in emotional autonomy by regaining the capacity to be alone.

The consequence of premature and impulsive re-engagement is that relationships are often tinged with desperation, wishes, and unresolved yearning for the lost love. Rather than feeling centered and anchored, the individual feels needy and vulnerable. This might be rationalized as a case of having been burned, but the reality is that impulsive re-engagement is a risky business, which at some level is often not recognized. The popular term is "rebound", which captures the sense that the energy derives from the former relationship casting a shadow on the new one.

Rebound, unremitting anger, and conflict or even referring to the new love by the old love's name is each suggestive of unresolved mourning. This is a common theme in divorce. The proposition is that unresolved mourning explains much of what can later go wrong in divorce. Although grieving is a key element of dealing with any loss, especially one as significant as marital or long term relationship breakdown, there can be a tendency to focus too much on the other and not enough on the self. As much as we must mourn the other, we must also mourn the self.

What does it mean to mourn the self? To be sure, the self is not actually lost in divorce although it can be badly decentered and depleted. Divorce requires us, though, to recognize the limits of the self—the limits of our capacity to make something happen, the limits of our wisdom and the limits of what we can actually control. The inclination is to impose a narrative that provides refuge from facing painful and humbling truths. It is easier to support a version that frees us from responsibility and is more about the other who usually figures large in most people's versions of broken relationships. Equally evading is the tendency to imply that the break-up had no meaning: "we drifted apart".

Certainly, people differ in terms of the amount of suffering or even truth they can handle. The problem is that mourning invariably creates helpless feelings and these are accentuated when we face humbling truths and loss. It is easier not to mourn for the other or for the self.

There is a plethora of techniques and strategies to avoid mourning. One way is to dispense with loss by falling in love with another while fading out of the original union. The hope is to create a seamless transition so that there is no loss at all.

Another is to deny that anything good has been lost. We see this when ex-couples come to hate and feel persecuted by each other. Glad to be rid of him or her goes the narrative—my enemy and not my friend.

There is also the approach that impersonalizes the break-up so that it is attributed to something other than the direct personal interaction of the two people. Examples include, blaming shift work, contrary interests or simply vague relational drift. The idea is that marital dissolution occurred without cause or casualty for that matter and therefore has no real significance nor represents a loss.

Finally, there is the partner who has left the other in a shambles of surprise and despair while saying after the fact that the other must have known something was wrong. The implication is that the union was so bad that leaving was the only reasonable path. The leaver implies that there was no loss to grieve because the relationship was already dead and the other was simply in denial.

Mourning is part of life and is not in itself pathological. Most probably, we never stop mourning major losses especially those that we gave up reluctantly. There is not a day that goes by, for instance, that I do not think about and feel some longing for my deceased parents. My mourning is intertwined with honoring my parents and stands as a testament to love and respect. Hence, it is unrealistic to expect that all mourning has a beginning and an end.

The same is likely true in divorce. Indeed, this is someone we loved enough to choose as a life partner with the promise that it should be forever. Is it realistic then to think that this could end so neatly and cleanly that we would miss nothing or not recall longingly what was once precious and shared?

In other words, mourning the other is not really the problem in most instances unless this mourning becomes pathological. Mourning the self, however, is often a pertinent and more complex issue. As already described, divorce is often a watershed moment that has major implications for the self. This includes failure and crisis management and its impact on self-esteem, confidence, sense of mastery, and mood regulation. The working through of the divorce experience, the recalibration of the self, the re-finding of an emotional center and capacity for healthy solitude comprise the essential divorce—work that will determine future capability and outcomes.

Conclusion

"Space for discovery" is an evocative term linking personal challenge with the notion of space. The spatial metaphor encapsulates the idea that we need an internal sense of space in order to be creative. It also implies that we have to be optimally present in that space to take full advantage of the opportunity. Being "present" is what is meant by terms such as agency or autonomy—the self is ready for psychological work and capable of functioning with independent judgment.

Space for discovery can be understood as having both internal and external referents. The two are connected. When we speak of being pressured by the demands of others or intruded upon, we are perhaps describing interpersonal space but also the way we feel emotionally. Indeed, what we are describing is outside and inside at the same time. Space also represents a potential for creative work. In other words, the idea of space in the human psyche is complex and conveys a sense of capacity, opportunity, and scope or maneuverability.

When identity first develops from budding strivings and early parental care, a sense of self-operating in its own space emerges. The young child gradually learns to function alone because of sufficient togetherness with a safe and protective parent. Inner security allows for curiosity and exploration. This capacity for autonomy provides the basic platform for creative enterprise in the future.

Paradoxically, acquiring autonomy and the capacity to be alone also means that our life space can be shared with others in intimate relation to us. This is where the best of romantic relationships are situated. They occur between two mature adults each with a capacity to be alone who willingly and passionately internalize each other's presence and share lives.

When marriages or relationships break down however, the traumatic rupture is felt at the deepest level of being. Even the capacity to be alone takes a beating when the rug gets pulled out from under. At these moments, a shaken self feels hobbled. We are more needy, vulnerable, destabilized and less at peace than we would ever want to be. It is a fallacy that only unhealthy people suffer major disruption after divorce. Breakdown of these encompassing, meaningful, and life defining relationships is shattering for most people.

Of course, the leaving spouse who orchestrated the breakup and is immediately re-partnered might look like they have cheated fate and survived unscathed. In the short term this might seem to be true but they have leveraged their life to a new mate to a compromising degree. Likewise, an illicit, secret relationship evolving in the shadow of an existing marriage or union cannot be wholesome no matter how it is rationalized. These new liaisons are at high risk of failing when they have to succeed on their own terms. The legacy of deception, subterfuge, and betrayal stamps these relationships and can be hard to shake.

Recovering from crises of many sorts requires a return to basics. Relationship breakdown and divorce is no different. Re-finding a stable inner solitude that fosters a space for discovery is paramount to achieving a healthy adjustment. First, making a space for the self automatically generates a space for thinking, relating and, as I have emphasized, taking stock and navigating through the many hurdles that divorce inevitably causes. Second, life-altering events such as divorce have much to teach those curious and open to its lessons. Discovering important truths while peeling away self-deceptions can be sobering but, in the end, self-knowledge is a powerful tool that will surely contribute to success and happiness in the future.

EPILOGUE

The image of two people intertwined in love conveys a powerful message of the importance of intimacy and togetherness in the human narrative. We are born into a world of others and immediately find survival and support in the embrace and care of parents. From these beginnings, relationships evolve within and then beyond the family and are eventually integrated with sexuality as we grow into our adult selves.

Divorce has likely been with us in some form as long as marriage but unlike marriage, it does not fit comfortably with the human narrative. Whenever it occurs, divorce rocks the foundations on which our lives and identities are built. In this sense, divorce is subversive considering that it undermines emotional and social security by provoking feelings of aloneness, vulnerability, abandonment, and betrayal.

Can there ever really be a good divorce? Certainly not, if we equate good divorce with happy divorce. These are rarely happy events. Nevertheless, it can mean that from decision to implementation and, finally, recovery, steps were taken to make the best of a very difficult and complicated situation. In this regard, divorce creates choice points and, as much as we might want to be driven by intuition and impulse, there are best practices to follow. This constitutes the good divorce.

Divorce must also include a component of forgiveness in order to be successful or "good". This could be discussed at the level of repair of a damaged link to another person. Psychically, however, it is less an interpersonal concern than one of recovering from the hurt, disappointment, and sense of disloyalty that are commonplace in divorce. Pride takes a beating and injuries run deep.

Failure of something as public and momentous as marriage is emotionally catastrophic and wishes for retribution can stand in the way of getting on with life. Bitterness and blame are telltale signs that forgiveness has not been reached. Behind the cover of resentment reside the pain, longing, guilt, shame, and sense of failure that can leave people feeling crippled for years.

When we mourn we can forgive and when we forgive we can work through the feelings, hurts, anger, and obsessive wishes for retribution that otherwise create emotional impasse.

Thus, the "good divorce" is also profoundly self-protective. It makes it more likely to reach a state of forgiveness, which in turn facilitates a working through of the many issues that must be faced. Although there is a tendency to focus on the other and the other's deeds, forgiveness of the self is just as important. Grudges keep us from remembering what we loved about the other, what drew us originally and what we shared during good times.

Successful resolution of a marital breakdown cannot be based on "hate" but must also recall love. In other words, the individual must capture what was good and loved in the other and in the relationship in order to give this up through mourning. Working through, mourning, and forgiveness overlap but describe interrelated processes that each contributes to the good divorce.

To those reflective and enquiring readers experiencing or facing the prospect of divorce, I hope that this book has given you something more to consider as you deal with this challenging and difficult experience. To those mental health, social service and legal professionals who have perused these pages, I hope that the themes and topics covered as well as the examples provided will assist you in your valuable work.

Individuals facing divorce are by definition in a disrupted state even when they have initiated the break-up. They need our compassion and support for sure but they also need to appreciate and be guided by their longer-term interests. The good divorce is an ethical divorce. Ethics are not simply principles. They provide important markers and guideposts that should inform behavior and inspire the choices we make.

Arthur Leonoff

NOTES

Introduction

1. Center for Disease Control (CDC). (2010). *Cohabitation, Marriage, Divorce, and Remarriage in the United States*. Center Series Report 23, Number 22. 103pp.
2. Statistics Canada. (2011). *National Household Survey 2011*. Canada: Government of Canada.

Chapter Two

1. See US census Bureau table at http://factfinder2.census.gov/faces/tableservices/jsf/pages/productview.xhtml?pid=ACS_11_1YR_S1201&prodType=table Accessed 13 November 2014.
2. Wallerstein, J. S. & Lewis, J. M. (2004). The unexpected legacy of divorce: Report of a 25-year study. *Psychoanalytic Psychology, 21*: 353–370.
3. Holmes, T. H. & Rahe, R. H. (1967). The social readjustment rating scale. *Journal of Psychosomatic Research, 11*: 213–218.

Chapter Three

1. Wallerstein, J. S. & Lewis, J. M. (2004). The unexpected legacy of divorce: Report of a 25-year study. *Psychoanalytic Psychology, 21*: 353–370.
2. Psychologist, Dr. Barbara Jo Fidler, and Law Professor Nicholas Bala, have provided, in my view, the clearest discussion of terms and the issues behind them in the literature to date. See: Fidler, B. J. & Bala, N. (2010). Children resisting post-separation contact with a parent: concepts, controversies and conundrums. *Family Court Review, 48, 1*: 10–47.

Chapter Five

1. Millar, P. (2009). *The Bests Interests of Children: An Evidence-Based Approach*. Toronto: University of Toronto Press.
2. Kelly, J. (1994). The determination of child custody. *Children and Divorce, 4*: 121–142.
3. Cyr, F., Di Stefano, G. & Dejardins, B. (2013). Family life, parental separation, and child custody in Canada: a focus on Quebec. *Family Court Review, 51*: 522–541.
4. My thanks to colleagues Drs. Margaret DeCorte, Sharon Francis Harrison, and Maggie Mamen who worked with me on a project for the Canadian National Judicial Institute and helped articulate these descriptions.
5. Human life is accommodating and same-sex couples and their offspring adjust very well to the circumstance. Attachments evolve and break-ups are disruptive along fault lines reflecting the couple in question rather than gender lines. Infants in this scenario are no different and their needs must be met in precisely the same way. As much as this applies across the board in terms of age range, it is not specific to any one developmental level.
6. Pruett, M. K. & Kelly, J. B. (2014). Parental separation and overnight care of young children, Part II: putting theory into practice, *Family Court Review, 52*: 256–262.

Chapter Six

1. Stewart, S. D. (2007). *Brave New Stepfamilies.* Thousand Oaks: Sage.

2. Cherlin, A. J. (2009). *The Marriage-Go-Round: The State of Marriage and the Family in America Today. New York: Alfred A Knopf.* pp. 8–24.
3. Parker, K. (2011). *A Portrait of Stepfamilies.* Pew Research Center report. http://pewsocialtrends.org/2011/01/13/a-portrait-of-stepfamilies/ last accessed 24 November 2014.
4. www12.statcan.ca/census-recensement/.../98-312-x2011001-eng.cfm.
5. Hetherington, E. M. & Kelly, J. (2002). *For Better or Worse: Divorce Reconsidered.* New York: W. W. Norton.
6. Andrea, J. Sedlak, et al. Fourth National Incidence Study of Child Abuse and Neglect (NIS-4) (2009–2010): Report to Congress (Washington, DC: US Department of Health and Human Services, Administration for Children and Families, 2010).
7. Freud, S. (1921). Group psychology and the analysis of the ego, *S.E., 18*: 67–144. London: Hogarth.

Chapter Seven

1. Brown, C. (1994). The impact of divorce on children: the Australian experience. *Family Court Review, 32*: 149–167.
2. Winnicott, D. W. (1953). Transitional objects and transitional phenomena. *International Journal of Psychoanalysis, 34*: 89–97.

Chapter Eight

1. Ogden, T. (1985). On potential space. *International Journal of Psycho-Analysis, 66*: 129–141.
2. Frankl, V. (1984). *Man's Search for Meaning*. New York: Washington Square Press.
3. Winnicott, D. W. (1958). The capacity to be alone. *International Journal of Psychoanalysis, 39*: 416–420.

REFERENCES

Brown, C. (1994). The impact of divorce on children: the Australian experience. *Family Court Review, 32*: 149–167.

Center for Disease Control (CDC). (2010). *Cohabitation, Marriage, Divorce, and Remarriage in the United States*. Center Series Report 23, Number 22. 103pp.

Cherlin, A. J. (2009). *The Marriage-Go-Round: The State of Marriage and the Family in America Today. New York: Alfred A Knopf*. pp. 8–24.

Cyr, F., Di Stefano, G. & Dejardins, B. (2013). Family life, parental separation, and child custody in Canada: a focus on Quebec. *Family Court Review, 51*: 522–541.

Fidler, B. J. & Bala, N. (2010). Children resisting postseparation contact with a parent: concepts, controversies and conundrums. *Family Court Review, 48, 1*: 10–47.

Frankl, V. (1984). *Man's Search for Meaning*. New York: Washington Square Press.

Freud, S. (1921). Group psychology and the analysis of the ego. *S.E., 18*: 67–144. London: Hogarth.

Hetherington, E. M. & Kelly, J. (2002). For *B*etter or *W*orse: Divorce *R*econsidered. New York: W.W. Norton.

Holmes, T. H. & Rahe, R. H. (1967). The social readjustment rating scale. *Journal of Psychosomatic Research, 11*: 213–218.

Kelly, J. (1994). The determination of child custody. *Children and Divorce, 4*: 121–114.

Millar, P. (2009). *The Bests Interests of children: An Evidence-Based Approach*. Toronto: University of Toronto Press.

Ogden, T. (1985). On potential space. *International Journal of Psycho-Analysis, 66*: 129–141.

Parker, K. (2011). *A Portrait of Stepfamilies*. Pew Research Center report. http://pewsocialtrends.org/2011/01/13/a-portrait-of-stepfamilies/ last accessed 24 November 2014.

Pruett, M. K. & Kelly, J. B. (2014). Parental separation and overnight care of young children, Part II: putting theory into practice, *Family Court Review, 52*: 256–262.

Statistics Canada. (2011). *National Household Survey 2011*. Canada: Government of Canada. www12.statcan.gc.ca/nhs-enm/index-eng.cfm, last modified 5 August 2014.

Statistics Canada (2012). *Portrait of Families and Living Arrangements in Canada: Families, Households and Marital Status—2011 Census of Population*. Canada: Government of Canada. www12.statcan.ca/census-recensement/2011/as-sa/98-312-x/98-312-x2011001-eng.cfm/.

Stewart, S. D. (2007). *Brave New Stepfamilies*. Thousand Oaks: Sage.

United States Census Bureau. (2011). *American Community Survey: 1-year estimates*. http://factfinder2.census.gov/faces/tableservices/jsf/pages/productview.xhtml?pid=ACS_11_1YR_S1201&prodType=table last accessed 27 November 2014.

Wallerstein, J. S. & Lewis, J. M. (2004). The unexpected legacy of divorce: Report of a 25-year study. *Psychoanalytic Psychology, 21*: 353–370.

Winnicott, D. W. (1953). Transitional objects and transitional phenomena. *International Journal of Psychoanalysis, 34*: 89–97.

Winnicott, D. W. (1958). The capacity to be alone. *International Journal of Psychoanalysis, 39*: 416–420.

Zemeckis, R. (2000). *Cast Away*. USA.

Made in United States
North Haven, CT
14 December 2021

12692617R00150